Degunking™ YOUR HOME

The Degunking 12-Step Program

Here is the basic 12-step degunking process that you should follow to fully degunk your home:

1. Understand what gunk is and why it builds up (Chapters 1 and 2).

2. Throw away what you can first (Chapter 3).

3. Apply the four box method to every room and closet (Chapter 4).

4. Put away, store, give away or sell, and (continue to) throw out or recycle collected items and clutter (Chapter 4).

5. Focus in on problem areas such as closets and kitchens, including pantries and the fridge (Chapters 5 and 6).

6. Organize bedrooms, bathrooms, offices, family rooms, and utility rooms (Chapters 7 and 8).

7. Create and manage long-term storage areas (Chapter 9).

8. Stay organized (and clutter free) by managing and completing daily tasks (Chapter 10).

9. Organize cleaning tasks for more efficient cleaning sessions (Chapter 11).

10. Learn how to express clean (Chapter 12).

11. Be prepared for cleaning emergencies (Chapter 13).

12. Maintain your organized home (Chapter 14).

Degunking with Time Limitations

To get the full benefits of degunking, I highly recommend that you complete all of the main degunking tasks in the order they are presented. Performing all of these tasks will require quite a bit of time though. If your time is limited, here are some suggestions for valuable degunking tasks you can perform in the time you *do* have—whether it's ten minutes, three hours, or an entire day.

Ten Minute Degunking

If you have a very short amount of time—less than half an hour, say—or if you have a hard time staying on task, you should focus on doing a few of these short degunking jobs:

1. Take out the trash or empty your recycling bin (Page 26).

2. Throw away leftovers stored in the refrigerator and wipe up spills (Page 27).

3. Empty a "Move" box (Page 48).

4. Throw away wire hangers, dry cleaning bags, mismatched socks, and anything else stored in a closet that you don't need (Page 55).

5. Put things that are on the kitchen counter back where they belong (Page 69).

6. Get rid of four coffee cups if you have too many (Page 70).

7. Empty the dishwasher (Page 76).

8. Carry something to the garage that does not belong in the house, like golf clubs (Page 91).

9. Get rid of two knickknacks (Page 100).

10. Throw away unnecessary papers and paper gunk (Page 119).

11. Gather a load of laundry (Page 158).

12. Fold a load of laundry (Page 159).

13. Take something out for dinner and set aside vegetables (Page 160).

14. Wipe kitchen or bathroom counters (Page 161).

15. Move newspapers to a recycle bin (Page 161).

16. Make a bed (Page 161).

17. Go through the mail (Page 161).

18. Set the dinner table (Page 162).

19. Gather household trash from trash cans (Page 163).

20. Make a to-do list (Page 166).

21. Use a disinfecting wipe to clean up a sticky spot on the floor (Page193).

Thirty Minute Degunking

If you only have thirty minutes or so, I recommend you perform a few of the ten-minute degunking tasks listed above or perform one of these:

1. Throw away expired foods, cleaning supplies, cracked drinking glasses, and bacteria-laden sponges in the kitchen (Page 27).

2. Throw away expired medications, lotions, hair dye, and creams in the medicine cabinets (Page 28).

3. Clean out a junk drawer (Page 28 and 38).

4. Create a space just for the junk you collect, such as newspapers, mail, catalogs, and magazines (Pages 33-34).

5. Apply the four box method to a single drawer or your wallet or purse (Page 37 and 40).

6. Tidy up a closet (Page 60-62).

7. Create a space for daily gunk such as cell phones, keys, PDAs, purses, and trash (Pages 74-76).

8. Throw away expired foods in the refrigerator, freezer, and pantry (Pages 80-83).

9. Group and store pet toys (Page 99).

10. Create a homework area (Page 107).

11. Figure out what problem areas exist in your home office and find solutions for them (Page 114-116).

12. Organize a utility room (Page 126).

13. Create a cleaning supply tote (Page 131 and in Chapter 11).

14. Create a toolbox (Page 131-132).

15. Walk the dog (Page160).

16. Make dinner (Page 162).

17. Create a system for dealing with weekly mail and bills (Page 169-172).

18. Express clean two bathrooms (Pages 192-194).

19. Express clean the kitchen (Pages 194-195).

One Hour Degunking

If you have an hour to degunk, I recommend you perform a couple of the thirty-minute degunking tasks listed above or perform one of these:

1. Throw away anything you haven't used in a year that can be considered trash as time permits (Page 27-29).

2. Help a packrat take control (Page 31-33).

3. Apply the four-box method to a small closet or small room (Page 37-39).

4. Take a box filled with charity items to your local drop off location (Page 48).

5. Organize kitchen drawers (Pages 71-71).

6. Encourage family members to pick up after themselves in family and living areas (Pages 93-95).

7. Rearrange a room for optimum degunking, cleaning, and maintenance (Pages103).

8. Make cleaning up easier for your kids (Pages 103-105) and teenagers (Pages 106-108).

9. Create a filing system (Pages 117-119).

10. Build a simple shelf in a utility or laundry room (Pages 123-124) or hang a wire organizer (Page 125).

11. Uncover problem areas in a utility room and rectify those problems (Pages 126-127).

12. Degunk a bathroom (Pages 132-134).

13. Create a chore list for you and your family (Pages 158-165).

14. Run an hour's worth of errands (Page 167).

15. Put tools in place to keep every room clean without any work at all (Page 183).

Half-Day Degunking

If you have a half a day to perform degunking tasks, instead of performing several less-time consuming chores, perform any of these:

1. Remove all of the trash from your home, including items in the garage, living areas, attics, bedrooms, kitchens, laundry rooms, and game rooms (Pages 27-29).

2. Spend some time adding a coat rack, wicker baskets, key racks, trash cans, door mats, shelves, and plastic hooks (Pages 41-43).

3. Apply the four-box method to a large clothes closet (Pages 51-59).

4. Degunk a dining room (Pages 90-95).

5. Degunk a family or living room (Pages 95-101).

6. Apply the four-box method to your kids' rooms (Pages 103-106).

7. Fix all problem areas in a home office (Pages 120-122).

8. Organize and create an area in the garage, basement, attic, or outbuilding for storing things long-term, such as bulk purchases, holiday decorations, and lawn equipment (Pages 142-145).

9. Organize and clean the basement (Pages 146-147).

10. Create a disaster preparedness kit and store it in long-term storage areas where it can be easily accessed (Pages 149-150).

11. Grocery shop, put away food, and create lunches and dinners for the week (Pages 156-157).

12. Dust, sweep, vacuum, mop, clean windows, mow, and change bed linens as time permits (Pages 163-165 and all of Chapter 11).

13. Run all errands (Pages 167-168).

14. Start degunking the garage, attic, or basement by applying the four-box method.

All Weekend Degunking

If you have an entire weekend to devote to degunking tasks, don't spend the time performing a scattered group of chores. Instead, devote the entire weekend to performing and completing one large degunking project:

1. Degunk the kitchen (Chapter 6).

2. Redo a utility room (Pages 127-130).

3. Degunk your garage (Chapter 9).

4. Perform as many monthly or yearly chores as possible (Appendix A).

5. Have a garage sale (Appendix C).

6. Set up an account on eBay, take pictures of your items for sale, and start an auction (Appendix C).

Spare Moment Degunking

There may be times when you have only a few moments to spare. Perhaps you're waiting for your kids to put on their shoes, for water to boil, or for a microwave dinner to complete. You can still use this time to perform quick degunking tasks. Some are repeated from the 10-minute degunking checklist to indicate their importance.

Twenty Useful Degunking Tasks

1. Carry one large item to the trash bin (a broken appliance, stuffed animal, or broken or outdated electronic equipment, for example).
2. Pick up the trash on kitchen counters and any other table within your line of sight.
3. Place dirty clothes currently on the floor in the proper hamper.
4. Make that quick phone call you've been putting off, like the one to make a doctor's or dentist's appointment.
5. Get rid of magazines at the bottom of the magazine pile.
6. Carry any item in the "move" box to its appropriate room and put it away.
7. Put shoes that have been left out where they belong.
8. Feed pets.
9. Empty the dishwasher.
10. Collect pets' toys, kids' toys, or feed fish.
11. Restack DVDs, CDs, or video games.
12. Read and update what's on the family calendar or whiteboard.
13. Move anything that needs to be in the garage to it.
14. Make tomorrow morning's coffee.
15. Make a bed.
16. Wipe down the kitchen counters and the stove with a disinfecting wipe.
17. Fold laundry.
18. Clean up a stain that's been bothering you.
19. Collect items family members have left out, even after being asked to put them away, and hold them for "ransom."
20. Set the dinner table.

Joli Ballew

President
Keith Weiskamp

Editor-at-Large
Jeff Duntemann

Vice President, Sales, Marketing, and Distribution
Steve Sayre

Vice President, International Sales and Marketing
Cynthia Caldwell

Production Manager
Kim Eoff

Cover Designer
Kris Sotelo

Degunking™ Your Home

Paraglyph Press, Inc.
4015 N. 78th Street, #115
Scottsdale, Arizona 85251
Phone: 602-749-8787
www.paraglyphpress.com

Paraglyph Press ISBN: 1-933097-11-6

Printed in the United States of America
10   9   8   7   6   5   4   3   2   1

ᐯ PARAGLYPH™
P R E S S

The Paraglyph Mission

This book you've purchased is a collaborative creation involving the work of many hands, from authors to editors to designers and to technical reviewers. At Paraglyph Press, we like to think that everything we create, develop, and publish is the result of one form creating another. And as this cycle continues on, we believe that your suggestions, ideas, feedback, and comments on how you've used our books is an important part of the process for us and our authors.

We've created Paraglyph Press with the sole mission of producing and publishing books that make a difference. The last thing we all need is yet another book on the same tired, old topic. So we ask our authors and all of the many creative hands who touch our publications to do a little extra, dig a little deeper, think a little harder, and create a better book. The founders of Paraglyph are dedicated to finding the best authors, developing the best books, and helping you find the solutions you need.

As you use this book, please take a moment to drop us a line at **feedback@paraglyphpress.com** and let us know how we are doing—and how we can keep producing and publishing the kinds of books that you can't live without.

Sincerely,

Keith Weiskamp & Jeff Duntemann
Paraglyph Press Founders
4015 N. 78th Street, #115
Scottsdale, Arizona 85251
email: **feedback@paraglyphpress.com**
Web: **www.paraglyphpress.com**

For mom, who is always amazed when she enters my pristine home, and who still comments occasionally on how messy I was in high school and college. Ah, I still remember the smell of spoiled food under the bed, my shoes sticking to the floor of my dorm room, and the happiness I experienced when finding my keys!

—*Joli Ballew*

ъ

About the Author

Joli Ballew, is a full time writer in the Dallas, Texas area. She has written over a dozen books, several with Degunking titles, including the critically acclaimed Degunking Windows with Jeff Duntemann. She loves working in the yard and planting flowers, remodeling her home, and biking and golfing on the weekends.

Acknowledgments

Degunking Your Home was created with the help of quite a few people. Of course, it would never have made it to press without the insight of Paraglyph Press big wigs Keith Weiskamp, Cynthia Caldwell, and Steven Sayre, and team members Kim Eoff and Dan Young. They helped me turn the idea for this book into reality, and I truly enjoyed working with all of them.

I'd also like to thank a few people for going beyond the call of duty. Cynthia Caldwell, Vice President of International Sales and Marketing at Paraglyph Press, offered helpful tips and a Gunkbuster's Notebook (One Woman, One Weekend, One Hundred Dollars, Chapter 8). She poured over every chapter too; made sure I didn't miss anything, and added ideas when she saw the opportunity. Garth Beard and his company, Scotland Yards, built the shed shown in Chapter 9 (Figure 9-5). It was completed in a single weekend, making it possible for me to finish the chapter on time. I really didn't know what I was going to do with all of the lawn equipment I had to keep! Aunt Doris and Uncle Harry allowed me to take pictures of their incredibly degunked kitchen and storage areas, one of which I included in Chapter 7 (Figure 7-2). Too bad I didn't have room to show the beautiful view of the Florida coast from their window!

Neil Salkind and Elsa Rosenberg, my agents at Studio B, should also get a round of applause. They've successfully kept me in books, generic writing projects, blog projects, and technical articles for many years, and I want to thank them for their persistence and tenacity.

Finally, my parents and my family continue to support me, and without them I have no idea if my writing career would have ever taken off, what I'd be doing now, or if I could ever have enjoyed life as much as I do now--being able to do something I love--every day.
—Joli Ballew

Contents

Chapter 14
Maintain a Degunked Home 211

Appendix A
Checklists 221

Appendix B
Must—Have Stain Removers 225

Appendix C
What to Do With Items You No Longer Want or Need 231

Index 239

Introduction

You remember moving in to your current home, apartment, or condominium, right? It was a blank slate, just carpet, linoleum, walls, and you, and it was yours for the decorating. Remember how proud you were the first time you had guests over? The place was sparkling clean and neat as a pin. Everything was in its proper place too.

Because you've picked up this book, I'm guessing you've come along way from that one moment in time when everything was just so. Your house is now not-so-spar-kling clean and not-so-neat-and-organized. In fact, you're probably reading this book while sitting on the edge of your couch because there are newspapers and magazines strewn over the rest of it. Or perhaps you're in your office reading, while also successfully ignoring a stack of mail or paperwork that needs to be filed. Maybe you're outside in a lawn chair because the inside of the house is just too chaotic. Or maybe, just maybe, *you're not the problem at all*; your spouse or your kids are the ones that keep messing things up and you have no idea how to take control. You could be reading this book while sitting amid their mess, all the while building resentment toward each and every one of them. Those slobs and packratties are really starting to drive you crazy. How hard is it, really, to hit the laundry hamper with your dirty, smelly, clothes? Can't you just put the ketchup back in the refrigerator when you're done with it? Whatever the case, if it's you or them, or all of you or only a few, it's working your last nerve.

Once you're to this point, bad things start to happen too. You can't find anything to wear in your closets, although they're filled to the brim. It takes longer to get out the door in the morning because you can't find your keys and cell phone. You start to develop problems with family members who leave messes everywhere. You're mad. You may even become indifferent to both the mess and your family. And that's just in the morning.

At night, you can't find the food processor when you need to fix dinner, but you have ample access to a million other appliances you rarely use, and thus no free counter space. You have broken appliances and electronics, and finding the one that works the best (or works at all) takes time. You might not even have what you need, because you can never remember what you should have bought at the grocery store. You can never find the to-do list you scratched on the back of that unopened bill either.

It may even go from bad to worse. You pay bills late and get slapped with fees. You miss deadlines for DVD and game rentals. You run out of gas. You purchase items you already have in the pantry or refrigerator. Food spoils before you can eat it. You forget to pick up junior from soccer practice. And there's more that's only specific to your home like pet messes and kid gunk. It's difficult.

One way to deal with this clutter and mess is to move. (You can also adopt out your kids or divorce your spouse.) That's all a little drastic. At least when you move, though, you have to look at everything you own and pack it up, and generally you can overcome current problems while doing so. This is especially true if you were born with the *lazy gene*. Who wants to pack up that stuff and then unpack at your new place when you can just put it in the front yard for the trash man or give it to friends or family?

You don't need to move though. You don't need to disown family members. You shouldn't to lock yourself in a room and ignore it either. The problem isn't with your home or family necessarily, the problem is with something I call "gunk." Think of gunk as bits of stuff just lying around in all the wrong places. Gunk is disorder among your belongings, and it increases over time. If you're not careful, all of this increased gunk can create a fire hazard, bring in pests, or cause a rift between family members. Of course, it causes you to have to work harder to do what you need to do too.

To gain control you need a plan. You need to get rid of the gunk. In this book that's exactly what you'll learn. You'll learn how, when, why, and where to get rid of the stuff you no longer need or want, how to organize what's left, and how to keep it organized (degunked), once you have it under control.

Why You Need This Book

Without a plan to get and stay degunked, you're doomed to fail in the long term. If you don't take control, the chaos in your home will build, causing problems from every possible angle. I don't want that to happen.

Degunking Your Home uses a unique approach that can save you countless hours of valuable time, and a bundle of money. It will help you regain control of your home, and allow you to mend fences with family members. You'll learn everything you need to know to degunk from top to bottom, and from inside out.

Here are some of the unique features of this book:

- An easy-to-follow 12-setp degunking process that you can put to work immediately.

- Explanations, in everyday terms, of how to easily fix common problems that create gunk in your home.

- Information on how degunking can help you save money.

- Helpful "GunkBuster's Notebook" sidebars in every chapter to help you solve specific problems related to everyday and long-term clutter and gunk.

- Degunking maintenance tasks that you can perform daily, weekly, monthly, and yearly to keep your home in top form.

- Before and after pictures, and images of what not to do.

- Instructions on how to express clean so you can get chores done more quickly, and thus stay degunked.

- Advice on how to position tools such as wicker baskets, coat racks, cleaning supplies, whiteboards, calendars, laundry hampers, shelves, and various bins and baskets to encourage family members to play along in your degunking strategies.

- Know when and how to play hardball with family members who insist on being slobs or packratties, or who simply refuse to clean up their own messes.

How to Use This Book

Degunking Your Home is structured around the order of the degunking process that you should follow. The book starts off by explaining the importance of degunking and why homes require it. Each subsequent chapter describes an important degunking task, explained in plain English, with step-by-step guidance and instruction. The book ends with some hard-nosed ideas for dealing with the worst offenders, from gathering up their stuff and holding it "hostage," to refusing to do laundry, or to simply throwing out the misplaced items.

NOTE: *This book is designed around a 12-step program (outlined in Chapter 2) that I recommend you follow, starting with Chapter 3 and continuing through the end of the book. I highly recommend you apply the process to your home in a room-by-room and closet-by-closet fashion until you've applied the 12-step program to every part of your house. This will result in the most benefit from the time you spend degunking.*

Once you've completely degunked your home, you should then perform daily degunking procedures, weekly degunking procedures, and monthly degunking procedures to keep your home from getting gunked up all over again. This is a very important concept. Staying degunked requires revisiting this book often, and staying on top of each and every degunking task outlined here.

The Degunking Mindset

The more you learn about degunking your home, the more you'll realize that degunking is a mindset, not just the act of performing the tasks outlined here and staying on top of daily and weekly tasks. I view degunking as mostly psychology; degunking and staying degunked involves a disciplined approach to managing your home and family, as well as your possessions and belongings. If you follow the approach and advice given in this book, you'll save yourself a lot of aggravation down the road. I also believe that *Degunking Your Home* will make your time at home more enjoyable, give you more time for fun with family members, and make any work you do at home more efficient and productive. Getting and staying degunked can be fun; I promise! With a little care and attention to detail, you can turn your home into the ideal living space you've always dreamed of! Happy degunking!

Chapter 1

Why Is My Home All Gunked Up?

Degunking Checklist:

√ Discover what gunk is and why it accumulates.

√ Understand that closets, kitchens, and living areas are three places where gunk will always build up.

√ See that organizing problem areas and creating long-term storage areas can reduce the amount of gunk in your home.

√ Learn that a gunked-up house can really affect the relationships between the people who live there.

√ Understand that performing daily chores efficiently is a necessity to (and a learned skill for) maintaining a degunked home.

√ Understand that speed cleaning and being prepared for cleaning emergencies is a key to maintaining a degunked home.

√ Find out why you need a strategy for degunking your home.

√ Learn that there are lots of things that can be done weekly, monthly, and yearly to keep your home in tip-top shape all year-round.

Because you've picked up this book, chances are you're (at least a little) frustrated. Your home lacks organization, you have piles of stuff every where, your closets are a mess, and you find yourself spending more time looking for what you need than actually using it (e.g., the remote control for the television). You might have a hard time working in the kitchen for lack of counter space, spend an undo amount of time cleaning because the supplies you need are scattered all over, or have trouble finding what you need in the garage because you have to sift through the holiday decorations to get to the Weed Eater. Maybe you have a hard time finding what you want to wear in the morning because your closet is disorganized. I'm sure you can never find your "good scissors" when you need them, either; that's a given. Your gunked-up home might even be becoming a sore point with the people you live with or with your friends who are scared to come over to visit. You've probably seen those wacky people on reality TV shows who have homes that are a mess and you're afraid that you might end up like them. Don't panic just yet; everyone has some level of gunk, and you can rest assured that you're not alone.

Unfortunately, a gunked-up home isn't just unsightly, stressful, inefficient, and energy draining, it can also be dangerous. Expired foods or medications can cause harm to humans and pets. Moldy plates under your kids' beds, teetering boxes in the garage, hazardous cleaning supplies and chemicals, and even frayed or overloaded extension cords can be dangerous, too. And if you're a compulsive hoarder, don't forget that five-foot piles of books and newspapers can fall. Some gunk, especially newspapers and old food, attracts pests, such as fleas, roaches, and rodents.

All of this stuff is gunk, and no matter what amount you've accumulated, it all collects dust, creates cluttered areas, makes cleaning more difficult, makes it hard to live with others, and undermines your attempts at taking control. Don't worry, though; you *can* take control. You just have to learn how. In this book, you'll do just that.

What the Experts Know

Yes, there are people in this world who have immaculate homes. Their Tupperware is always stacked and they can always find a lid, they know what's in their junk drawers, and their house is always clean. They can have guests over any day of the week, and they throw dinner parties. They know 50 ways to use a Ziploc bag and can unload their dishwasher in under two minutes. Think June Cleaver or Martha Stewart. Sometimes you may want to classify these people as obsessive-compulsive or anal-retentive, though, perhaps because you feel there is no way any "normal" person could maintain such an organized home and life. But in reality, these people are quite normal; they've simply learned how to manage their home and possessions efficiently. They follow a system, and by doing just a little here and a little there, they make it look like it takes very little effort. The tricks they know are the tricks I want to teach you in this book. They are easy to follow and you won't need a lot of time. I'm a firm believer in the principle that a little bit goes a long way. In the long run, I'll actually show you how to save a lot of time by doing some important things on a regular basis. You'll save time because you won't keep wasting time looking for the car keys, trying to find some important tool in the garage, or trying to work in a kitchen that could be classified as a disaster area.

You may feel you do not have the time or energy to devote to getting here, though. Perhaps all you want out of this book is to be able to find a matching pair of socks in your sock drawer, learn how to make your spouse put their dirty laundry in the hamper instead of the floor, or organize a closet or two. If you put your mind to it, though, you can get much more than that out of this book. I'll show you a proven 12-step program for controlling clutter and taking control of your home that will work for something as small as a sock drawer, or something as large as your entire kitchen or garage. You don't have to take time off from work to do it or take any time away from your family. You just have to work through the steps, one at a time, and devote yourself and some time to the specific task at hand.

Besides not knowing if you have the time or energy to devote to degunking completely, you may also feel that you can ill afford to go out and buy all sorts of home organizing goodies that are supposedly a cure-all for clutter or new tools that allow you to clean your house faster. While fancy tools for organizing and cleaning can be helpful (and you'll learn when it's appropriate to use them), you can actually put to use many items you have already. For instance, while a rechargeable bathroom scrubber tool might make quick work of scrubbing the dirt out of the tub, the process of charging, using, cleaning, and then putting away the electric scrubber takes longer than if you just cleaned the tub with a sponge and some Comet. And while storing your garbage bags in a nice little $40 plastic organizer may seem like the right thing to do, it's faster if, when you take out the garbage and replace the old bag with a new one, you place two empty bags underneath the new one you put in. The next time you take out the garbage, there will be another one right there! Tricks like these are the ones that the experts know, and they are tricks that I'll show you in this book.

Understand How You Got So Gunked Up

Look around your house and you'll see the signs of gunk. Dirty dishes, spoiled food, plastic and paper bags, and old newspapers and magazines accumulate quickly because you don't have a daily strategy in place for controlling the daily clutter. Forgetting to take out the newspapers and the trash for a week can make a place unlivable. Forgetting to load or unload the dishwasher, do the laundry, or otherwise perform daily (and basic) cleaning tasks has the same effect.

It isn't just stuff that must be thrown away, put away, or cleaned daily, though. Closets are often filled with clothes that don't fit, clothes you don't wear, and shoes that have outgrown their usefulness, all of which makes getting ready in the morning or putting away clean clothes difficult and time consuming. And stacking all of those things you never use on the mantle, the coffee table, or countertops makes doing anything with or on those spaces almost impossible. Clutter like this will accumulate over time; that's inevitable. Therefore, you must devise a plan to control it.

Is There Something Wrong with Me?

Gunk and clutter are normal and are proof you are alive and well. It's easier to leave appliances you use on the kitchen countertop instead of putting them back under the counter where they belong. That's human nature. You'll out-grow your clothes and you'll wear out shoes, too. That's the way things are. Unfortunately, you'll often think you'll wear those clothes when you lose weight, or you'll want to keep the shoes for yard work. (FYI: You only need one pair of yard shoes, and if you actually do lose that weight, you're going shopping and you know it!) You'll take a shortcut or two when putting things away in a closet, and it'll get messy. And, on occasion, you'll leave stuff where you know it doesn't belong and fail to put it away later (or maybe never put it away).

How Can I Better Live with Others?

You might be struggling with your gunked-up home and lifestyle so much that it is really becoming an obstacle for how you share your house and live with others. Many people have different levels of "gunk tolerance," and this can lead to frustration around your home. For example, you might be a pack rat who saves everything that comes in the door, but your spouse is a neat freak who walks around the house with a polishing rag 24/7. Or you might be trying to keep your house in order but your spouse can't walk five extra steps to put dirty clothes in a hamper, and instead leaves them on the floor and insists on wearing clothes multiple times (leaving you with the problem of where those half-clean-half-dirty clothes should be kept). You might have a pet that sheds, and vacuuming every day just isn't going to work for you. You might have a teenager. Enough said. Keeping your house organized and clean is much harder under these circumstances and will require a plan and help from family members. The bottom line is that learning to deal with gunk isn't a solitary thing, especially if you have a family, kids, and/or pets. It takes a team effort—and one that requires a little planning and discussion with everyone involved.

Throughout this book, I'll try to provide tips so that you don't feel that you have to be a hero and do it all yourself. If you take the lone wolf approach, you'll likely get frustrated and throw in the towel at some point or become impossible to live with. The hardest thing about degunking is getting everyone to see eye to eye about what needs to be done, but with a little effort, you can do it.

What You Can Do to Take Control

To take control of your home and your life and all the clutter and gunk that surrounds it, you have to first understand how you got where you are today. Whatever the cause of your gunk, it likely started for one of four reasons:

√ You collect, buy, find, and acquire stuff regularly but never get rid of anything (throw away, give away, sell).

√ You don't have the time (or you think it takes too much effort) to put things away after you've used them or acquired them.

√ You claim that it's not your fault, it's your family's; they're all slobs or pack ratties, or you simply have too many family members.

√ You don't have the necessary space to organize what you have.

So, make a decision, and be honest, about what category you're in and let's go from there. And remember that you'll need to get everyone involved. If your kids are slobs, you'll have to work on them, too. You are the parent, after all. If your husband is afraid of the dirty clothes hamper, counseling may be in order. No matter what, everyone has a little of the pack-rattie thing, so the first thing you'll do, no matter what type of person you are, is throw away stuff you don't want, don't need, or can't use. From there, degunking will flow from one step to the next.

Working the Program

The 12-step program, outlined in Chapter 2, introduces you to the degunking process. You don't have to buy 20 books on organizing, 15 books on speed cleaning, and 30 books on creating organized spaces. It's all right here, in a simple easy-to-follow guide. By following the 12-step program introduced in this book, you'll have control in no time.

Here are the five key areas of the 12-step degunking program:

1. *Throwing Stuff Away*: Here you'll focus on getting rid of clothes that don't fit and things you don't use, don't need, and don't want. This can be the most difficult step, especially for those who have been collecting things for years. Knickknacks, old newspapers, stuffed animals, love letters, old sets of plates or silverware, extra coffee cups (where do all of those cups come from anyway?), clothes you've "grown out of but will certainly be able to wear when this new diet starts to work," and books you've read are the worst culprits. Old appliances and broken electronics are also gunk. At best, all of this stuff takes up room in closets and bookcases, attracts dust, and gets in the way of your being productive and uncluttered. At worst, they become fire hazards, dangerous stacks of gunk, or closet-hoggers. The first thing you'll learn, then, is how to throw stuff away, give it away, or sell it.

2. *Organizing Problem Areas*: Once you've gotten rid of everything you can part with *for now*, you'll learn how to organize what's left. While that's simple enough to say, it must be tackled one drawer, one cabinet, one closet, or one room at a time. Closets, for instance, attract gunk for multiple reasons, but mostly because they're an easy target for hiding and storing stuff and have doors that close, so you never have to look at the mess in there for very long. The kitchen and the family room are problem areas because these rooms are where you cook, eat, do homework, talk about the day, and relax at night. They're also where you keep DVDs, watch TV, and entertain guests. (Face it, guests and family members mostly stay in the kitchen, or wherever the food is.) The kitchen and living areas are where your keys, cell phone, pagers, PDA, hats, coats, shoes, purses, and other daily items fall. You can think of organizing these problem areas as an extension of organizing your life—if you can organize where you cook, eat, watch TV, do homework, complete projects, dress, and, well, *live* every day, you'll be taking a gigantic step toward organizing your home as well as your life.

3. *Creating Long-Term Storage Areas*: With living areas manageable, you'll focus on creating places to store things long term. Holiday decorations, bulk purchases, lawn equipment, fine china, books and magazines you *have* to keep, and sentimental memorabilia are just a few of things you might need to store. There will always be sports equipment, too: bicycles, skis, basketballs, soccer balls, baseball mitts, snowboards, and sleds. But wait! There's more! Kitty litter, dog food, fertilizer, paint, bulk food purchases, toilet paper, and things you simply have to box and store take up time and space, too. (Just wait until your oldest heads off to college or your elderly parent moves in.

You'll be storing stuff in boxes, take my word for it, so it's worth it now to create a space.) I'm also going to ask that you get rid of treadmills and stair steppers you don't use instead of trying to store them indefinitely.

4. *Cleaning Efficiently*: Once your house is organized and you don't have a lot of unnecessary "stuff" around, you'll focus on cleaning. You'll see that it'll be much easier minus the clutter. However, you won't clean if you can't find the supplies easily. And you won't clean if you have a lot of stuff to clean "around," which is why you spent so much time getting rid of stuff and organizing what's left. And it will also take you less time to clean if you know some basic tips and tricks for making it go faster. In the final steps involving cleaning, you'll learn how to speed-clean, and you'll learn what supplies are must-haves for emergencies. You'll also learn how to schedule daily tasks so that you can stay on top of the gunk you'll inevitably collect and never feel overwhelmed or get completely gunked up again.

5. *Maintaining a Degunked Home*: Finally, with your home in your control, you'll learn how to keep it that way. There are tasks you should schedule to perform every day and some to perform weekly and monthly. There are also yearly tasks, like having your air conditioner serviced or your fireplace swept. And it isn't a crime to ask family members to help and give even the youngest daily tasks. In the end, I'll show you some tricks for *sharing the wealth* with your family when it comes to chores.

The point of these steps is this: You must develop a plan to take control of your gunk, get rid of clutter and dirt, and organize what's left. Once that's done, you *must* have a strategy for managing clutter and gunk every day and for performing everyday chores. You can't just throw away some stuff, box up the rest, throw it in the garage, and promise yourself you'll keep it that way. Gunk has a way of sneaking back into your life. By working through our proven 12-step program, you can get control and keep control.

Ready for Degunking?

The most difficult part of getting your home back to where it should be involves dedicating a little time and getting everyone in the household involved. As you move forward through this book, remember that it isn't going to be an overnight fix. In fact, don't assign any timeline to it at all. Just work through the steps, chapter by chapter, first getting rid of stuff you don't need, then organizing what you want to keep, and then completing a strategy for managing and maintaining problem areas and creating long-term storage areas. Performing small steps, even performing all of the previous tasks on a single closet, will keep you motivated by your successes and keep you focused on getting and staying degunked. It might take you a full Saturday to clean your first closet. It may take another day to build additional shelves or organize your shoes. That's okay; you'll get better at it with practice. Once your home is degunked, cleaning will be easier, too. There won't be so many obstacles to clean around, there won't be so much to dust, there won't be so many things to put away each day, and you'll be able to find your cleaning supplies quickly. The object is to take each step and each chapter one at a time. As long as you keep making progress, you're good to go.

Chapter 2

Learn the Degunking 12–Step Program

Degunking Checklist:

√ Understand that the best degunking results can be obtained by performing program tasks in a specific order.

√ Know you can obtain results even with limited time or limited willpower.

√ See why getting rid of things you don't need is the first step to degunking your home.

√ Understand that the kitchen and family rooms are two places that will always attract gunk.

√ Know that your family must be involved in degunking efforts; without their assistance, the program will not work as well as it should.

√ Learn the 12-step program for degunking your home.

√ Understand that a long-term strategy must be put in place to maintain your degunked home.

W e could have called this chapter "Degunking: The 12-Step Program to Success" because our ultimate goal is to introduce you to our proven 12-step program, which can really help you get control of your home, your possessions, and even a little part of your life. Before we go there, though, we need to focus on the strategy behind the degunking process. This chapter is designed to help you get into the degunking mindset. Once you understand the psychology of degunking, we'll be able to move into the basic techniques.

After introducing the psychology here, in the chapters that follow, I'll show you, step-by-step, how to roll up your sleeves and complete the 12 essential steps of the degunking program. The best part is that even if you have limited time, limited energy, limited willpower, or even a short attention span, any step you perform or any effort you make, no matter how large or small, will go a long way toward helping you make your home more enjoyable and more livable (and less cluttered).

The Strategy behind Degunking

The strategy behind degunking is to rid your home of unnecessary "stuff," organize what you want to keep, and then create a long-term strategy for keeping your home in order. The last part, keeping your home in order, also includes applying tricks for cleaning your home and performing daily tasks quickly; storing things in optimal places so they can remain organized, neat, and easy to get to; and creating areas that can be gunked up and degunked daily. (There will always be gunk!)

This strategy behind degunking is based on how your home is used (and abused) on a daily basis:

√ Newspapers, magazines, school papers, mail, coupons, insurance papers, health forms, user guides, bills, owner manuals, bank statements, warranties, tax records, contracts, loan papers, and similar documents are a part of life and often become gunk on the dining room or kitchen table.

√ Clothing, shoes, belts, scarves, ties, sweaters, coats, and hats get old, go out of style, get stained, and get torn, or you simply don't like them anymore, but we all have problems getting rid of these items when we should.

√ Partaking of breakfast, lunch, coffee, condiments, sodas, and whatever is for dinner is an everyday, and sometimes every hour, activity for a family. Trash, leftovers, failure to pick up after oneself, and the related dish-mess are daily gunk-makers.

√ Broken or unnecessary appliances and electronic equipment are space hogs; blenders, food processors, crock pots, fondue pots, woks, and other minimally used appliances take up limited counter space, usually because people do not put them away after using them.

√   Keys, cell phones, jackets or coats, PDAs, briefcases, purses, pens or pencils, organizers, homework, notebooks, and backpacks are items your family members take out of and bring into the house every day. These items usually do not have a designated place and end up on counters, on the floor, on a dining room table, or on the fireplace mantel, all creating gunk.

√   Dirty towels, clothes, sheets, and dishes are daily gunk, as are pet hair and dust and stuff that accumulates on countertops. This type of gunk is often not dealt with in a regulated manner. By the time you get around to cleaning, the task is overwhelming.

The idea is simple: Because you and your family live in and use your home on a daily basis, the gunk that accumulates will build on a daily basis. As you'll learn in this book, though, you can take control with a little bit of effort. You only need a program and a plan for success.

Questions to Ask Yourself

To further make the point about the psychology of degunking, and to sell you even more on the degunking mindset, ask yourself the following questions, keeping mind how many times you answer yes:

√   Will it be difficult to locate my keys, cell phone, medications, kids, spouse, and coat if there's an emergency?

√   Do I often have trouble finding what I want to wear or look at a full closet and claim there's nothing to wear?

√   Do I cook less because the task is no longer pleasurable; because I can't find the proper utensils, pots, pans, spices, appliances, or food items; or because there isn't enough counter space?

√   Can I see mold in the bathrooms or in other rooms of the house?

√   Has it been longer than a week since I've vacuumed, swept, cleaned the bathrooms, loaded or emptied the dishwasher, or taken out the newspapers?

√   Do I have magazines that are more than three months old?

√   Do I have paperwork that is unfiled or unanswered, or have I been late paying a bill recently? Have I failed to return a movie on time or missed a similar deadline? In other words, are my disorganized piles of gunk costing me money?

√   Have I ever gone to the store, only to realize I had the items I needed in the back of the freezer, refrigerator, or pantry?

√   Do I ever purchase things I already have because I want a "newer" model and then fail to get rid of the older one?

√ Have I relegated a certain room for junk, such as an office, garage, attic, or basement, but I rarely go in there?

√ Do I pay for a storage building?

√ Do I keep "perfectly good items" that I'll never use again in the garage or attic, such as old VCRs, computers, televisions, game systems, mowers, edgers, Weed Eaters, blenders, rusty circular saws, and furniture?

√ Do I have duplicate shovels, hammers, screwdrivers, drills, saws, or mowers?

√ Is it hard to find the makeup I want, the jewelry I want, and the accessories I want quickly?

√ Do I cringe when I have to go into my kids' rooms, the linen closet, or the hall closet for fear of what I might find?

√ Am I constantly picking up after my kids or my spouse and feeling resentful about it?

√ Do I have various household cleaners under the kitchen sink, in the bathroom, in a storage closet, in the garage, and in the yard?

√ Do I have dishes, silverware, china, fancy tablecloths, linens, bedsheets, comforters, blankets, pillows, place mats, shoes, purses, pet toys, books, knickknacks, figurines, electrical equipment, yard supplies, over-the-counter medications, magazine subscriptions, wine openers, paper clips, catalogs, golf clubs, sports equipment, food no one will ever eat, photos, or paper products that never (and will never) get used?

√ Do I keep stuff because someday "it may be worth something" or because I might need it?

√ Do I save items that I don't use or even look at because "someday" my children, grandchildren, or others may want them?

√ Does my family have pairs of shoes that they have outgrown, used once because they don't feel good, or are worn out?

√ Do I insist on hanging on to items that are out of style or uncomfortable just because they were "expensive" and I don't want to lose my investment?

√ Do I have pests, such as roaches, fleas, or mice?

If you had to answer yes to very many of these questions, you should not only degunk for your own sake (and sanity), but also for your family's. By taking control, you can improve the relationship you have with them, remove existing barriers to decluttering your home, and improve your family's safety and mental health.

A Little Psychology behind Gunk

I'm no psychologist, but I've read quite a few books on the psychology of acquiring things and have formed some opinions of why we let ourselves get as cluttered as we do. For the most part, being cluttered and disorganized isn't a medical problem, and it isn't genetic. We're not predisposed to collect stuff as far as I can tell, and the majority of us don't need medication or a therapist to help us get our home out from under the gunk heap. However, this isn't to say that we don't have problems when it comes to clutter either. Our clutter is often an extension of who we are, perhaps defining us as successful because we have more "things," or openly offering up our hobbies or interests to anyone who visits our home.

Unfortunately, with the accumulation of stuff almost always comes the inability to deal with it all effectively, which in turn can produce feelings of depression, guilt, failure, or create conflict with family members. Gunk may also prevent you from having guests over or otherwise encourage you to become isolated. Once covered in clutter, you may feel overwhelmed, too, a sensation that may lead you to become a pack rat or a slob or simply give up completely. These can be real problems.

Procrastination as a Cause

It is my opinion that clutter and a gunked-up home is the direct result of being a procrastinator and/or being unable to make vital decisions quickly. When the top to the coffeepot melts in the dishwasher and you purchase a new coffee machine the same day (because you can't find the user guide to order a new one), do you throw away the old coffeepot? If not, the old one, the one that is in perfect working order except for the top, is still taking up space in your home. You've procrastinated about getting rid of it.

While you may say you have chosen not to make a decision about the old coffeepot, or that you have put off making that decision, in reality you have. You have firmly decided that this coffeepot is in fine working order, minus the top, and you're going to keep it. Maybe you plan to give it to a charity, minus the top, or to your kids, minus the top, or maybe you plan to reuse a part from it later (as if you'd be able to repair a coffeepot anyway).

It's this kind of non-decision you have to watch out for. You also have to watch out for the dreaded "I'll do it later" statement. Don't put off cleaning up that spill or it could leave a stain. At the very least, it'll be harder to clean up later. And don't put off throwing away something for fear you may need it later. Chances are you won't.

Procrastination is often a problem of perfectionists, too. They either cannot make a decision for fear of making the wrong one, or get so wrapped up in the small details of cleaning the medicine cabinet that they don't notice that the rest of the house is a disaster. Sometimes the most exacting people are the biggest slobs. Sometimes, it's just hard to stay focused, and that's what some of the chapters in this book will address.

Whatever kind of person you are, it's important as you work through this book to recognize that decisions must be made quickly when it comes to degunking, especially when degunking has to do with getting rid of things before they become clutter or cleaning up something before it causes permanent damage. If you put off making a decision or taking action, chances are good the thing you're hesitating about will become gunk or cause permanent problems. It's okay to get rid of that perfectly good coffeemaker (the one that doesn't have a top), and it's okay to expect your children to clean up the Kool-Aid they just spilled. And, it's okay to insist that your spouse take a look at that leak in the bathroom; putting it off could cause a water disaster.

Pack Rats as a Cause

If you've ever kept something because you think you might need it someday, because it holds sentimental value, or because you can't find anything like it anymore, you might have some pack-rattie tendencies. You'll want to get over that before it gets over you! Sure, you might be able to use that spare tire that you kept from your last car someday, but chances are you won't. And yes, that ashtray you bought from the French Quarter in New Orleans is nice with the alligator on it and all, but you don't smoke. Oh, and sure, you can't find that perfume in stores anymore, but did you know that perfume goes sour after a couple of years? You do now.

Living with the Opposite Type

Here's a little more psychology. If you are a pack rattie (or a slob) and you live with a totally neat person, you'll have your own share of unique problems. For one, you are likely totally oblivious of the work they do keeping the house in tip-top shape, which will put a strain on your relationship. You may also be completely unaware of how much it bothers your neatnik when you leave your clothes on the floor or pile all of your stuff on the kitchen counter when you come home. They probably don't like your teapot or tool collection, either. And I'd venture to guess that you have no idea just how important it is to them that the house be neat and organized.

If you're the neatnik and your spouse is the slob or pack rattie, you may be totally oblivious that all of that nagging you do really does bother them. The nagging bothers them almost as much as it bothers them when you take the newspaper to the recycle bin before they've finished reading it, or when you vacuum while they're trying to relax and make them pick up their feet. And this pales in comparison to cleaning up the table while they're still eating or putting something in the washing machine that could have been worn again.

The idea is this: unless you talk about it openly with your spouse or other family members, this underlying problem may escalate. The slob may leave their stuff everywhere out of spite, or the neatnik may become quiet, cold, and distant because they are resentful of the spouse's behavior and lack of help. As you work through this book, try to keep your family members in mind, and try to see through their eyes, and try to talk openly about what you plan to do before you do it.

So, let's continue by examining the 12-step program. I'll introduce each step with a paragraph or two, and in the next chapter, we'll move on to the applying the first step of the program.

The Proven 12-Step Program

As mentioned earlier, the steps outlined in the 12-step program should be performed in order. "In order" can mean several things, though. For instance, the first few steps in the 12-step program help you decide what gunk is; what to throw away, give away, recycle, or sell; and what to do with what you want to keep. You can perform these steps on a single drawer, on every closet, or even on every room before moving forward. When you finish, you can then move ahead to the next area or to the next step. This may mean you perform all 12 steps on a single closet before doing anything else, or it may mean you perform the first few steps on your entire house before moving up the 12-step ladder. You'll have to decide what option is right for you after reading through the steps.

The steps I'll introduce are listed here:

1. Understand what gunk is and why it builds up.
2. Throw away what you can first.
3. Apply the four box theory to every room and closet.
4. Put away, store, give away or sell, and (continue to) throw out or recycle collected items and clutter.
5. Focus in on problem areas such as closets and kitchens, including pantries and the fridge.
6. Organize bedrooms, bathrooms, offices, family rooms, and utility rooms.
7. Create and manage long-term storage areas.

8. Stay organized (and clutter free) by managing and completing daily tasks.

9. Organize cleaning tasks for more efficient cleaning sessions.

10. Learn how to speed-clean.

11. Be prepared for cleaning emergencies.

12. Maintain your organized home.

Understand What Gunk Is and Why It Builds Up

This is the first step, and I think I've explained clearly what gunk is and why it builds up, so I won't add much here. In a nutshell, though, gunk collects because of the things you do every day, such as make coffee, read the newspaper, get the mail, eat, cook, and shower. Every day, each member of your family brings in something, too. It could be homework, a toy, an electronic device, an appliance, or simply the usual: keys, cell phones, purses, backpacks, and iPods. Each family member produces their own dust, share of dirty clothes, and dirty dishes. Your pets create gunk as well, so we can't leave them out. Gunk is acquired on a daily basis.

Throw Away What You Can First

This is the second, and by far the most important, step. It should be done before any of the other steps, whether you apply the 12-step program to your junk drawer or your entire garage. This is not recycling, this is not moving stuff from one place to another, this is not deciding you might need it later; this is the simple act of putting a large cardboard box by the door of a room (or single drawer), going through the room, and throwing as much stuff away as you can bear. You'll learn to apply this step on a daily basis, too. You'll learn to stand by the trash can when you go through your mail, or throw away that old, broken blender when you get a new one. Throwing away the "obvious" garbage first (old newspapers, magazines, junk mail, expired food, and so on) allows you to make decisions next about what is really important. It also gives you a great feeling to see what you have accomplished so quickly.

Apply the Four Box Theory to Every Room and Closet

Applying the four box theory is what you do after you've thrown away what you can and is the fourth step. In Chapter 4, you'll tackle each room or closet with four boxes:

√ Give Away, Recycle, or Sell

√ Move

√   Store Long Term

√   Throw Away

With the items that don't belong in the closet or room in a box, you can then go through each box, putting things where they belong. This will help you understand what things are useful but no longer needed, what things are stored improperly, what things should be in a storage area, and what things you still need to throw away that you missed the first time around. (There are tricks to putting things away, too; I'll talk about that throughout the book.)

Put Away, Store, Give Away or Sell

Unfortunately, this step is the hardest, and it's also covered in Chapter 4, as well as Appendix C. For some reason, it's pretty easy for people to apply the four box theory and put things in boxes once they've set their mind to it, but it's really difficult to do anything with the boxes once they're done. No, you're not supposed to stack these boxes in the garage or in a corner of the closet. You're supposed do something with them.

In Chapter 4 and Appendix C, you'll learn that you should make giving, recycling, or selling items in boxes a top priority so they themselves do not become gunk. Any items that should be stored somewhere else, well, go ahead and put them where they're supposed to go. (Don't do this until the end of your four box process or you may get distracted in other rooms.) If you're tired and want to quit for the day, take the items to throw away to the trash bin, put the items to donate in your car, and leave the ones to put somewhere else in the hallway. Promise yourself you'll get to those tomorrow.

TIP: It may be tempting to start on another room or drawer when you get the momentum going, but **do not do this** until your first area is completed or the entire house will become a disaster area, defeating the whole purpose

---

Focus in on Problem Areas

After you've thrown away what you can and removed items from your drawers, closets, garage, attic, or entire home—or at least from the areas that you deem worthy—you can now focus on problem areas. Closets and kitchens are the worst. In Chapters 5 and 6, you'll learn how to get control of these problem areas, including how to organize your closets so they won't get gunked up again and how to create a kitchen space that works for you and your family.

Everyone's needs are different, and some kitchens are not only a place to cook, but a place to eat, do homework, entertain guests, and play games. You'll explore those possibilities when you get to these chapters.

Organize Bedrooms, Bathrooms, Offices, Family Rooms, and Utility Rooms

In Chapters 7 and 8, I'll guide you through organizing other areas of your home. For the most part, what you'll do here is move things around so you have better access to the things you need, and you'll organize the parts of these rooms that are driving you crazy. As with the other steps, this should be done only after completing the steps prior to it. There's really no point in organizing your bedroom closet if you've yet to clean it out and get rid of things that don't fit or you'll never wear. There's no need to organize your office if you've yet to go in there with a box and fill it with stuff you need to throw away or file.

In these chapters, you'll also learn how to increase available space by building shelves, bookcases, or magazine racks and how to make the most out of the space you have, such as under the bed and in the tops of closets. You'll learn how to keep these areas degunked, too, by creating "Move" boxes; creating places for remote controls, newspapers, and magazines; and labeling specific items in your home.

Create and Manage Long-Term Storage Areas

Creating effective long-term storage areas is another incredibly important task. You need a place to store bulk items, tools, holiday decorations, out-of-season clothes, sentimental items, fertilizer and yard items, and sports equipment. Long-term storage areas aren't just sheds and outbuildings, though, and it isn't always your garage. Long-term storage can be created in utility rooms, bedrooms, attics, or even closets. You'll learn about long-term storage in Chapter 9.

You also should know how to increase the capacity of a small room, such as a dorm, or studio apartment. You can increase the space by utilizing long-term storage options, such as employing stackable bins, adding bookcases, installing extra cabinets, or purchasing beds with drawers underneath.

TIP: As mentioned, performing these steps in order is important, though. You would not want to organize your long-term storage area before deciding what things in your home need to be stored long term.

Stay Organized (and Clutter Free) by Managing and Completing Daily Tasks

The things you do every day create the greatest gunk magnets. Where are you, your spouse, and your two teenage boys going to keep your keys and cell phones? Where are you going to leave the newspaper all day, every day, until everyone has read it? And who is going to perform these additional daily tasks, and how and when:

√   Load and empty the dishwasher

√   Take out the trash

√   Take out the newspapers or recyclables

√   Dust

√   Gather, wash, dry, fold, and put away laundry

√   Clean up after the pets, including vacuuming up pet hair

√   Run errands

√   Put away stuff that accumulates

In Chapter 10, you'll learn how to streamline these tasks so they get done. This will include requiring family members to participate, creating a checklist and schedule for daily tasks, restructuring your morning routine, and learning some tricks for performing these tasks faster. Just because a task has to be done each day doesn't mean you have to do it yourself or spend unnecessary time on it.

Organize Cleaning Tasks for More Efficient Cleaning Sessions

In Chapter 11, you'll learn how to clean quickly and successfully. Often, you sabotage your own cleaning sessions without even knowing you're doing it. If the supplies you need aren't easily accessible, if you don't keep a to-do list, and if you don't arm yourself with tools that make cleaning easier, you're making your cleaning sessions unproductive. In addition, you'll learn that tools that are supposed to make life easier often don't. Those high-tech, rechargeable, bathroom cleaning tools are more work than they're worth. And why purchase a product that is supposed to scrub your tub with scrubbing bubbles if you still have to get out the Ajax to get rid of the bathtub ring?

Learn How to Speed-Clean

Speed-cleaning is the wave of the future. In Chapter 12, I'll show you what I know and teach you how to clean your house in half the time it takes you now. This will include some psychology, such as staying focused and only making one pass at a room, but it will also include technology, such as having the right supplies and carrying them with you. Finally I'll answer the age-old question, Should I dust first or vacuum first?

TIP: Kids and spouses can be quite a help with speed-cleaning chores. You'll learn some tricks for them in Chapter 12, too.

Be Prepared for Cleaning Emergencies

Vomit. Pee. Hair balls. Blood. Mustard. Red Kool-Aid. These words send shivers up the spine of anyone in charge of removing these types of stains for their household. In Chapter 13, you'll learn the tricks for removing such stains and what to do about other cleaning emergencies, such as unexpected company, a busted water heater, or a red wine spill during a dinner party. Being prepared for these emergencies is an important part of degunking because a stain that sits for a while usually becomes a stain that's there forever.

Maintain Your Organized Home

The last step in the 12-step program is maintaining your degunked, clean, and organized home. The following tips and topics are included:

√   Keeping your family involved

√   Creating working clutter areas

√   Performing daily tasks every day

√   Sharing the wealth of the chores with family members

√   Creating and following a cleaning, organizing, and task schedule

√   Throwing stuff away daily

√   Knowing what tasks to perform when (Appendix A)

√   Knowing when to call the experts (see Appendix A)

Decide Where You Should Start

Everyone is different and everyone will have a different measure of success with our 12-step program. Look at Table 2-1 to help you identify the area in which you are best suited to start the program for optimal success.

Table 2-1   Decide where to start based on your personality and needs

Personality, trait, or specific problem area	Where you should start	What areas, chapters, and steps to focus on first
You classify yourself as a "hoarder," or you think your condition is a medical one. You find that even the thought of throwing anything away causes extreme anxiety, your home is a fire or health hazard, you are so afraid of people seeing your home that you have become isolated.	Consider seeking outside help. This could be a friend, family member, or perhaps a therapist. There are organizations like Clutterers Anonymous (clutterersanonymous.net) and community resources that will help you get control. Understand that you are not a bad person; you may simply need some extra support and help. Do your best to give things you don't need or want to a charity or to family or friends.	Concentrate solely on Chapters 3 and 4.
You keep things because they may be of value someday.	Using the Internet, research what you have, and see if there's any fact behind your beliefs. If things are of value, consider storing them in a storage unit or temperature-controlled environment to preserve them. *If these items are not valuable enough to store properly, they are probably not valuable enough to keep.*	Concentrate on Chapters 3 and 4 when working in the problem areas. Continue with the 12-step program in other areas of the home.
You keep things because you don't know what they are or what they go to or you think you can use their parts to repair something someday.	Try to identify the items you're keeping. If you can't recall what a key is for, throw it away. If you no longer own the vacuum cleaner that you still have the attachments for, throw them away. If you don't know what a part goes to, throw it away. New things come with their own new parts.	Concentrate on Chapter 3 in the problem areas and throw away anything you can't identify or anything that belongs to something you no longer own. Work through the other steps throughout the home.

(continued)

Table 2-1   Decide where to start based on your personality and needs *(continued)*

Personality, trait, or specific problem area	Where you should start	What areas, chapters, and steps to focus on first
You have a spouse with one of the previous conditions.	Warn the family member that you will be degunking the home. Give that family member one week to gather up the things they want to keep. Tell them these things must be put away and out of sight, in an area of the house designated just for them. Make sure the family member has a place to keep their stuff. Degunking with a family is a compromise, not a takeover.	Work through the entire book in each area of your home, alone or with a friend. Do not work through any steps with the spouse present. Box up anything you think your spouse might have missed, but get rid of the rest. If they ask for an item, tell them where it is and why you put it in a box. Try to keep the item boxed for as long as possible, and then throw away the box when appropriate (if it hasn't been used or looked at for a year, it can probably be thrown out).
Your kids are messy and you can't get them to help with degunking.	First, teach them the four box method and make it fun. Play music, and hold degunking "speed" contests. Be sure that children can store their things in place where they are easy to reach and use. If this tactic doesn't work, warn children that a new rule will go into place in one week. *Put it away or lose it.* During scheduled cleaning sessions, box up anything left out where it should not belong, and leave it in that box for a month. Make sure the kids are aware of these sessions, whether they occur each night at bedtime, or every Saturday.	Work through steps 1 through 12 at your own pace and with the help of your family. Reward kids for performing tasks as required.

(continued)

Table 2-1   Decide where to start based on your personality and needs *(continued)*

Personality, trait, or specific problem area	Where you should start	What areas, chapters, and steps to focus on
You have a short attention span and have problems staying on task.	Make each task short. For instance, degunk a drawer, then a cabinet, then one side of a closet. Make sure you can finish any task before your attention span has lagged. Remember, you have to do something with the things you'll get rid of, too, so allow time for that. It's okay if you move slowly, as long as you're moving forward.	Work through the 12-step program but focus on one area at a time. Degunk an entire closet using all 12 steps before starting on any other room in the house.
Your entire house is a disaster area and you're ready to start tossing stuff out.	If you're fed up, get a large trash bag and a few large cardboard boxes. Work through every room, throwing anything and everything in there you don't use, don't need, and don't want. Then, throw it or give it away immediately.	For every room in the house, work though Chapters 3 and 4 first. Get everything out of the house you don't want. Then, continue with the 12-step program in each area as desired.
You have a few problem areas that are driving you crazy, such as a closet or kitchen, but for the most part, the rest of the house is okay.	Write down what the problem areas are, in order of their frustration level. Start with the one that's driving you the craziest.	After applying the techniques in Chapters 3 and 4, look for the chapter and section that addresses your particular problem area. Follow the guidelines there. Once problem areas are clear, continue by creating long-term storage areas as detailed in Chapter 9.
You have a week off from work and are eager to degunk your home.	Start with the four box theory and apply it to every room, closet, and drawer, one project at a time, until each one is completed. Deal with the boxes immediately.	Focus on Chapters 3 and 4, and apply those techniques to the entire house. Continue with the degunking process from there.

Summing Up

Degunking isn't just rolling up your sleeves and getting to work; there's a lot of psychology involved. We become attached to our stuff as if it was an extension of ourselves, and it is often hard to get rid of things. Sometimes, though, there's so much gunk it's hard to know where to start. That's why I devoted an entire chapter to learning about the 12-step program.

In a nutshell, you'll get rid of stuff you don't need, organize what you want to keep, create long-term storage areas, and learn some tips and tricks for cleaning your home quickly and keeping it organized with minimal effort.

Chapter 3

Throwing Stuff Away You Don't Really Need

Degunking Checklist:

√ Discover why throwing stuff away is the first, and most important, step to degunking.

√ Adhere to the one-year rule for keeping things.

√ Learn how to live with a pack rat.

√ Perform the most important step: throwing stuff away.

The first step to gaining control over your house, and ultimately your life, is to get rid of all of the junk you've accumulated that you really don't need. Specifically, in this chapter, it's about taking out the trash. Once you get going, you'll to be amazed at how much trash you have and how much you can throw away. So get ready to fill up some trash bags. This isn't going to be a long chapter by any means, although it certainly may be the toughest one to get through.

Why Taking out the Trash Is So Important

It's a given that you take out the trash a couple of times a week, but I'll bet the trash you take out comes from an actual trash *can*—usually situated in a kitchen or office, a bathroom or bedroom—and it's gotten full. This chapter is not about that kind of trash; it's about a more concealed type. The trash you're going to collect while working through this chapter will be inside desk drawers, in mail piles, in medicine cabinets, under sinks, and in similar places throughout your home.

Taking out this kind of trash is the first and most important step because in many cases, this kind of trash is the gunk that started you on the clutter path in the first place. It's probably also what causes half of the clutter in your home now, and what causes most of your current headaches. Failing to deal with the waste you collect, including broken appliances, junk mail, cleaners with only a drop or two left, plastic butter tubs you've saved, catalogs, and sentimental knick-knacks, is one of the main reasons your home is disorganized and hard to manage.

Here's what you can do by simply getting rid of the trash:

√ Overcome chronic disorganization by creating new, usable spaces where there once was clutter.

√ Live with less "stuff," which requires dusting, putting away, moving, storing, working around, or otherwise managing daily.

√ Save money and time by not purchasing duplicates of things you can't find.

√ Save money by not allowing food to spoil.

√ Save time by not having to look for everyday, every month, or seasonal items when you need them.

√ Downsize required cleaning and organizational chores, saving time and stress.

√ Make your home safer by getting rid of expired drugs, unsafe cleansers, and precariously stacked clutter and having keys, purses and wallets, medication, and cell phones accessible in an emergency.

√   Discourage rodents, roaches, ants, and moths from coming into your home.

√   Encourage yourself and your family to continue to keep the home clean and organized.

Adhere to the One-Year Rule

If you haven't used it in a year, seriously consider throwing it away. That's the rule for today, but for now, I'm talking only about trash. I'm not talking about things that work that can be donated to charity, given to family members, or sold. This rule, as it stands here, *does not* have to do with skis, basketballs, blenders, or juice makers, or anything else that is functional, such as good clothing or shoes. All you want to deal with in this chapter are the trash and things that don't work. For instance, junk mail is trash, you can't use the Tupperware that has no matching lid (unless you plan to use it later to organize a junk drawer, to store keys by the door, for items in a medicine cabinet, for make up in a bathroom, or for small toys in your kids rooms), and you can't use the power supply from the digital camera you lost two years ago. That's the trash I'm talking about.

Table 3-1 lists a few things you may have had cluttering up your home for a year or more, all of which you can get rid of. (Keep in mind that you may find the items listed in multiple rooms.)

Table 3-1   Items to Look For and Throw Away

Room	Dangerous	Broken	Unusable	Old-Fashioned Trash
Kitchen	Expired foods; cleaning supplies under the sink; bacteria-laden sponges; cracked drinking glasses	Broken appliances, chipped dishware; working appliances with missing parts	Plastic containers with no lids; stained napkins and kitchen towels; stained coffee mugs or plastic ware	Expired coupons and batteries; junk mail; newspapers; old homework; broken or stained utensils, pots, pans, or cookware
Living or Family Room	Spills; newspapers on the floor; anything that could be tripped over and cause a fall	Dead plants, broken remote controls; broken furniture	Toys that pets or kids no longer play with; old TV guides; remote controls to equipment no longer owned	Newspapers; catalogs; junk mail; papers

(continued)

Table 3-1   Items to Look For and Throw Away *(continued)*

Room	Dangerous	Broken	Unusable	Old-Fashioned Trash
Pantry or Utility Room	Expired foods; easy-to-reach poisons; cleaning supplies	Irons; ironing board; stored appliances	Cleaning supplies you'll never use; coffee filters that don't fit the coffeemaker; opened, stale food products	Empty or nearly empty bottles of cleansers; too many saved grocery bags or cleaning rags; expired telephone books
Dining Room	Piles of bills, correspondence, and movie rentals; cardboard boxes; anything that can be tripped over; moldy food from last week's dinner; ants, roaches, mice, rodents	Furniture; knickknacks; window blinds; dishes; stained or broken dining room chairs you've replaced	Duplicate wine or bottle openers; old homework papers and report cards; used plastic or paper products	Junk mail; dead plants, including centerpieces; empty cardboard boxes; wine corks
Bathrooms	Expired medications, lotions, and creams in the medicine cabinet; expired hair color products; moldy bath mats; mold	Lipstick and other makeup; costume jewelry; electric toothbrushes and their brush heads; curling irons; hair dryers	Makeup and perfumes older than two years old; ragged toothbrushes; toothpaste with one squeeze left	Soap slivers; magazines and catalogs; empty toilet paper rolls; torn and ragged towels and washcloths
Closets	Dry cleaner's plastic bags; piles of clothes and other items that could topple; vacuum cleaner attachments or anything else that could be tripped on	Loose clothes rods; lightbulbs or lighting appliances; mechanical tie racks	Socks with no match; clothes with holes, tears, or stains; bed linens in triplicate; linens that don't fit any bed	Dry cleaning tags and bags; paper and notes; shoes with no match; stuffed animals; sentimental knickknacks
Junk Drawers	X-Acto knives; sharp pens, pencils, and sewing needles; medications; rusty screwdrivers, nuts, bolts, and nails; leaky batteries	Eyeglasses; sewing kits with no needles; tools; and about half of the rest of the stuff in the drawer	Keys that don't go to anything; parts of old appliances; old batteries; old cell phone chargers	Instructions for things you no longer own; recipes; to-do lists; catalogs; grocery lists; receipts

(continued)

Table 3-1   Items to Look For and Throw Away (continued)

Room	Dangerous	Broken	Unusable	Old-Fashioned Trash
Garage	Chemicals; piles of boxes that could topple; sharp objects; oil and gasoline; open containers; old oils, paints, and poisons	Mowers and other lawn equipment; garden tools; stored appliances and electronics; sports equipment such as bicycles and motorbikes	Cardboard boxes; line for a Weed Eater you no longer own; VCRs, computer monitors, and other electronics that have been replaced with newer models; old oils, paints, and poisons	Old newspapers; catalogs; cardboard boxes; garden shoes, rusty and broken tools, flat tennis balls; pieces of rope, cord, or twine; broken appliances and electronic equipment; actual trash in trash bags; old pet supplies including doghouses and cat boxes; a broken hammock; used saw blades; dried-up paint; rusty nails, screws, brads, bolts, and dried-up wood glue; rugs; bath mats

So get out the trash bags, the big ones, grab yourself a couple of cardboard boxes for the bulky stuff, and move on to the next section.

Make a Move: Throw It Away

As mentioned earlier, this is a short chapter, and that's because it's up to you to take it from here. Get your trash bags and start wherever you feel the most comfortable. If you want to start with a junk drawer, start with the messiest one. Take everything out of the drawer and put it on the counter, go through each item, and throw away what you deem trash but keep what you think you need. Once you've taken out the trash, you can leave everything on the counter and move on to Chapter 4, complete the organizational tasks and return here, or throw everything back in the drawer.

What I want you to do here is to ultimately go through your entire house, inch by inch, drawer by drawer, closet by closet, and room by room, and throw away as much as you possibly can. If you can tackle only a drawer at a time, that's just fine, though. Just make some kind of move. Whatever you decide, whether it's throwing away what's in a single drawer or working through your entire house, you'll make progress. And don't worry: We'll deal with all the things you don't consider trash in the next few chapters.

If you're starting to feel stressed, that's normal. To lighten the mood, I'll include some fun tips to help you through the process and to help you distinguish trash from the real thing.

TIP: If you think you'll find so much trash that you'll need to put it out on the curb for bulk pickup, plan your cleanup time based on the day bulk pickup comes by your house.

You Know It's Trash If

You know the item you're holding in your hand is trash if

√ It's making you break out in a rash or the smell is making you want to puke.

√ It's growing something green or yellow, or it has hair.

√ It stinks, stings, or stains.

√ You don't know what it is, what it goes to, or what it opens.

√ It's rusty, it's leaking, or it's already caused damage to the inside of your junk drawer, cabinet, or bathroom.

√ It has a date on it, and it's more than a year old (but it isn't wine).

√ It's in your handwriting but you don't remember writing it.

√ You don't like it or won't wear it, or it turns your finger, wrist, or neck green.

√ It doesn't have a lid, a top, or a match, or is missing an extremely important part or piece.

√ It is a cable, cord, or power supply for an item you no longer own.

√ It is something you already have more than two of (such as computer mice, wine openers, empty key chains, or broken cell phones).

√ It's been tacked to your bulletin board for more than a year.

√ It's a newspaper, magazine, catalog, or clipping that's more than a year old (preferably no more than three months old).

√ It's broken, such as an appliance, calculator, printer, scanner, blender, pizza oven, mower, edger, cell phone, or juice maker.

√ It belongs to your grown children and you warned them months ago you'd throw it away if they didn't come and get it.

√ You found it in your yard while mowing.

√ It has a crust on top of it, like an opened paint can, spoiled food, or your kid's sneakers.

√ It's dead.

So hop to it. Time to get out the trash bag and start going room to room. If you have time, allot a day for it. Once you get started, I can almost guarantee you'll see such great results you won't want to stop! It could take longer than a day though; it all depends on just how much trash you have.

TIP: *Take full bags to the trash bin or to the curb immediately. You don't want the bags to become gunk or give your family members any time to go through them. In fact, it's best to use trash bags that aren't see-though.*

GunkBuster's Notebook: Living With a Packrat

If you purchased this book because you're pretty neat but you live with a pack rat (I like to call them pack ratties), you've got a challenging task ahead of you. Some people have real problems when it comes to throwing stuff away, and it isn't because they're trying to drive you crazy. Really, they're not. They just view gunk differently than most people.

There are all kinds of pack rats. There are those that keep stuff because they "might need it" someday, some that keep only things that hold "sentimental" value, those that are simply lazy (and a few that are just spiteful), and some that claim they will use the stuff for crafts or hobbies at some unspecified date. Some feel items may be worth a lot of money someday, and some have an underlying medical problem. I think the latter is rare, and therefore, I believe most pack ratties can be helped to overcome their tendencies to hold on to unnecessary things.

If you live with a pack rat, consider these actions (which are all independent from one another to offer multiple ways to tackle the problem). Choose one of the following and give it a go, making sure to take into consideration your pack rat's personality and the nature of your relationship with them:

√ Make throwing stuff away a joint activity. Every Saturday, promise to spend an hour or two together throwing things away. Let your pack rat watch you throw away an old pair of shoes and convince them to do the same. Small steps can eventually lead to big ones, as long as you don't come across as a nagger, a bully, or a control freak.

√ Convince the pack rat, with you by their side, to box up anything that hasn't been used in two years. Put those boxes in the attic or garage. Start with a small area, such as a closet or single room, to make the task easier. Next year, convince your pack rat to throw those boxes away. (It's about patience.) Repeat this step every two months.

√ Tell your pack rat you'll purchase that <insert item here> they've been wanting or do <insert activity here> next week, but they have to throw away five things and pick up all of their clutter from the <insert room here> first.

√ Volunteer for the Salvation Army or another needy cause, and let your pack rat come along. Clean out your closets for the cause, and ask your loving spouse to donate, too.

√ In the same vein, tell your pack rat that there are needy people all over the world, and even in your community, who would really appreciate and wear all of those clothes that are of no use here. There are libraries and schools that would love to have their collection of *National Geographic*, and there are plenty of places to recycle all of the books they've read. They can even sell their used books for a few bucks. There are nursing homes, charities, and churches that could really use the items that are not useful, too.

√ Be honest with your pack rat. Tell them you are simply overwhelmed with the clutter. Talk about different gunk tolerances, and explain that yours is low. Ask for a compromise, create one, and stick to it.

√ Let your pack rat have a room all their own. Keep the door closed. This is a good way to start and will allow you to take control of the rest of the house while giving your pack rat their own room.

√ Sit down with your pack rat and help them make a reasonable list of goals that you are both comfortable with. It's important to make your goals achievable and get everyone's input so they won't feel bullied. Tell your pack rat to fix it, store it, sell it, or throw it away. Give them a month, and then throw it away yourself.

√ If your pack rat collects knick-knacks, consider a rotation system for displaying them. Box up all but a few, display those for a while, and then put them away and display another group.

√ If you think your pack rat is being a pack rattie out of spite, you probably have a larger, perhaps, marital or parental problem. Once the root problem is solved, so may be the pack rat problem.

√ If you think your pack rat is really a slob in pack rat's clothing, try not washing their clothes for a month unless they make it into the clothes hamper. Throw other clothes in a pile in the closet. If the pack rat is a slob in disguise, they will eventually get the message.

Everyone has a different gunk tolerance. While your gunk tolerance is low, a pack rat's is quite high. In fact, as comfortable as you feel when you're free of gunk is about as comfortable as they feel in a mound of it. So living with a pack rat poses its challenges, and it's ultimately about compromise and patience.

Use Everyday Maintenance Tasks for Throwing Stuff Away

As you've learned, trash is a big reason behind the cluttered home syndrome. Old telephone books, junk mail, broken appliances, newspapers, catalogs, and other items pile up quickly and become gunk. So once you've finally thrown everything out, what can you do to manage the new gunk that will make it into your home on a daily basis? Table 3-2 will help you stay on top of it all.

Table 3-2   Staying on Top of Daily Trash to Avoid Clutter Buildup

In	Daily Solution	Out
Newspapers	Create a space just for the newspaper, such as a wicker basket, the bottom shelf of a coffee table, or an area of a bookshelf. If the paper is not being read, that is where it should be.	Assign a member of the family to put the previous day's paper in the recycle bin or trash can each morning on their way out the door.

(continued)

Table 3-2   Staying on Top of Daily Trash to Avoid Clutter Buildup (continued)

In	Daily Solution	Out
Mail	Read and open mail daily, at the same time every day. Preferably, open mail in an office, next to a trash can, file cabinet, inbox, or shredder. Put mail for other family members in their room, in a specified and agreed-upon area.	Throw junk mail away immediately; file coupons, insurance papers, and bank statements; put bills in an inbox created specifically for correspondence that must be dealt with immediately.
Catalogs and magazines	Create a space just for these, such as a magazine organizer, the bottom shelf of a coffee table, or an area of a bookshelf.	Put new magazines and catalogs on top of old ones. Go through the stack when it's getting large, starting at the bottom and throwing away anything more than three months old.
Appliances, electronics, toys	Assign a space for the new addition immediately. Remove what is being replaced, if anything. Decide immediately what to do with the old item: throw away, give away, or sell. If there isn't room, get rid of something else so there is.	After deciding what to do with the replaced item, do it.
Cleaning supplies	Keep cleaning supplies together, in a carrying case with a handle. Use this to carry the supplies from room to room when cleaning. Try to purchase cleaners that serve more than one purpose to keep cleaning supplies to a minimum. Keep supplies on a high shelf.	If it has three drops left it in but you can't get them to come out, throw away the bottle. Don't repurchase cleansers that don't work.
Broken items	When things break, throw them away (or get them repaired) immediately. This includes appliances, electronics, glasses, toys, dishes, and computer equipment.	Do not replace an item without throwing out the broken one.
Food and medicine	Check expiration dates on refrigerated food once a week. Check expiration dates on medication every two months.	Throw away expired food and medication immediately.

Summing Up

In this chapter, you learned that trash is a major problem in any home. But the trash introduced in this chapter isn't the trash that makes it to your trash cans. It's the trash that remains in drawers, cabinets, medicine chests, pantries, and closets and never finds its way out the door once it's made its way in. Getting rid of the trash in your home is thus the first step to degunking it. In this chapter, you learned how to identify this hidden trash and how to get rid of it.

Chapter 4

Getting Rid of Clutter Using the Four-Box Method

Degunking Checklist:

√   Put the four-box method into place to help you quickly declutter and get organized.

√   Know that dealing with the items you put into boxes is part of the degunking process, not a temporary (or permanent) solution for clutter control.

√   Learn how to live with an Oscar Madison.

√   Apply everyday tricks for maintaining degunked areas using an adaptation of the four-box method.

The four-box method is a popular one for organizing, decluttering, and taking control of your home. It works because applying it forces you to pick up an item and decide immediately what you want to (or should) do with it. You will have to decide if the item in your hand should be thrown away, put in another room, placed in long-term storage, sold, given away, or recycled. You'll then have to put that item in the appropriate box. Forcing you to handle an item and immediately make a decision about it helps you instantly see, deal with, and eliminate the gunk in your home.

With the four-box method, sessions can be short, too. It only takes a few minutes to bring four cardboard boxes into the house, a few minutes to label them, and then a half hour or so to work through a small closet, a couple of drawers, or a cabinet or two. Another 15 to 20 minutes dealing with the boxes, and you're done!

TIP: *When you're out shopping, ask retailers if you can take home some empty cardboard boxes; many give them away happily. This not only helps you prepare for degunking sessions, it will also keep you focused on degunking while you're shopping. (Be careful not to let the boxes become gunk, though—use them quickly!)*

Understand How the Four-Box Method Works

As mentioned, when you apply the four-box method, you'll have to look at each item and decide straight away what to do with it. It forces an immediate decision. If you can look at an item, hold it in your hand, understand that you haven't used it in a year or more (or you don't like it or won't wear it), and then put it in the box of items to give away or sell, you've made progress. If you can hold an item in your hand and understand it's clutter, like a stack of magazines or books you've read, perhaps you can get rid of those, too. Maybe you can even get rid of that old computer or printer that hasn't worked in years. Whatever you do, everything you get rid of is one less thing in your home you have to deal with.

The four-box method is also designed so that a single session can be completed in a few minutes for a small area, in an hour for a larger one, or in an entire day or weekend for a room or garage. The immediate gratification you'll get from cleaning out a drawer or closet will also motivate you to continue to other closets, cabinets, drawers, or rooms, if only to simply fill up a box that will be donated to charity. Finally, the four-box method works because it's about moving stuff around. As you start to move things around, you'll start to feel the freedom of having less to dust around, store, wash, pack if you move, trip over, and clean.

NOTE: *Make sure you've completed Chapter 3, gathered up a few empty cardboard boxes, and thrown away everything you can before continuing.*

Apply the Four-Box Method

The easiest way to get started with the four-box method is to gather four boxes and, with a marker, label them as follows:

√   Give Away, Recycle, or Sell: This is the box for items that work, are usable, are wearable, or are functional but that *you* no longer use or want.

√   Move: Use this box for items that you want to keep but which belong somewhere else in the home.

√   Store Long Term: This is the box for items that you rarely use, such as holiday decorations or off-season clothing.

√   Throw Away: Finally, this is the box for items that you find that are trash, such as dried-up rubber bands, stained or torn clothing, screws or bolts that don't go to anything, and broken appliances or electronics.

Now, locate a junk drawer (everyone has at least one of those), and get to work (hopefully, you have already been through this drawer, throwing away anything that was trash, but if you haven't, that's okay, too):

1. Pick up every item in the drawer, one at a time, hold it in your hand, and give yourself no more than 60 seconds to think about which box it should go in.

    a. If you don't use it or don't like it and it still works, put it in the Give Away, Recycle, or Sell box.

    b. If it should be somewhere else in the home and not in this drawer, put it in the Move box.

    c. If it's a seasonal item or something you rarely use but have to keep, put it in the Store Long Term box.

    d. If it's trash, put it in the Throw Away box.

    e. If the item actually belongs in the junk drawer (scissors, tape, pens, pencils, a screwdriver, eyeglass cleaners, batteries), leave it on the counter.

2. Once the drawer is empty and you've gone through everything, decide how you want to place the items that go back into the drawer. Consider these tips:

   a. Purchase inexpensive drawer separators by Rubbermaid or use short, plastic Tupperware bowls or other organizers that you already have to keep things separate.

   b. Spend $5.00 on a junk drawer organizer and put everything in its place. A sample is shown in Figure 4-1. Many of these organizers even come with stickers that allow you to label where each item belongs.

   c. Recycle take-out containers, plastic tubs, metal tins, candy boxes, or even old jewelry boxes to organize the drawer.

   d. Put the items you use most toward the front of the drawer.

   e. Consider making a place in the drawer for your keys and cell phone, or consider creating a larger, designated place by the entryway for these items and purses, briefcases, backpacks, and wallets. You'll always know where they are.

Figure 4-1

Junk drawer organizers, such as this one, can be purchased, or made on the cheap with recycled plastic ware, metal tins, or take-out boxes.

3. With all of the items organized in boxes, look in the Give Away, Recycle, or Sell box. If you have a mix of items in here, such as items you want to give to your kids, items to take to the office, items to give to charity, items for your church, and items to give to parents, you'll likely need additional boxes to sort it out.

   a. If you plan to give items to charity, tape up the box and circle the words *Give Away* with your marker. Write the name of the charity or church on the box. Immediately put the box in your car and drop it off at the appropriate place on your next outing, or immediately call your favorite charity for pickup.

   b. Put things that can be recycled into the proper recycling bins, or contact the proper company to donate.

   c. If you're going to sell the items at a garage sale, bazaar, on eBay, or even on Amazon, make a date to do that now. Box and seal the items and label them appropriately. Move them out of the house into the garage or other storage area. For now, you can let the garage be your holding area. If you really plan to have a garage sale, it's okay. If you're just putting off getting rid of the stuff, be honest and reclassify the items you're keeping.

TIP: *Appendix C contains phone numbers and addresses for charities, information for eBay, a how-to-guide for having a successful garage sale, and phone numbers for recycling household goods.*

---

4. Look at the items in the Move box. Drag or carry the box from room to room, closet to closet, and put everything where it belongs. Although these areas may be pretty cluttered and you may feel you're adding to it, it's okay. You'll tackle these problem areas soon enough. The issue still remains; everything does have a proper place, and it's your immediate job to put everything in its place.

5. Look at the items in the Store Long Term box. Put this box in your current long-term storage area. This may be a shed, your garage, or the basement. At least you've put the items where they belong, and later, in Chapter 9, you'll learn how to create working, long-term storage areas and organize the mess.

6. Take the Throw Away box to the curb or to the outside trash bin to avoid the temptation to open the box and drag stuff back out, or to allow family members to do so.

TIP: *You're going to have a lot of items in boxes for charity and such, and you're going to find a lot of items you want to keep and store long-term. It may be in your best interest to clear a space in the garage or basement for those boxes before continuing.*

GunkBuster's Notebook: Taming Your Wallet and Purse

You can (and should) apply the four-box method to your wallet or purse. You might have to adapt it a bit, perhaps call it the *four-pile method*, and maybe be a little more lenient about the category titles, but whatever you call it, cleaning and organizing your wallet or purse is a simple and fast way to gain some clutter control. It's important for health reasons, too. A heavy purse or bulging wallet can cause posture problems and aches and pains, leaky pens can ruin a good purse, and expired makeup or sharp objects might even cause harm.

Cleaning out your wallet or purse is also an important security issue, especially if you have expired credit cards, carry your social security card or original birth certificate, or have notes about security keys or PINs for ATM cards, your home security system, answering machine, or safes. Table 4-1 offers a list of things to look for.

Table 4-1   What to Look for When Degunking Your Purse or Wallet

Keep (and Organize)	Move out of Your Wallet or Purse	Store Long Term (File)	Throw Away
Driver's license, ATM card, and car insurance cards	Home security system PIN and ATM PINs	Original Social Security card or birth certificate	Expired driver's licenses and car insurance cards
Health insurance cards, medical information cards, and donor cards (Update medical information cards.)	Anything with your Social Security number on it	Safe combinations, lock combinations, and warranty information and receipts	Expired health insurance cards and medical information cards
Credit cards (Write *Check For ID* on the back of each credit card you carry.)	Credit card PINs and blank credit card checks	Business cards and phone numbers and credit cards you don't use often	Expired cards, including credit cards (make sure to cut into small pieces)
Discount store cards, library cards, and frequent shopper cards	Discount cards, credit cards, frequent flyer cards, and frequent shopper cards you rarely use	Information related to credit cards, such as rates and privacy statements	Cards you no longer use for grocery stores, libraries, or discount stores

(continued)

Table 4-1   What to Look for When Degunking Your Purse or Wallet (continued)

Keep (and Organize)	Move out of Your Wallet or Purse	Store Long Term (File)	Throw Away
Money and a checkbook (Organize money by denomination.)	Coins	Used (duplicate copy) checkbooks and full registers	Leaky pens, broken pencils, and broken calculators
Small makeup bag (emphasis on the word *small*)	Makeup you don't use *daily*	Extraneous pictures and papers	Old candy, gum, wrappers, paper clips, rubber bands, and broken makeup items
Cell phone	Cell phone chargers	Cell phone statements	Broken electronics

Make the Four-Box Method a Part of Your Daily Life

A friend of mine complains that when his wife comes home from a full day at work and another half day at school, she "explodes" in the entryway. In 60 seconds their pristine entryway becomes a combat zone, filled with a backpack, purse, mail, cell phone, key ring, shoes, socks, and coat. Sometimes included in the explosion are other items, too: trash from the car, an empty fast food bag, a to-do list, various papers, an umbrella, a hat, and even groceries. The cats must greet her, of course (and she, them), so there's always cat hair on the floor, along with any mud she's tracked in. It's driving him crazy.

While there's likely no changing his wife completely, he can concede that this is a problem area, understand that he has a lower gunk tolerance than she does, and make an attempt to work some "boxes" into the area that can keep things from escalating from "That's getting on my last nerve" to "I want a divorce."

As you can probably tell, to her, the entryway is an extremely appropriate place to drop her things. She can access the items she needs very quickly now and in the morning, and she doesn't have to deal with putting them away after a long day at work and school. To him, it's the first thing people see when they enter the house, and he wants it to look nice all the time. There is a way to make peace, though. He can organize the entryway using "boxes" from the four-box method, and work to incorporate them into both of their daily lives.

"Boxes" can be created by entryways to organize what must come in and out of the house every day. Depending on your particular circumstance, most of these will be short-term or long-term holding areas or holding areas where things can be moved to their appropriate places later. Here are some ideas for the entry area of your home:

√ A coat rack for coats, hats, purses, backpacks, umbrellas, and other hanging items. This acts as both a short-term and long-term storage solution and keeps things organized, off the floor, and within reach.

√ Wicker baskets mounted on the wall or on a table for incoming and outgoing mail. This acts as an area to hold things (mail) until they are ready to be moved to the appropriate room, bill paying area, or mail box.

√ Wooden key racks on the wall for each person's keys. If you can obtain one that also holds mail, cell phones, or other items, you're making even more use of the space. This acts as a short-term holding area as well as an organizational tool. With a multipurpose key rack, you can store DVDs that need to be returned, signed school papers, and checks that need to go to the bank.

√ A trash can for items brought into the house that should be immediately thrown away, such as junk mail, catalogs, empty fast food bags, and flyers that were placed on the door. This is the trash "box" and, being easily available, will usually work quite well.

√ A doormat both inside and outside the house to trap daily dirt on shoes.

√ An umbrella stand if you live in a rainy climate. You may want to consider placing it outside the door if the door is covered by a patio.

√ A shelf inside the door or a table or small stand with wicker baskets or other organizational tools.

√ Plastic hooks halfway down the wall for children's coats and backpacks.

I have a myriad of other tips for dealing with clutter-prone areas, problem scenarios such as the one detailed earlier, and areas of the house such as entryways, where gunk will always accumulate:

√ Don't leave items that could be stored somewhere else in this area, such as newspapers, dog or cat dishes, skateboards, or golf clubs.

√ If you have a hall closet, refer to Chapter 5 for more hints on how to organize it effectively. If you're lucky enough to have a closet by the entryway, you can work miracles by building shelves and using available wall space for organizing.

√ Use walls to hang baskets, hooks, and small organizational bookcases or shelves.

√ Don't let shoes accumulate. Insist that if shoes are muddy, they stay outside. If they aren't outside, put them outside yourself. Create an area for them on the patio or porch. If shoes are a real problem, insist that all shoes be put away each night before bed time.

√ Install a family bulletin board/calendar/dry erase board in the entryway and attach markers using string so they can't get lost. Use this as a way to communicate with your family about appointments, to leave messages, and to remind kids what they need to take with them every day (backpack, lunch money, iPod, and so on).

√ Put items that you need to return and their receipts in your car, and handle them the next time you're out. This includes items to give to charities or churches.

√ Be patient with family members as they learn the new system.

You can apply this method to any area that is a daily gunk magnet. (Take note that I'm using the term *entryway* liberally, though. An entryway is where most family members come into the house, and it may be the back door or where the garage meets the house.)

GunkBuster's Notebook: Living with Oscar Madison (a Slob)

If your spouse is an accomplished slob, it's going to be a little harder to take control of your home. Slobs are the Oscar Madisons of the bunch. They make a sandwich and leave the bread, mayonnaise, meat, and cheese on the counter and expect someone else to clean it up. They spill something and never wipe it up and then wonder why it stained. They open a cabinet for a glass and don't close it. They drop their dirty laundry on the floor, have incredibly messy closets, and are always asking you where something is. They use your stuff and don't put it back. Understandably, this bothers you. Unfortunately, you need to make peace with one thing right now: You're not going to be able to turn your slob into a neat freak.

Just because you can't change them, though, doesn't mean you can't be creative and get some results. You can try to make tasks easier for them. For instance, my spouse leaves dirty clothes and wet towels on the bathroom floor, so I installed plastic hooks on the door for the towels and put a plastic dirty clothes hamper in the dressing area right outside the shower. Without me saying anything at all, clothes started appearing in the hamper and towels started appearing on the hooks.

The same creativity can be applied elsewhere, too. You just have to find the problem areas and see if there is anything you can do to make them go away. Let's say your slob opens the mail and leaves all of the torn envelopes, junk mail, unwanted catalogs, and other items on the counter. You have a few choices. Put a small office-sized trash can in the area, create a new area for opening mail (one that is close to an existing trash can), or get the mail yourself, separate it yourself, and put their mail in their office or slob-room. These areas are all really just boxes from the four-box method, adapted to meet the needs of your particular problem.

As a final example, let's say your slob is always using your scissors, tape, stapler, calculator, or pens and pencils and never returns them, leaves them open, or uses them all up. Again, you have several choices. You can lock the items in your desk drawer and make them ask, you can purchase duplicates and create a small office for your slob in another room (preferably one that has all of their other stuff in it), or you can create an area in the house that you both use and create a public space for everything using an organizer. While it might be difficult for your slob to put everything back in its place, it will be easy for you to, and you can keep an eye on things in the meantime.

TIP: As harsh as it sounds, living with a slob is a choice you made by either raising it, marrying it, or allowing it to move in, so you'll have to live with it. This means you'll need to be prepared to do more of the chores than should be your "fair share."

If you've tried to make things easier by adding additional dirty clothes hampers and applying other creative ideas but it isn't working, you'll have to take it a step further. As Figure 4-2 shows, a slob may still be a slob even if the opportunity is there to improve their habits.

If this is the case, you'll have to understand some underlying issues and try a few things to see what works:

√   Almost all slobs had or have a mother who has nagged them their entire lives about their messiness. It didn't work. Nagging will therefore get you nowhere.

√   Slobs aren't (usually) being messy to annoy you; they just don't think messiness and clutter is an important thing to worry about. They'd rather do something fun, like play video games or watch TV. That, to them, is more important than a neat home. In the case of Figure 4-2, perhaps you're dealing with a creative type who always has his mind elsewhere.

Figure 4-2
Sometimes, a slob is not easily reformed.

√ Sharing your feelings sometimes works. Tell them their sloppiness is really getting to you and you don't know how much longer you can take it. Explain that the sloppiness is causing friction in your relationship and offer a compromise. State the most important things to you, write them down, and ask your slob to work to complete them or resolve the issues.

√ Slobs usually do better with lists of chores instead of vague references to them, so sit down and create a list together, along with a timeline for doing them. If it doesn't work after a couple of weeks, revisit the conversation, stating again how this is affecting your relationship. People do get divorces over these issues, and your spouse must understand this. Their failure to help or to try to change is disrespect to you and your relationship.

√ Taking the gross-road works occasionally. Tell your slob they can have one room of the house to slob around in, but you want the rest of the house clean. Any slob-stuff they leave around is going in there, including anything they leave on the counter from their sandwich-making spree, dirty laundry found on the floor, and stinky shoes. Once they run out of clean clothes, they might get at least a partial clue.

√ Don't do any laundry that is on the floor. Ever. If you do laundry and their closet is a mess, just put the laundry on the floor in the closet and close the door.

√ Although it's a gamble, sometimes being a slob yourself works. If you're a gambler, don't pick up anything for a few weeks, don't do any dishes, don't do any grocery shopping, and see what happens.

√ Slobs are going to take offense if you nag them to perform chores. Try to set a time, say Saturday morning, where you both work together to perform basic tasks.

√ Realize that some slobs have specific personality issues or traits that make it nearly impossible to get with the program. Those with attention deficit disorders, those who are perfectionists, and those that are creative, extremely intelligent, or have a highly stressful job are sometimes simply unable to keep their attention on tasks as insignificant as hitting the clothes hamper with their dirty laundry.

Use the Four-Box Method Maintenance Tasks for Controlling Your Clutter

You can keep clutter from building up again by applying the four-box method on a daily basis, only on a smaller scale. Just create areas in the house where you can keep "boxes," preferably in places that attract the most gunk. These boxes may be wicker baskets, a cardboard box in the garage, under-the-bed storage, or even a plastic bowl by the front door. As an example, I keep a wicker basket behind our bar for stuff that collects in the kitchen and family room and needs to be moved somewhere else. This includes mail, paperwork, GameBoys, iPods, CDs, DVDs, and even shoes. When I pass it, I pick up what's in it and take it with me to its appropriate place.

I also use wicker baskets to store everyday items, such as toilet paper, newspapers, magazines, pet toys, and towels. Figure 4-3 and 4-4 show examples. In Figure 4-3, the space in which the wicker basket is positioned is an unused area of the dressing area, where one usually sits and puts on makeup. We don't do that much here, so the space is now used for storage. Figure 4-4 shows a wicker basket on the fireplace, and the cat knows to get his toys from there when he wants to play. (I've yet to teach him to put them back, though.)

I also keep a lot of trash cans around the house. There's one in every room, one by the entryway, and one on the back patio. All of these trash cans make it easy to keep trash where it belongs. It's easy to empty the trash, too; I just grab a new bag, walk around the house, and empty the cans in it. In Table 4-2, I'll detail some other ideas for applying the four-box method.

Figure 4-3
Wicker baskets can be used to hold toilet paper in a bathroom.

Figure 4-4
Wicker baskets can be used to hold pet toys.

Table 4-2   Everyday Maintenance Tasks for Controlling Clutter by Applying the Four-Box Method

Box	Location	Adding Items to the Box	Dealing with Items in the Box	Keeping the Box from Becoming Gunk Itself
Give Away, Sell, Recycle	Keep three labeled boxes in the garage, storage shed, or long-term storage area. Create a recycle area for cans and bottles that is easily accessible, preferably with the trash can in the kitchen.	Put items in the boxes as acquired.	When any box is full, tape, label, and get rid of it by either selling the items or giving them to charity immediately.	Store boxes where they can be easily accessed but where they're not in the way. Do not stack full boxes; get rid of them.
Move	Place "move" boxes between the family room and the bedrooms, by the entryway, and in the kitchen.	Place items in the box as they accumulate. Teach family members to do the same.	Every time you pass the box, carry an item with you to the appropriate room and put it away. (You might even want to create a box for each family member.)	Make sure the box is aesthetically pleasing and large enough to hold the items you accumulate.
Store Long Term	Under the bed, in the attic, in the top shelves of closets, in a storage shed.	Add items during spring, summer, fall, and winter cleaning sessions.	Four times a year, go through the box when adding or moving items to or from them and get rid of items you don't need or haven't used in a year or more.	The box should be hidden away yet accessible. Stackable items are best, as are shelves in the garage or in closets.
Throw Away	Put a trash can in every room.	Any time there is trash, put it in a trash can. Never leave trash on the counter, in drawers, or in the entryway.	Assign the task of taking out the garbage to a family member, and have them take out the trash when it's even with the top of the can.	Consider purchasing a trash can with a lid, putting trash cans in plain sight, and choosing trash cans that are easy on the eye.

Summing Up

In this chapter, you learned how to use and apply the four-box method for controlling clutter. The four-box method works because it forces you to hold each item from a drawer, cabinet, closet, or room and decide whether it's worth keeping or not. The four boxes are generally Give Away/Sell/Recycle, Move, Store Long Term, and Throw Away. You can apply the four-box method to your entire home, too, allowing you to keep your home degunked once it's in order.

Chapter 5

Degunking Problem Area: Closets

Degunking Checklist:

√ Use the four-box method when cleaning out a closet.

√ Understand there are different types of closets, and thus, different strategies for dealing with them.

√ Move rarely-used items to long-term storage areas.

√ Organize your clothes, ties, shoes, and other items by color, size, use, and type, based on the type of organization strategy you need.

√ Keep items you use often in stackable bins, dresser drawers, and storage containers to help keep your closet organized once it's clean.

√ Consider closet organizers and shoe racks for long-term degunking.

√ Use special degunking techniques to maintain a degunked closet.

Closets, especially closets used for accessing and storing clothing, are gunk magnets because you use them every day. As noted in previous chapters, the entryway, the kitchen, and closets will always be the hardest areas in your home to get (and keep) degunked. That's because when you access them, you're usually in a hurry. If things are in disarray, it makes matters worse, because finding and putting things away is harder than it should be, therefore enabling gunk to accumulate even faster.

Clothes closets are also problem areas because they offer an easy way to keep, store, or hide items you should really get rid of. These include clothes that don't fit, clothes that are torn or stained, clothes that are out of style, and shoes you'll never wear. They also allow you to store items that should really be put in long-term storage, such as furs, winter coats or summer dresses, tuxedos, and wedding or cocktail dresses. With clothes closets, you're also able to easily store items that should go somewhere else, like old textbooks, games, pictures, exercise equipment, and vacuum cleaners. This chapter, therefore, will be mostly about the closets in which you store clothes.

Types of Closets

There are lots of closet types, including linen, pantry, utility, junk, clothes, hall, coat, toy, storage, and office. You may have others I haven't named here. Dealing with different closet types requires different strategies. Throughout the book, I'll address some of these types and the strategies that work best. For instance, in Chapter 6, I'll address organizing kitchen pantry closets; Chapter 7, china cabinets and linen closets; and Chapter 8, utility rooms and storage closets.

One closet that seems to be common to most households is the junk closet, so it deserves special mention here. It's where you put stuff that doesn't really have a place anywhere else. Often, it's a closet in an office or guest room. If you have a "junk closet" like the one shown in Figure 5-1, you'll have to tackle that using the four-box method as if it were a *room* in your home. For that type of closet, you should refer to Chapter 4.

Figure 5-2 shows what we're working on in this chapter, and in this picture, it's gunked-up closet shelves. Figure 5-3 shows another mess, although some attempt has been made at organizing previously. You can see the plastic drawers, plastic organizer, and wicker basket. Unfortunately, the applied organizational strategy didn't work in the long term, and thus, was not a successful attempt at degunking. This is the type of stuff you'll learn about in this chapter.

Figure 5-1

Most people have a junk closet that should be tackled using the four-box method; this one could certainly stand some improvement.

Figure 5-2

If your closet shelves look like this, you've got some work to do.

Figure 5-3
Sometimes, even the best-laid plans go awry.

The First Steps to Tackling Closets

Hopefully, you've worked through Chapters 3 and 4 before finding yourself here. If you haven't, you'll want to read through those chapters before continuing. In a nutshell, though, and in case you don't have time to review those chapters, or if you just really need and want to get to your most problematic closet, I'll outline those chapters briefly.

First, you need to take everything out of your closet, throw away anything that is trash, and then filter unnecessary or unwanted items into four boxes. Use the method outlined in Chapter 4 for doing this, including handling things only once and being ruthless when discarding things you know you'll never use again.

TIP: *Boxes are better than garbage bags because they can be stacked in a garage for a future garage sale, easily distributed to charities and churches, and labeled descriptively, and what's more, the contents are hidden from nosy (and worried) family members.*

You'll need four boxes, labeled as follows:

√ **Give Away, Recycle, or Sell**: For things that are usable, worthy of donation, too big or small to wear, or out of style.

√   **Move**: For things that belong elsewhere (or can be stored elsewhere), such as vacuum cleaners and attachments, coats, newspapers and magazines, dirty clothes, long-term storage boxes, old computers and monitors and printers, books, linens, towels, games, and similar items.

√   **Store Long Term**: For items that should be moved to long-term storage areas, such as out-of-season clothes, fur coats, clothes you want to keep but don't wear (coach's jackets and team jerseys, for example), and wedding dresses. Chapter 9 discusses strategies for long-term storage.

√   **Throw Away**: For items that are not usable or are trash, such as dry cleaner plastic coverings, broken appliances, old coat hangers, and shoes or socks without matches.

Once everything is out of the closet and the boxes are filled with unwanted or misplaced items, you must do something with the boxes before continuing. Refer to Chapter 4 and Appendix C for help there.

Now what's left—all of the stuff that isn't in a box, must be put *back* in the closet in an organized and maintenance-free fashion. (Don't forget to scrub and vacuum before replacing the items in your closet.) Putting the stuff back is what I'll discuss next.

TIP: *There's no way to organize your closet without first working the four-box method!*

Put It Back: Tips and Tricks

If you've just spent most of the day buried underneath the ton of gunk you found in your closet, I'm sure you are tired, sweaty, hungry, and mentally exhausted. I'll also bet you just want to put (throw, stuff, cram) all the things you want to keep back in the closet as quickly as possible. It's tempting just to toss all the stuff back in there and hope for the best. However, if you're too tired now to do the job right, put it off for a day and come back to it. My motto is "If you don't have time to do it right, you'll never have time to do it over."

If you *do* have the strength now, sit down for a few minutes and actually think about what you want to do with this particular space (which is now empty). By putting a little thought into it, you can create an area that works for you not only at the present, but also in the future. By creating a *working* plan, you can create a space that makes it easy to keep the area degunked in the long term. So before you begin, read through table 5-1 and see what areas you should focus on.

Table 5-1   Workable Solutions for Problem Areas

Problem Area	Long-Term Solution
You have too many things on the floor, including shoes, hats, purses, and shoe boxes.	Purchase an inexpensive hanging shoe bag for the shoes, get rid of the shoe boxes, and hang hooks on the wall for the purses or hats. If you use the purses or hats often, consider devoting a shelf to them.
You wear some of your clothes two or three times before laundering them, but don't want to mix clothes you've worn with the rest of your wardrobe.	Create one area in which to hang clothes you've already worn and want to wear again before laundering them. You can do this by adding another clothes pole in the closet or dedicating an existing space. You can even use a small coat rack or plastic hooks. Put a wicker basket on the floor for folded items.
Your folded clothes never stay organized.	Put like items together, such as sweaters, sweatshirts, T-shirts, work shirts, undershirts, tank tops, and pajamas. If possible, separate them into dresser drawers, wicker baskets, or plastic bins. Label the areas using Avery labels and Sharpie markers. Also, consider creating or purchasing shelf dividers that clamp onto a shelf and act as a "book end." This way, items will not be able to migrate to other areas.
Some clothes you rarely wear take up valuable closet space.	Store rarely-used items on top shelves, under the bed in plastic storage containers, or in the garage in boxes, properly labeled. Consider cedar chests and trunks, as well.
Hangers are always getting tangled up.	Decide on one type of hanger you want to use, such as wire or plastic, and convert your whole closet to it. Plastic hangers can be purchased on sale for less than a dime each and are well worth the cost. Get rid of the other hangers.
You can never find what you want to wear in the morning.	Organize hanging clothes by type, such as suits, jackets, pants, shirts, ties, jackets, blouses, skirts, and pants. You can also keep entire outfits together or organize items by color. If you share a closet, halve it. Keep your things on one side, organized as you like. Put folded items you use most often at eye level, put rarely used items on higher shelves, and keep folded items organized by type. If you have time, consider laying out your clothes the night before. You'll save lots of time in the morning.
The closet is simply too full to be functional.	Move out as many items as possible. Put sweaters in a dresser or bureau, put coats in a hall coat closet, and move rarely worn and seasonal items to long-term storage.

(continued)

Table 5-1   Workable Solutions for Problem Areas (continued)

Problem Area	Long-Term Solution
There is a lot of wasted space in the closet.	If you have unused wall space, add shelving, hooks, or additional clothes poles. If you have unused closet door space, add hanging door organizers. If you have empty floor or shelf space, add stackable bins, modular drawers, spinning caddies, or pull-out shelves.
There are always pajamas, towels, nightgowns, and bathrobes on the floor.	Add hooks for these items inside the closet. Label if necessary.

Here are some other tips you might want to incorporate:

√   Keep a small step stool in the closet to reach items stored on top shelves. This will keep you from toppling piles of folded clothes when you want the item on the bottom of the pile.

√   Hang a full-length mirror on the closet door.

√   Move boxed items out of the closet and into long-term storage areas, freeing up room in the closet.

√   Fasten the top button of any hanging item to keep it on the hanger.

√   Make use of organizational items you already own, such as milk crates, an old dresser stored in the garage, large Rubbermaid or Tupperware containers, cedar chests, trunks, old filing cabinets, and shoe boxes (for rolled-up belts or ties).

√   Employ your dual clothes pole system effectively by grouping blouses, skirts, and shirts on the top tier and pants and longer items on the bottom.

√   Add metal or plastic shelving, or install wire closet organizers.

√   Put a small trash can inside the closet door for trash in clothes pockets and dry cleaning tags.

√   Store out-of-season clothes somewhere else.

√   Remove the doors from a small closet with bifold doors and replace them with full-length curtains. This will add much more space for you to reach in and hang items.

√   Paint the inside of your closet your closet your favorite color, or add wild wallpaper. Buy hangers and bins in your favorite color. If it's as nice as the rest of your home, you'll be less likely to gunk it up.

Figures 5-4 and 5-5 show examples of what can be done in an afternoon. Comparing Figure 5-4 to Figure 5-2 (shown earlier) demonstrates quite an improvement. Notice that the shirts are grouped by color and are all on plastic hangers, and folded clothes are categorized by type, with a little breathing room between piles. This may or may not work in the long term, though, and if it doesn't, I'll have to add separators between the piles of clothes to keep them

Figure 5-4
Compared to Figure 5-2, this is quite an improvement.

apart. If separators don't do the trick, labeled baskets or bins on the shelves can be added to hold the stacked items. For now, though, this is an organized and functional space, with long-term strategies to keep it that way.

Figure 5-5 shows the improvement made to the area shown earlier in Figure 5-3. Again, it's a work in progress because this may or may not work in the long term. However, all wire hangers have been removed, unwanted shoes have been given away, and the plastic bins have been reorganized. Often-used items are readily available, making obtaining them and putting them away after they're laundered quite easy. Belts and hats are easily accessible and have a specific space, and shirts are categorized by type. The wicker basket shown in Figure 5-3 is now in the lower-right corner of this image and will be used to hold lightly worn clothing, which definitely was a problem area. There are hooks to hold sleepwear on the walls, shown in Figure 5-6, and it seems to be working. There's also a mirror on the closet door. All in all, not bad for a day's work.

Figure 5-5
What didn't work before might work now, with boxes and boxes of stuff removed and organization made simpler.

Figure 5-6
With no prompting at all, the pajamas found their way onto the new hook in the closet.

Use Everyday Maintenance Tasks to Keep Closets Organized

Keeping your clothes closet degunked and organized won't be simple, especially if the mess wasn't your fault to begin with, but it can be done. The idea is to watch for things to go awry—such as shoes becoming disorganized, dirty clothes accumulating on the floor, items showing up there that don't belong, or folded clothes piles turning back into a big messy pile—and dealing with those issues immediately. To help you stay on top of problem areas you come across, then, consider the tips in Table 5-2.

Table 5-2   Everyday Maintenance Tasks for Keeping Closets Organized

Recurring Problem	Short-Term Solution	Long-Term Solution
Shoes are all over the place.	Move outdoor shoes outside, including garden shoes, golf shoes, baseball or soccer cleats, and boots. Create an outdoor or garage space for them. Get rid of shoes you no longer wear if you haven't done so already. Consider purchasing a shoe rack or over-the-door shoe organizer or putting rarely-worn shoes in shoe boxes you can stack.	Purchase a shoe holder to hang on the closet door or a shoe rack for the floor of the closet. Box shoes that haven't been worn in a year or more, and put them in long-term storage until you can get rid of them completely. If you buy a new pair of shoes, vow to get rid of one pair in your closet. (The same goes for purses and hats.)
Dirty clothes accumulate on the floor.	Don't launder anything that's on the floor of the closet and hope that someone runs out of clean clothes and takes the hint, or launder everything you find on the floor, thus irritating those that enjoy wearing things twice (or more) before laundering and can't find them on the floor where they left them. Place a laundry basket or hamper in the closet or right outside the door.	Find out what works in the short term. If the laundry basket or hamper works for the short term, create a place for that unit long-term. If a particular laundry strategy works, go with that.

(continued)

Table 5-2   Everyday Maintenance Tasks for Keeping Closets Organized *(continued)*

Recurring Problem	Short-Term Solution	Long-Term Solution
Gently worn clothing has no dedicated space in the closet, or the dedicated space doesn't work.	Ask the culprit where they would like to store these lightly worn clothes, and create a temporary but workable space there. Use a wicker basket, plastic bin, coatrack, an area of the clothes pole, or even a separate hamper.	Evaluate short-term strategies and find what works. When one is found, create a permanent place in the closet for whatever unit is needed.
Folded piles of clothes don't stay folded.	Try making piles shorter, moving what isn't being worn to long-term storage, adding shelf separators, and straightening the piles each time you take clean laundry into the closet. Be especially careful when removing clothes from piles, and have a stepladder so items on higher shelves can be reached easily.	If short-term solutions don't work, put folded items into drawers. Label the drawers so items remain in the proper places. Do not overfill the drawers. Categorize drawers by clothing type, size, or color. Additionally, sometimes this problem works itself out, as often-worn clothing ends up on the tops of piles after laundering, making the problem of pulling items from the bottom of the pile disappear.
Hanging clothes become a jumble quickly.	When something is out of place, move it to where it should be, as you notice it. Each time you bring laundry to the closet, spend three or four minutes making sure you put things in their proper place.	If your hanging strategy isn't working, change it. Consider grouping shirts on the left, pants on the right, and skirts and jackets in the middle. Keep trying until something clicks.
The closet continues to attract gunk that doesn't belong, including trash and items that should be somewhere else.	Put a trash can and a "Move" box in the closet or just outside of it. Place things in here as they accumulate and deal with the items in these two containers weekly (or better yet, daily).	If the short-term solution works, create a permanent space for these containers. If the strategy doesn't work, close the closet door and put a "clothes only" sign on the front to remind yourself and your family what does and does not belong there. As things migrate there, put them in a box and move the box to the garage. Chances are, they won't be missed.

(continued)

Table 5-2 Everyday Maintenance Tasks for Keeping Closets Organized *(continued)*

Recurring Problem	Short-Term Solution	Long-Term Solution
The closet becomes gunked up quickly because new clothing, purses, belts, coats, and shoes are constantly being purchased and stored in the closet.	Put off making a purchase for one day after deciding you must have it. If you still want it the next day, return to the store to purchase it.	Each time you bring a new item into the home (or closet, specifically), get rid of two items. It doesn't matter how small; it could be a pair of socks and a hat. The idea is to get into a habit and to stay aware of possible future gunk problems.

Summing Up

In this chapter, you learned how to take control of your clothes closets. As with Chapters 3 and 4, the strategy is the same. Gather up four boxes, work the four-box method, and then replace things in such a way as to facilitate long-term degunking. Long-term degunking strategies include organizing items by type, size, color, or use; creating dedicated spaces for shoes, purses, ties, and hats; and hanging clothes the best possible way. As with any degunking task, maintaining a degunked area is a high priority, too, so remember the tips and tricks you learned for keeping your closet organized.

Chapter 6

Degunking Problem Area: The Kitchen

Degunking Checklist:

√   Apply the four-box method *before* you start organizing your kitchen.

√   Arrange the items in cabinets by most used, by category, or by type.

√   Organize cabinets and drawers by how and when the items in them are used.

√   Free up counter space by removing items that aren't used every week.

√   Create a space for baking pans, dehydrators, juice makers, and bread makers in long-term storage or on higher shelves.

√   Determine the source of "paper gunk" and create a system for managing them.

√   Organize the pantry, refrigerator, and freezer.

√   Understand the shelf life of foods, and get rid of things before they go bad.

√   Learn how to maintain a degunked kitchen.

The kitchen is the hub for most family and entertaining activities, and therefore, is a problem area. As with closets and entryways, the kitchen sees action every day and quickly becomes a gunk magnet. Kids do homework there, dishes accumulate there, and people cook and eat there. Besides being the center of many family activities, though, the kitchen also has a lot of counter space for stuff to accumulate, and a lot of cabinet and drawer space for things to be hidden away and forgotten about.

Another reason the kitchen gets so messy so quickly is that there's usually too much stuff and not enough room for it. Crock-Pots, bread makers, pasta makers, woks, ice tea machines, espresso machines, and food sealers take up a ton of space and are often rarely used. The space these items take up could be the main reason your kitchen is gunked up. There's nowhere to put the food processor, the can opener, the toaster, the coffee machine, and other items you use often because all of the good real estate is taken up with rarely-used, large, bulky items.

In addition to large cooking gadgets like these, though, there's often a huge amount of little stuff that isn't needed or used (like cake-icing sets), stuff that doesn't work (like a rusty rotary cheese grater that won't turn anymore), items that don't match (such as dishes or mugs), and things that cause more problems or take up more space than they're worth (like the homemade pasta maker your grandmother gave you or the bread basket you don't use). You need to take control!

Apply the Four-Box Method First

Hopefully, you've worked through Chapters 3 and 4 before finding yourself here. If you haven't, you'll want to read through those chapters before continuing. In a nutshell, though, and in case you don't have time to review them, or if you just really need and want to get to the kitchen, I'll outline those chapters briefly.

First, you need to remove everything from the cabinets and drawers and throw away all of the trash. Kitchen trash includes anything that's broken, chipped, or cracked; paper gunk such as grocery store receipts, homework papers, to-do lists, and expired coupons; and plastic ware that is stained or is missing a lid. Expired foods and leftovers are also trash. Use the method outlined in Chapter 3 for getting rid of the trash and Tables 6-1 and 6-2 later in this chapter to determine the shelf life of foods in your pantry, refrigerator, and freezer.

Once the trash is taken care of, you'll need to go through everything that remains and decide what you can give to charity or sell, what needs to be moved elsewhere, and what needs to be stored long-term. As noted in Chapter 4, handle everything on the counter and in each drawer or cabinet only once, and be ruthless when discarding things you know you'll never use again. You can't organize your kitchen if it's all gunked up with things you can't use, won't use, or don't need. Figure 6-1 shows a work in progress; all of the items in this picture are things to give to charity.

Figure 6-1
First, throw away anything that's trash; then, separate what you can give to charity (or sell in a garage sale) and box it up.

TIP: If you haven't performed the tasks in this section, return to Chapters 3 and 4 and work through them in the kitchen before continuing. This is extremely important!

Organize Cabinets

The best strategy to taking control of the kitchen is to organize the cabinets first. If you degunk the cabinets correctly, you'll create extra space where you can put items you'll need to deal with later, such as larger items that are currently on the kitchen counter and don't belong there, but don't belong in long-term storage either. If you can create a space in a cabinet to hold the blender you use only use on Fridays to make margaritas, you can get that appliance off the counter and still have easy access to it when the weekend comes around. Creating more counter space and ease of access is a good step toward degunking.

Start Fresh and Have a Plan

Right now, everything should be out of the cabinets (or drawers, depending on the magnitude of this particular degunking session). Before moving forward, sweep out the inside of the cabinets and clean them with a moist cloth and a mild cleanser. A DustBuster is often a good tool for this, especially if you have the smaller attachments (Argh! Gunk!). Replace the shelf paper if needed, and then sit down for a moment and think about how you use your kitchen.

You need to decide now where you want things to go before putting them back. If your coffeemaker is on the left side of the kitchen, don't put the coffee mugs on the right. Try to minimize movement. Figures 6-2 and 6-3 show

Figure 6-2
Decide how you can maximize each area in the kitchen and minimize movement at the same time.

Figure 6-3

Careful degunking in the kitchen can lead to small improvements in degunking your life.

before and after pictures of a coffee area. In the before picture, you can see that the family had to travel across the kitchen for a coffee cup and coffee and fight the other items in the cabinet for sugar and stirrers. In the after picture, the morning coffee routine is streamlined and much more efficient. There's even a new sugar holder so there are no empty sugar packets to pick up afterward.

Spices, pots, pans, lids, and pot holders can be stored close together to make cooking more efficient, too, as can plates and bowls and flour and sugar. To decide what works for you, think about how you use your kitchen and how often you walk back and forth to perform a task, such as baking cookies. Figure 6-4 shows an example of an organizational technique.

Figure 6-4
Put items you use often on lower shelves, put things you use less often on
higher ones, and put spices next to the stove and oven to minimize movement.

This is a good time to readjust the shelves as well. Most cabinets have shelves
that can be raised or lowered, and you can adjust them depending on what's
stored there. If one cabinet shelf is only for glasses and there's a lot of free
overhead space, there's no reason not to lower the shelf above it to maximize
the room you have.

Additionally, really think hard about the items you rarely use. Those items should
be placed on a top cabinet shelf, in the back of a bottom one, or moved to a
long-term storage area. To motivate you to do the latter, note this: About three
months ago, I boxed up several appliances I rarely use, wrote on the box what
was inside, and moved that box to the garage. It still sits there today, untouched.
That box is going to Goodwill if I don't use any of the items in it over the next
holiday season. You could do the same.

Finally, make sure your kitchen is organized around where the dishwasher is (or
the sink). You should be able to empty the dishwasher in the time it takes a
frozen dinner to heat in the microwave; that's about 5 minutes. If it takes longer
than that, your kitchen is not arranged effectively.

Putting Things Back

Once you have a plan, it's pretty easy to put things back into the cabinets. Put like things together. That includes plates, saucers, coffee cups, bowls, salad dishes, pots, pans, spices, medicines, cleaning supplies, towels and napkins, vases (do those really belong in the kitchen?), baking pans, muffin pans, pizza pans, Pyrex, Tupperware, lids, recipe books, Saran Wrap and foil, and other items. While putting things away, though, keep the following in mind:

√ Arrange spices in alphabetical order. If a spice has lost its smell, toss it.

√ Arrange cleansers by name or type.

√ Keep the dishwashing detergent and soap under the sink and/or next to the dishwasher. (Install kid-proof locks if needed.)

√ Put rarely-used items (but items you still want to keep in the kitchen) in the back of cabinets or on high shelves of cabinets.

√ Label shelves if you live with children or an adult that acts like one.

√ Stack smart by nesting items.

√ Purchase a lazy Susan for smaller items such as spices, salt, pepper, and other seasonings. Look back to Figure 6-4.

√ Purchase foil and plastic wrap holders for inside cabinet drawers.

√ Consider adding pullout shelves.

√ If you don't use your large pans often, get rid of them and use disposable ones when you need one.

√ Box up items you haven't used in three months, label the box, and put it in the garage or in long-term storage. If you don't use the items after the next holiday season, get rid of them.

√ If you don't have enough cabinet space, consider hanging pots and pans, leaving clean dish towels in the laundry room and using the stove handle for the towel currently being used, purchasing an island for extra cookware or tableware, and elevating cookbooks to a shelf in the kitchen.

GunkBuster's Notebook: Do You Really Need 20 Coffee Cups?

My guess is that you don't need all the coffee cups you have. Coffee cups accumulate the same way key rings, refrigerator magnets, take-out restaurant menus, and busted pens do; they just sort of show up out of nowhere and start gunking up the place. Figure 6-5 shows an example of a coffee cup fiasco.

Figure 6-5
Living with a coffee-cup pack rattie can be difficult.

You can see in Figure 6-5 that the cups don't match, some are chipped, and there are multiples of the larger, white cups. They're stored inappropriately, too, with excess space above the top row and no organization in the bottom one.

Unlike many people, though, I know where this mess came from. The white cup-bowls came in a package of a dozen, a dozen seeming like an appropriate number for my pack rattie. The colored mugs were a dollar each; again, a dozen seemed to be a fair amount to purchase. Behind the mess are "commemorative" coffee cups from events, from Campbell's Soup (they may be valuable someday), and from charity fund-raisers. (The small blue and white bowls also came by the dozen, but we're talking about cups here.) You may have a similar problem.

The solution to this is again a simple one. First, hope that the restaurant supply store down the street goes out of business. Then, box up all but the amount of coffee cups you'll need. Two per coffee drinker seems appropriate, with an extra four for guests. Move the unnecessary cups to a storage area, which will likely be okay with your pack rattie since they'll still be available. Box up commemorative cups for "safekeeping." After enough time has passed, donate the coffee cups to a local nursing home or shelter.

Organize Drawers

Organizing drawers is like organizing cabinets. Remove everything first, then apply the four-box theory. Take what's left and put the items back into the drawers, keeping a close eye on where you'll store the items you need and use the most. As with cabinets, there are some things you can do to stay gunk free:

√ Minimize movement by making the drawer next to the sink or dishwasher the silverware drawer. This will make quicker work of emptying the dishwasher or putting away washed and dried silverware.

√ Use the drawer next to the stove for cooking utensils. If you're right-handed, use the drawer to the right; lefties, use the drawer to the left. If you don't have enough drawer space, consider a utensil holder on the counter.

√ Have a separate drawer for knives only. Choose a drawer for knives that is near where you cut up meat, vegetables, or fruit, and also near the cutting board (or hang a magnetic strip close to the stove).

√ Purchase or create drawer organizers to keep things separate. Rubbermaid makes drawer organizers that are extremely inexpensive.

√ Use larger drawers for items like cheese graters, blender and mixer attachments, measuring cups and spoons, whisks, wooden spoons, thermometers, and skewers. Consider using inexpensive plastic shoe or sweater boxes to keep these items together and in easy reach. Don't forget to throw away attachments for appliances you no longer own

√ Have a drawer for clean dish towels, sponges, and napkins.

√ Remove manuals for appliances from drawers and file them in a filing cabinet.

√ Designate a drawer for plastic wrap, foil, and baggies if you have the room. They'll stay organized that way and will be easy to access, or use hanging racks.

√ Have a junk drawer for rubber bands, twist ties, tape, pens and pencils, coupons, and small tools. You can even buy inexpensive "junk drawer" organizers with labels for these items.

Free Up Counter Space

The kitchen counter is often a family sore spot. Different people have different views about what the kitchen counter should look like and what it should be used for. Kids think it's a great place to do homework; working spouses think it's a great place to dump their change, purse or wallet, keys, sunglasses, cell phones, and paperwork; and guests think it's a great place to gather, even when there's an entire living and dining room available for mingling. And the cook, well, the cook thinks it's a great place to store appliances, no matter how large or small, so they'll be available when they're needed.

Unfortunately, each family member produces (and wants) their own amount of kitchen counter gunk, making it hard to control. And when the kitchen counter is cluttered, the kitchen loses its appeal and its functionality.

Organizing and decluttering the kitchen counter is very important, then, and should be a high priority. I've saved the counter for last because I know that after successfully degunking the cabinets and drawers, you'll have lots of extra space there for the items currently on your counter.

Start Fresh and Have a Plan

As with the previous degunking sessions, you'll start degunking your kitchen counters by removing everything from their current places. This may mean moving everything to the center of the countertop, to the floor, or to a table, but if you want to start fresh, you need to start with a blank slate.

Next, clean the counters with good cleanser and get up all of the dirt and dust. While the countertops are drying, make a list of the things you use on a daily basis (or at least three times a week). The list will likely include the coffeepot, can opener, toaster, and microwave, and maybe a specialty appliance like a pizza oven, juicer, or food processor. Put those items in their proper places, either in the same place or a new one, concentrating on the location, accessibility, and functionality of each item.

Finally, go through everything that's left. If you've used the item in the last month, put it in a cabinet that's easily accessible. If an item hasn't been used in three months, move it out of the kitchen completely, or store it in the back of a deep cabinet or in a high cabinet designated for long-term storage. (When you get to the long-term storage chapter, Chapter 9, you'll learn how to create a mock pantry in your garage, attic, or basement where you can store and access these items when you do need them.) If you haven't used the item in a year, and won't need it for the next holiday season, get rid of it.

Figure 6-6 shows a degunked, deep cabinet. This cabinet used to be filled to the brim with unnecessary items, but now that it's cleaned, it offers a place to store the iced tea maker, the food processor, the blender, and pans and serving dishes that aren't used very often. There's still room for other things, too.

Figure 6-6
After the cabinets are degunked, there's usually lots of room for items that used to be on the counter, such as the iced tea maker, food processor, and blender.

Tips for Eliminating Physical Kitchen Counter Gunk

There are lots of other ways to eliminate kitchen counter gunk and clear the counter of unused appliances to create a space that is workable, cookable, and mingleable. (Okay, I made up those last two words, but you get the idea!) Here are some of the best tips around:

√   Hang what you can, including cutting boards, utensils, and pots and pans, on a wall or from the ceiling. You'll free up both cabinet space and drawer space, as well as counter space.

√   Move appliances you haven't used in three days or more to lower cabinets with plenty of room for easy access and easy manageability. If you make these appliances hard to get to, you'll be less motivated to put them back when you're finished using them the next time.

√   Purchase hanging wire baskets for fruit and vegetables normally stored at the bottom of the pantry, on the counter, or on a window sill. (Storing in the refrigerator is better, though, if you have the room.)

√   Mount the can opener, coffee maker, or toaster underneath the cabinets.

√   Purchase a rolling cart or an island if you have the room.

√   Add small shelves underneath the cabinets (and above the countertops) to hold spices, herbs, salt and pepper, and other small items.

√   Purchase a lazy Susan for items you leave on your counter all the time, such as spices or medications.

The idea is to remove as much as you can from the counters, making the kitchen counter a place for *living* instead of a place for *storing*.

Tips for Eliminating People and Paper Gunk

You and your family members are responsible for much of the daily kitchen counter gunk that accumulates. Some of this gunk is in the form of paper, some is trash, and some of it consists of utensils or appliances that have been taken from their hiding places, used, and then not put away.

Other gunk is the result of the end-of-the-day "explosion factor" detailed in Chapter 4. An entryway (which is often the kitchen) can go from *pristine* to *combat zone* in 60 seconds. The combat zone is made up of backpacks, purses, mail, cell phones, key rings, shoes, socks, and coats. Explosion items also include trash from the car, empty fast food bags, to-do lists, papers, umbrellas, hats, gloves, and even groceries. It can really get on a degunker's nerves. To help control and eliminate this people gunk, refer to Chapter 4. There are a couple of bulleted lists in that chapter that offer more than two dozen tips for taking control of this kind of clutter.

As for paper gunk, you first need to figure out the source of the gunk. If it's little pieces of paper with items you need to get at the grocery store, you can solve that problem by mounting a whiteboard inside your pantry door. If it's recipes or coupons you collect, the solution lies in a system for organizing those things using notebooks or folders. It it's homework, permission slips, field trip notices, report cards, lunch menus, and sports notices from your kids, you'll need to create an area for that specific type of gunk and manage it there. That may mean designating a specific office area or creating a filing system.

Here are a few more ideas along the same lines:

√ Purchase a recipe box and index cards, convert a three-ring binder, or purchase a plastic-coated photo album for storing, organizing, and saving recipes.

√ Purchase and use a coupon organizer for the coupons you collect, or use something as simple as an envelope. You can even keep the envelope or organizer in the car and keep it out of the kitchen altogether.

√ Designate a box for things that don't belong in the kitchen. Put stuff there as it accumulates and move it to the proper area of the house each night before bed. Figure 6-7 shows a wicker basket behind the bar that works quite well and is mostly out of sight.

Figure 6-7
Wicker baskets are good for holding things temporarily.

√ Post a calendar by the door. Transfer information from the papers that arrive to the calendar, and then immediately file, put away, or throw away the paper the information was written on.

√ When deciding whether to display an item in your home, ask yourself if it can also be used *for* something. Trunks, magazine holders, coat racks, wicker baskets, and cedar chests are nice to look at and display, and they also offer storage options. For the kitchen specifically, wicker baskets are great for keys, glasses, and cell phones.

√ Use a collapsible file folder for storing papers that must be in or near the kitchen, such as instructions for the bread machine or Crock-Pot, and keep that file folder in a bottom or top cabinet.

GunkBuster's Notebook: Tips for Emptying the Dishwasher

I mentioned earlier that if you can't unload your dishwasher in the time it takes for a frozen meal to cook in the microwave (5 to 7 minutes), something isn't right. Either your kitchen isn't organized efficiently, or you need tips on how to empty the dishwasher quickly. Hopefully, your kitchen is so organized now that you'll meet this 5-minute time limit with room to spare. Here are some tips, though, just in case you're not quite there yet:

√ Make your kids do it. They have more time than you do. When your kids do it, you spend zero minutes, a world record!

√ Load items in the dishwasher so they are grouped together. It is usually possible to pick up multiple items and put them away in a single move.

√ Organize the cabinets by the dishwasher so that you can reach into the dishwasher, get a glass or plate, and put it away without taking a step.

√ Organize the cabinets and drawers by the dishwasher to minimize having to put items on the counter, close the dishwasher door, and then put the items away after.

√ Load the dishwasher after unloading it and before closing the dishwasher door. Never close the door on an empty dishwasher; there's always something that you can put in there.

√ Unload (or load) the dishwasher while your food is in the
microwave, during a commercial break on TV, while your
kids are getting ready for school, or while waiting for a
phone call or fax. It should only take 5 minutes. Knowing
that, you can do it almost anytime at all.

√ Wait until the dry cycle has completely finished so plastic
ware will be dry enough for stacking.

√ If something comes out of the dishwasher that's still dirty,
spray it with cleanser and soak it in hot water. Run it
through the next time.

Organize the Pantry

The pantry gets a lot of action, just as the countertop does. Fortunately, though,
it's pretty easy to keep the pantry organized once you've degunked it because
most of the time you're taking stuff out of the pantry or replacing what you've
just used, such as oil and vinegar. You really only have the opportunity to gunk
up the pantry when you get home from a trip to the grocery store. If your
pantry's organized, though, it will make putting things away easy and you'll be
more likely to follow your own lead to keep it that way.

You degunk your pantry the same way you've learned to degunk everything
else. As with cabinets and drawers, first remove everything from the pantry,
apply the four-box method, clean the dirt and grime, and then replace the
items you want to keep. The only extra knowledge you need here is to know
when to throw what away. Did you know spices lose their potency after a year?
I'll outline things like that later in Table 6-1.

TIP: *Write down everything you throw out so you can replace it on your next shopping trip.*

You may be wondering just how long an item can live in your pantry before
it goes bad. If you've ever opened an old can of vegetables and gotten a
wicked surprise (perhaps the yams that didn't make it to the table at the
Thanksgiving dinner you served three years ago) you need to take a look at
this table. If you're not sure what should or should not be thrown away while
degunking, Table 6-1 will come in handy for you, too.

NOTE: *Pantries are dark and have doors because most pantry food should be stored in a cool, dry area, out of
direct sunlight.*

Table 6-1: **Pantry Food Shelf Life in General Terms**

Food	Opened and Stored Sealed	Unopened
Baking supplies, including baking powder, biscuit mix, bread crumbs, brownie and cake mixes, semi-sweet chocolate, chocolate chips, coconut, flour	6 months	1 year
Baking soda	6 months	2 years
Bread	1 week	2 weeks
Candy opened three months	6 months	1 year
Canned fruit and vegetables, canned fish, canned meats, canned olives	Once opened, should be placed in a different container in the refrigerator.	1 to 3 years, but loses nutritional value as time passes
Cereal	3 months	6 months
Coffee	2 - 3 months	2 months
Crackers and chips	10 days	6 months
Herbs and spices	6 months	1 year
Mayonnaise, jams and jellies, peppers, pickles, sauces, condiments	Once opened, should be placed in a different container in the refrigerator.	1 year
Pasta	6 months	1 year (although some people believe indefinitely)
Peanut butter	6 months	6 months
Rice	6 months	2 years
Stuffing, potato, and dinner mixes	3 months	6 months
Tea bags, sugar substitutes	1 year	2 years

Disclaimer: All foods and pantries aren't the same. A food will last longer or expire sooner depending on the manufacturer, how it was packaged, and the temperature of the pantry itself. *If ever in doubt, throw it out.*

You'll find lots of other items in your pantry, though, and your best bet is to look at the dates on those items. If it's expired, throw it away, and if it's been opened longer than six months, get rid of it. Some things seem to last indefinitely, though (although manufacturers of the products may state otherwise):

√ Salt

√ Vinegar

√ Wheat

√ Sodas (although it loses some flavor)

√ Granulated and brown sugar

√ Honey

√ Liquor like whisky, scotch, vodka, and other distilled spirits

√ Beef jerky (although it loses some flavor)

√ Vegetable oils

√ Dried corn

√ Soybeans

√ Bouillon products

√ Dry pasta

√ Cream of tartar

Putting Things Back

After you've applied the four-box method, you can apply the same organizing techniques when organizing the pantry as you did for the cabinets and drawers. It's pretty much the same: put taller items in the back and shorter ones in the front, put often-used items at eye level and rarely-used items on the top and bottom shelves, use lazy Susans for cans and spices, stack "like" items, and add additional shelves or shelf helpers if you don't have the space you need.

Specifically, in the pantry you can group foods by use or by type, or even alphabetically. I prefer grouping items by type because it seems to make everything easier to find than when you use other methods. If items are organized by type, you don't have to think about the name of the product to find it in an alphabetical list or make a connection between the food you're looking for and the "use" group it belongs to. Here's an outline of what seems to work best for most people.

Group the following items together at eye level:

√ Canned vegetables organized in subgroups by type such as corn, green beans, baked beans, carrots, asparagus, tomatoes, and others.

√ Canned meats including tuna, chicken, and fish. Stack them.

√ Cereals

√ Soups

√ Crackers, chips, nuts, popcorn, and other treats

√ Breads

√ Boxed soup and dip mixes

√ Boxed dinners

√ Pasta

Group these items on higher shelves:

√   Sugar, flour, and other baking supplies

√   Items purchased in bulk that can be stacked (these items can also be stored in a utility room)

√   Tea and coffee

√   Glass items, including bottles of vinegar and oil, and unopened extras (in glass), including jalapeños, mushrooms, hot sauce, salsa, and olives

Group these items on lower shelves:

√   Onions, potatoes, and other fresh vegetables that should be stored in cool, dark, and dry places

√   Bags of dried beans

√   Trash bags

√   Pet foods and treats (if there's no other place for them)

√   Trash can

Group these items on a shelf on the left or right side of the pantry, if one exists (if not, choose a higher shelf):

√   Cans of cooking soups, cooking tomatoes, and other items required for making casseroles and dinner dishes

√   Breakfast bars, power bars, granola bars, and diet bars

√   Refrigerator replacement items like ketchup, mustard, mayonnaise, and salad dressings

Figure 6-8 shows a pantry with foods organized by type. Although this pantry varies some from the bulleted suggestions in this section, it is still fully functional, organized, and secure. You should organize your pantry in a way that follows the tips in this section but also meets your specific needs.

TIP: *Incorporate shallow organizers, wire or plastic baskets, and Tupperware for storing smaller items.*

Degunk the Refrigerator and Freezer

The only thing left to degunk in the kitchen is the refrigerator and freezer. I saved this for last because once you degunk the panty, refrigerator, and freezer, you'll probably need to make a trip to the grocery store to restock your kitchen. You should also plan to degunk the refrigerator around the time the trash man comes to pick up the garbage, and I'm betting your garbage cans are pretty full

Figure 6-8
An average pantry, organized by type.

now, so you may have to wait. You're not going to want those expired eggs to sit in the trash for a week before they leave the kitchen or get picked up by the trash man.

It's also the best part of kitchen degunking; it's fun and will make a nice reward for finishing up the kitchen tasks outlined in this chapter. Make it a game to find the items you've been missing or to identify spoiled food. I love going through the refrigerator because it's always full of surprises.

Getting Started

As usual, remove everything and clean the fridge. Use mild cleansers to wipe up the gunk so you don't leave a smell in there. (You probably already know that one strong smell can linger in the refrigerator long after the offending product has been removed.) Spray the cleanser on a paper towel and wipe the refrigerator down with it; don't spray anything directly in the refrigerator. Once it's clean (and if you need help, refer to Chapter 12), put an open box of baking soda in there. It isn't just a marketing ploy by Arm & Hammer; it really does work.

Once it's clean, it's time to start throwing stuff away. You may be wondering just how long an item can live in your refrigerator before it goes bad, though. Table 6-2 will outline some of the basic rules for refrigerator and freezer shelf life to help you decide what you should and shouldn't keep. Remember though, *when in doubt, throw it out!*

TIP: *If you've ever opened a Tupperware container and gotten a smelly surprise, you may need to take a longer look at this table.*

Table 6-2:   Refrigerator and Freezer Food Shelf Life

Food	Refrigerator	Freezer
Baby food	1 to 2 days	Do not freeze.
Breads	Storing in refrigerator may promote spoiling. If you do, though, 1 week is a good rule	1/2 year
Butter and margarine	1 to 2 months	1/2 year
Casseroles, soups, and stews	3 to 4 days	2 months
Cheese (hard)	1/2 to 1 year	1 to 2 years
Cheese spreads	1 month	1 month
Condiments: ketchup, mustard, pickles, relish	1/2 year	Do not freeze.
Eggs	4 weeks	Do not freeze.
Fish sticks	Not applicable	1 1/2 years
Frozen dinners and frozen pizza	Not applicable	4 months
Fruit	3 days to 2 weeks	1 year
Ice cream	Not applicable	2 months
Juice	2 weeks	3 months
Meats (raw)	1 to 3 days	3 to 4 months for lamb, turkey, and variety meats; 1/2 to 1 year for hamburger, pork, duck, goose, and steaks
Meats (processed) including hot dogs, lunchmeat, and ham	1 to 2 weeks	2 months

(continued)

Table 6-2: Refrigerator and Freezer Food Shelf Life *(continued)*

Food	Refrigerator	Freezer
Milk and cream	5 to 7 days	3 weeks
Pies	1 to 2 days	1 month
Salad dressings, mayonnaise	2 to 3 months	Do not freeze.
Seafood (most)	1 to 3 days	3 months
Sour cream	1 month	2 months
Vegetables	3 days to two weeks	1 year for commercially frozen
Waffles, pancakes, quick breads	(usually stored in the freezer)	1 to 2 months
Yogurt	1 week after "sell by" date	2 months

TIP: *Write down everything you throw out so you can replace it on your next shopping trip.*

Putting Things Back

After you've applied the four-box method, you can apply the same organizing techniques when organizing the refrigerator as you did for the pantry. It's pretty much the same: put taller items in the back and shorter ones in the front, put often-used items at eye level and rarely-used items on the top and bottom shelves, stack items that can be stacked (like sodas), and use the shelves and door organizers efficiently.

As with the pantry, I prefer grouping items by type because it seems to make everything easier to find. If items are organized by type, you don't have to think about the name of the product to find it in an alphabetical list or make a connection between the food you're looking for and the "use" group it belongs to.

Group these items together at eye level on a shelf:

√ Leftovers in see-through containers with lids, stacked

√ Leftovers from delivered meals or restaurants

√ Prepared meals such as casseroles or lasagna to be cooked later

√ Healthy foods, including fruit you'll eat in the next couple of days, low-fat Jell-O or pudding, and yogurt

√ Prepared foods with a short shelf life, such as mayonnaise-based salads, guacamole, and homemade or pre-cooked pastas

√ Meat or fish that will be cooked in the next three to five days (kept in a separate pullout bin to avoid contaminating other foods or dripping on the shelf)

√   Dairy items such as eggs, butter, sour cream, cottage cheese, and margarine. These foods need to be kept cold, and the refrigerator door is the warmest part in the refrigerator. They're best stored on a shelf with easy access.

Group these items in the meat and cheese drawer, and put them in a Ziploc baggie after they've been opened, unless they come in a package that can be sealed:

√   Hot dogs and lunchmeat

√   Cheese and cheese products

√   Sausage, bacon, and pepperoni

√   Small on-the-go snacks

TIP: *Keep raw meats separate to avoid contamination. Either store them in the bottom drawer or shelf or keep them in a separate container, such as a pullout bin.*

Group these items on the inside of the refrigerator door:

√   Jams, jellies, and preserves

√   Condiments such as ketchup, mustard, and mayonnaise

√   Pickles, pepperoncini, relish, and peppers

√   Sauces such as Worcestershire sauce, steak sauce, soy sauce, hot sauce, and barbecue sauce

√   Drink mixers such as Bloody Mary mix, tonic water, and lemon and lime juice

Group tall or bulky items together, preferably on a top shelf or door:

√   Juices, sodas, and water

√   Milk, half-and-half, and other taller dairy products

√   Soups and stews

√   Iced tea

Here are some other hints and tips:

√   Make it a rule that before every trip to the grocery store, you get rid of anything that might be old or spoiled and wipe up any spills. Doing so makes it *much* easier to maintain a clean fridge when you are dumping new stuff in with old things, and you'll know exactly what you need. This will also help you avoid buying more items at the store that you don't need. Don't forget to dig down deep and look through the fruit and vegetable bins. Things that spoil quickly tend to like to hide down in there!

√ Group fruits together in a fruit drawer, if you have one. They'll stay fresher longer, especially compared to leaving them on the kitchen counter or windowsill.

√ Fruits and vegetables emit gases that cause each other to spoil. Grouping like items together minimizes this effect.

√ Do not wash fruit or vegetables before storing them in the refrigerator. They'll deteriorate faster.

√ Group vegetables in a vegetable crisper. Most vegetables come in the bag they should be stored in, and most of the time that is a perforated bag or a loose plastic one. Don't just dump veggies in the drawer without their bag.

√ Some vegetable leftovers, like cucumbers and onions, should be stored in an airtight Ziploc bag once they're cut open to avoid spoiling and to keep them from sharing their scent with the rest of the items in the bin. When in doubt, if it has a smell, put it in a baggie.

√ Do not store leftover canned fruits or vegetables in their can in the refrigerator. Transfer them to a plastic container.

√ Meats that won't be used in the next three to five days should not be stored in the refrigerator; instead, these items should be stored in the freezer when you bring them home from the store. Group the meats together in the freezer, though, on the same shelf or bin.

√ Overfilled fridges may not stay cold enough to keep food at proper temperature, so don't let yours get too crowded.

√ Throw away leftovers that are more than two days old.

Once the kitchen is degunked, organized, clean, and rid of papers, things that don't belong, and unworthy, broken, duplicate, or useless kitchen items, how do you plan to keep it that way? With Table 6-3, I hope to keep you and your family on track by helping you find problem areas and dealing with them before you get gunked up again.

Table 6-3:   Everyday Maintenance Tasks for Keeping a Clean Kitchen

Problem Area	Solution
When items such as blenders, mixers, or fruit smoothie machines are used, they are not put back in their proper storage places.	Make sure the storage solution is easy to reach and accessible. Ask the family member who uses this item where they would like it stored.
The morning coffee area is littered with sugar packets, coffee stains, filters, and stirrers.	Place a small "trash can" on the counter to collect small trash items. There are many decorative ones available. Also, get away from packets of sugar and creamer. Put those items in a holder specifically created for them.

(continued)

Table 6-3: Everyday Maintenance Tasks for Keeping a Clean Kitchen

Problem Area	Solution
You dread emptying the dishwasher because it takes so long.	Reconsider the location of the items in your kitchen. Move silverware drawers closer to the dishwasher, and organize plates, cups, bowls, and glasses around that area, too. Minimize movement.
You can never find the necessary knife or cooking utensil when you need it.	Consider a container for the counter that holds the cooking utensils you use often or a butcher block knife holder.
The kitchen counter is always covered in paperwork, homework, keys, cell phones, and other gunk, making cooking dinner each night a clean-then-cook chore.	Create an area in or near the kitchen where family members can "explode" when they get home. Refer to Chapter 4 for help. Hang wicker baskets for each member, build or purchase a key ring/cell phone/mail holder, and create a specific area for kids to sit and do homework and parents to read the paper, mail, and pay bills. Make sure this area is as close to the kitchen as possible.
Your kids are still messy, especially when making their own snacks.	Put items the kids use often in their reach. Make it easy for them to return the items they use, such as condiments, and insist they put used dishes in the dishwasher or sink. Consider paper plates and plastic spoons, and put a trash can in plain sight until they are trained.
You often look for something and realize you're almost out of it or don't have any at all.	Put a whiteboard inside the pantry or on the side of the refrigerator. List things there you need to purchase on your next shopping trip.
Your coupons, recipes, and other paperwork still cause gunk.	For a while, leave the notebooks, photo albums, recipe box, and filing system in plain sight. Once you're trained, move those items underground. Post a calendar for all family members to use, to transfer what's on all of that paper to a central location.

Once the pantry and refrigerator are degunked, organized, clean, and rid of spoiled and expired foods, how do you plan to keep it that way? See Table 6-4 for tips on everyday maintenance for those areas.

Table 6-4:   Everyday Maintenance for a Clean Pantry and Fridge

Problem Area	Solution
You're not sure how old the canned goods are that are stored in the pantry, or which ones you should eat first.	First, throw away any cans with expiration dates that have passed. Then, when returning from the grocery store, put duplicate items behind the ones that already exist. That way, you'll always be using the oldest ones first.
You or your family members don't put things back into the pantry (or refrigerator) where they belong.	Consider labeling the shelves or putting pictures up for kids (they could even draw them), and make sure the spot you've chosen to house the coffee, cookies, crackers, and chips is easy for all family members to reach.
Smaller items get lost in the pantry or refrigerator.	Use open baskets, plastic containers, or glass bottles to hold loose items.
You often find spoiled food in the refrigerator.	Keep all leftovers in plain view, and throw leftovers away after 48 hours. Make a thorough search through the refrigerator once a week, perhaps while you're waiting for water to boil on the stove or the night before the trash goes out.
Food spoils more quickly than is outlined in Table 6-2.	Change the settings on your refrigerator to make it colder, read the refrigerator manual, and use a thermometer to test the temperature. It should be between 35 and 38 degrees Fahrenheit.
Sometimes you look in the refrigerator expecting to find ketchup, but none is there.	Put a whiteboard on the refrigerator door. When any member of the family has finished an item, have them write it on the whiteboard's grocery list.
Apples taste like onions, and onions taste like olives.	Store like things together. Fruits stay with fruits, and vegetables with vegetables.

Summing Up

In this chapter, you learned how to degunk, declutter, and organize your kitchen. You learned that applying the four-box method works here, too, and that getting rid of stuff is again the best thing you can do to degunk. Degunking the kitchen not only means cleaning cabinets, drawers, and countertops, though; it also means cleaning the pantry, the refrigerator, and the freezer. You can refer back to the tables in this chapter for the shelf life of the most common foods so you'll know when to throw them out and when to keep them.

Chapter 7

Organizing Living Areas

Degunking Checklist:

√   Create a dining room you can dine in.

√   Use long-term and deep storage for seasonal or rarely used items.

√   Create an organized area in family rooms and living rooms for everyday clutter, such as remote controls, magazines, and pet toys.

√   Make your bedroom a place to relax by organizing and decluttering it.

√   Control the disorder in your kids' rooms by making it easy for them to put things away and keep things organized on their own.

√   Apply everyday maintenance tasks to keep these rooms degunked.

In the past few chapters, you've tackled problem areas including the kitchen and closets, and hopefully, you've made progress. You dealt with all of those areas using similar tactics, specifically applying the four-box method to get rid of things you no longer need or want, laying out what you want to keep, and then creating an organizational plan to put those items back to discourage gunk from accruing again. You're now going to apply those same principles to the most-used rooms in your house. Here, you'll focus on the dining room, living areas, bedrooms, and kids' rooms. (In the next chapter, you'll focus on smaller areas, including bathrooms, utility rooms, and offices.)

Make Your Dining Room a Place to Dine

The dining room, whether it's a separate room or in the form of a breakfast nook or eat-in kitchen area, is truly a gunk magnet. Family members find the kitchen (or dining room) table simply too enticing because it's a great place for spreading out projects and jigsaw puzzles, going through the mail and paying bills, collecting things that need to go out (like checks for the bank, coupons, DVDs, or grocery lists), and storing things until they're needed. It's also a great place to keep magazines and newspapers or do homework, and it offers a handy place to throw all of the day's paperwork. All of this can make dining in this area impossible or, at the very least, uncomfortable. The idea in this section, then, is to make this area a place you can eat in again.

As you did with the other chapters, go through this room and apply the four-box method first. Get rid of things you don't need, don't want, or don't use; move things that don't belong; and then decide how you're going to deal with the rest. Unfortunately, though, you also have to deal with what goes *on* there too, not just what goes *in*. If the dining room table is where your kids do their homework and you like it that way because you can keep an eye on them, then you'll have to take that into consideration when you start to organize the area. Figure 7-1 shows some things that don't belong in the dining room; including golf balls and golf clubs, the fan, which needs to be put away, and the leaves to the table, which should be stored out of sight.

Living without a Closet

Most dining areas don't have closets, so many people employ a piece of furniture for storage. Dining room furniture can include a china cabinet, armoire, or hutch. If it's a breakfast nook, you may use built-in cabinets or storage under a seating area. If you have any of these things, go through them and get rid of what you can, and then use these areas to organize what you need to keep. If you don't have anything like this, you'll have to improvise by adding your own

Figure 7-1
Golf clubs don't belong in the dining room.

storage, such as a trunk or a seating area that also serves as storage via a lift-up seat. You might also build shelves. Some dining areas also have cabinets or drawers, especially if there's a wet bar attached to the dining room or if the eating area is part of the kitchen. Again, this is a good place to incorporate dining room storage. Figure 7-2 shows a small eating area in the kitchen of a condominium, with cabinets underneath the breakfast nook for storage.

To use the storage areas you have (or will create) effectively, you have to consider what *exactly* it is that you need to store there. For instance, you probably don't need to store your holiday tablecloth and napkins; you can put them somewhere else, where you'll have easy access to them during the holiday season. You probably do need your everyday place mats and napkins, salt and pepper shakers, coasters, a wine opener, and a tablecloth for the times guests arrive for dinner on short notice. You have to decide what can stay and what should go.

Here are some tips to help you get the most from your non-closet-dining-kitchen-breakfast-nook space:

√   Use a cedar chest or trunk to store rarely-used items, like the tablecloth your
    grandmother knitted and willed to you. You can leave the trunk in the
    dining room area if you like the look and have the space.

Figure 7-2

Even the smallest of areas can offer storage options.

√   If you never use your "good" china or silver and are only keeping it to will to your kids, go ahead and give it to them now. Perhaps they'll enjoy it. At the very least, they'll store it.

√   Stack dishes and store silver in a china cabinet or hutch in the most space-saving way possible. Box up anything you haven't used in two years and put it in the attic. The space you'll clear will likely be all you'll need to store the stuff you use.

√   Put items you must have but rarely use in the dining area on high shelves if those exist. Consider building additional shelving.

√   Remove items from hutches, china cabinets, and armoires that don't belong in the dining room. Linens, photos, newspaper clippings, and "things that may be worth something someday" belong elsewhere.

√   If the dining area is next to a hall closet, use that closet for storage.

√   Hang attractive pieces of dishware on the walls instead of in china cabinets. You can hang ceramic bowls or plates or larger serving plates.

√   Consider a freestanding wine rack if you have lots of wine and a free corner of the room.

√   Dedicate a drawer if you have one for small candles and matches, napkin rings, and coasters.

√   Rid yourself of knick-knacks you have to dust around.

Making Peace with the Dining/Working Area Phenomenon

While freeing up the dining room table makes eating with the family, visiting with friends, and simply looking at the room a much more pleasurable experience, actually making that happen can be nearly impossible when the dining room or eating area also doubles as a work area. The eating area is often the only available place in the home where mom and dad can cook dinner while also watching junior surf the Web or do his homework. In small apartments, it may also be the only choice. If you have to live with this setup, then, at least make it as organized and functional as possible.

First, the dining area must remain a place to eat. That's the main goal, and keeping the table free of clutter is going to take some doing. While it's fine to have coffee and read the paper here in the morning, the paper should never remain on the table once it's read. There must be a tool in place for facilitating that, such as placing an attractive recycle bin nearby. This can be as simple as a plastic bin or as elaborate as a large, decorative bowl. Figure 7-3 shows an example.

Figure 7-3
Something as simple as a large, decorative storage bowl or attractive basket could keep your dining room or kitchen table free of newspapers.

Next, make sure family members have other options for picking up after themselves:

√   Add a "move" box, such as a wicker basket or plastic bin, where anything left on the table is stored until it can be moved to the room in which it belongs.

Encourage family members to remove items from the box daily. Have a rule in effect for items left in the move box for more than two days, such as dumping the leftover (and obviously unimportant) items in a cardboard box in the garage or in the newspaper or magazine recycle bin.

√ Place a centerpiece on the table, or leave place mats and napkins on the table to remind family members that this a place to eat and not a final resting place for their junk.

√ If extra coins are a problem, use jars to hold loose change, as shown in Figure 7-4.

Figure 7-4

Jars make great options for loose items like change.

√ Consider adding a filing cabinet if the dining area also serves as an office or bill-paying area. A small filing system, especially a plastic collapsible one, can be hidden in a cabinet or hutch.

√ Designate a drawer for pens, pencils, tape, a small stapler, stamps, envelopes, and other "office" items. Put a plastic organizer in there to keep the drawer organized. Encourage family members to put things away after using them. You could also consider using an attractive utensil and napkin holder such as the ones made for picnic tables for these items if you don't have a drawer.

√ Designate a table in the dining area if room exists to hold homework, projects, and paperwork temporarily while dinner is served. Transfer back to the table to finish and then onto other areas such as, backpacks or offices, before bed.

TIP: *Cancel subscriptions for magazines or newspapers you no longer have time to read.*

What you're trying to do here is to figure out what causes the problem of gunk in the first place. If it's paperwork, a filing system may be needed. If it's homework, a homework area may be designated. If it's newspapers, a recycle bin is needed. Whatever the problem areas are, though, identify them and create a solution. Don't get discouraged, though; as you learned in previous chapters, even putting a clothes hamper in the exact spot where your spouse dumps their clothes on the floor doesn't mean they won't drop them on the floor next to it. The idea is to create solutions and try to help your family use them.

Create Livable Family Rooms

Family rooms (or living rooms) can have a lot in common with dining rooms, because they are often attached and part of the main dining area. Therefore, it's important to re-read the dining room section of this chapter, keeping one eye on the section's highlights and another eye on the living room. The same concepts can be applied here as in the dining area, including adding a "move" box, canceling unwanted magazine subscriptions, designating a table for homework and work projects (which must be cleared before bed), and removing items from the room you no longer use. And yes, this includes knick-knacks, videos, CDs, books, and keepsakes. Once you've applied these concepts to your family room, you can continue to degunk by applying the family-room-centric ideas in the following sections.

Add, Remove, or Modify Furniture

One way to degunk a living area is to add or remove furniture or modify what you already own. If there's a beanbag chair your kids grew out of, a love seat only the cat uses, or a recliner that no longer reclines, get rid of it. The space you'll free up might be just what the doctor ordered. If the item you remove is in a corner, for instance, you can use the space for a new corner shelving unit. The chair's replacement can now house the telephone, CDs and DVDs, photos, and plants.

Adding furniture (or replacing furniture) with more functional pieces makes a room more sensible, too. Traditional coffee tables, for instance, are really quite useless. They don't have drawers or compartments, and most don't even have a shelf underneath. Replacing one of these tables with a more functional one with built-in storage can easily solve the coffee table nightmare (remotes, pens, paper, magazines, telephone, etc.). The same can be said for lamp tables. Usually, these tables have a single, and quite small, drawer that doesn't hold anything. Replacing this type of table with an item that can store things can work wonders. You can create an attractive side table with a small two-drawer filing cabinet and an inexpensive round table top from one of those accent table kits, top with an attractive tablecloth, and you have an elegant storage solution for videos, CDs, and such in the family room. Also consider making a sideboard with a plank and two sturdy sawhorses. Cover with a large rectangular tablecloth and store items underneath it in baskets. In a dining room, you could use the top to hold your centerpiece and dining items while you are using the dining table for work.

If you can't afford to replace your traditional coffee or lamp table, though, it is possible to modify what you have. You can cover a table with a nice linen skirt and store things underneath it. This is an especially good tactic with round lamp tables. You can do the same with a coffee table, or purchase a hanging shelf that hooks onto the table itself and offers storage underneath. (These are not unlike pullout keyboard trays you find in computer desks.) Of course, you can always purchase a nice wicker basket that fits the table or recycle an old drawer or plastic tub.

Finally, if there's room under the sofa, again consider your storage options. If you can fit a drawer, basket, or similar storage container under the couch that can be pulled out and pushed back under easily, you've found a new place to store your magazines and books!

TIP: *Don't forget about the walls. Hanging photos on the wall or creating a new shelf for knick-knacks keeps those items off of the one or two tables available in the room.*

Rearrange the Room

If your living area feels crowded, is physically uncomfortable, is hard to navigate, or difficult to clean, you'll have a rough time getting and staying degunked. It won't matter what you do initially, if the room doesn't "feel" good to you or your family, chances are you won't care enough about the room to put in the effort required to keep it organized. It's the family room; it should fit your family's needs and personalities.

Having this room fit all of your family members' needs and personalities can be a little tricky, though. This is especially true if one member collects something. Porcelain frogs, thimbles, shot glasses, commemorative golf balls, family photos, DVDs, CDs, tapes, and electronic equipment are common collectibles. These things can really gunk up a room, make it hard to navigate, make it hard to dust, and make it look, well, cluttered.

You'll also have a problem if this room is where junior plays video games, where mom knits, where dad builds model cars, and where sis does her homework. The idea is to sit down and decide what the purpose of the room is now, what you want the purpose of the room to be in the future, and how you're going to arrange the room to meet these needs.

The Room Should Be Easy to Navigate

First and foremost, the room should be easy to navigate. Making a small or cluttered room easier to navigate often means getting rid of furniture or replacing larger furniture with smaller pieces. Making a larger room easier to navigate often means rearranging the furniture. I personally think for most people and most rooms, the couch is best situated against a wall, not in the center. When a couch is against a wall, there's no additional space required for walking around the back of it. Putting the couch against a wall frees up the space that would be needed to walk around the entire thing. The same is true of larger TVs, stereos, and electronics. There's no need to lose valuable real estate by putting larger things anywhere but against a wall. (Of course, if you have a huge room, this won't necessarily be a problem.)

With the larger items against the wall, take a look at the smaller ones. Lamps and tables should be situated where you need them, at the ends of couches and beside chairs. A coffee table, if you have one, should be placed in front the couch, and some sort of under-the-table storage should be employed to hold remote controls and other items. CD and DVD racks, magazine racks, and shelving can also be a big gunk buster and don't take up much space. Consider purchasing these items.

Create a Hobby Center

Finally, when rearranging a room, spend some quality time thinking about what you do there and what you will continue to use the room for. If it's mostly for watching TV and playing video games, work the room around that. To encourage neatness, make sure you create an organizational unit for the items that must stay in the room, such as DVDs and video games.

If you currently use the room as a hobby room—for instance, for building model ships, quilting, working jigsaw puzzles, or scrapbooking—remember, this is your family's room, too, not just yours. It's also where guests will congregate and it is usually where you'll entertain. It really should not look like a hobby shop or a flea market. You could consider creating a designated hobby area in a section of the room with storage, lighting, and a work table and chair, if necessary. Or seriously consider using another room or, at the very least, a rolling cart to keep supplies on, and bring out the cart only when you're working on your projects. You can always store the cart in the hall coat closet or in an office. Rolling carts are wonderful for anyone who has ongoing projects and hobbies.

Create a Place for the Clutter You Will Always Have

Remember, you'll always have clutter. There will always be remote controls, magazines, pet toys, nail files, pens, pencils, mail, and phone messages. But, is this stuff really clutter? Not necessarily. It's only clutter if it takes away from the look or functionality of the room or interferes with daily living. It is for that reason you need to create places for these things. Here are some tips for dealing with everyday clutter:

√ Use a decorative cup, flower pot, or vase to hold pens, pencils, nail files, and similar items. This is a good way of making a previously unused knick-knack an asset. See Figure 7-5.

√ Clean out cluttered drawers and find new ways to use them more effectively. See Figure 7-6 for an example of a useless drawer.

√ Store pet toys in a basket and place the basket out of sight. You're pets will find them. See Figure 7-7.

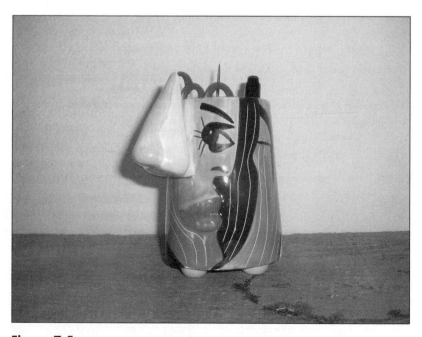

Figure 7-5
Artsy cups can hold the small stuff.

Figure 7-6
Drawers, even small ones, should be cleaned and used effectively.

Figure 7-7
Group and store pet toys out of sight.

√ Build or purchase a remote control organizer.

√ Consider a media armoire.

√ Use a cedar chest or trunk for storage; it can double as extra seating if you have a crowd.

√ Use a wicker basket or trunk for kids toys. Insist that all toys be put there or put away before bed.

√ Get rid of DVDs, video games, and CDs you haven't viewed or listened to in over a year. Consider trading them for new ones, donating them to the local library, or giving them to friends or family.

√ Don't let photos, birthday cards, holiday cards, knick-knacks, and similar items clutter up the room. If you must, pick three and rotate them with others as you tire of them.

√ Hang speakers and photos, and put plants on shelves to keep them out of the way.

GunkBuster's Notebook: Parting with Knick-knacks and Memories

Getting rid of things you've spent years collecting can be traumatic. In fact, it can be so upsetting for some that it brings tears to the eyes or creates a sense of panic. If you're one of those people, it's going to be tough to get rid of your collectibles, family "heirlooms," your kid's old schoolwork and artwork, and duplicate photos in order to declutter the fireplace mantle. I know that, and while I can't help you in the physical sense, I can try to help you in the emotional one.

If you're having trouble getting rid of things (the ashtray your kid made in summer camp back in 1982, the keys to your first car, or items that belonged to a relative who's passed on), here are some tips to help you get started:

√ Put everything you can part with temporarily into a large cardboard box and tape it up. Move the box to the garage or another long-term storage area. Promise yourself you'll keep the box, and if things get too hard for you emotionally, you'll open the box and dig out one or two of your favorite items for comfort. At some point, you might be able to consider getting rid of the box.

√ Choose your favorite three knick-knacks and box up the rest. Rotate among your favorites as often as you'd like, never having more than three out at a time.

√ Give items to your children, especially if you deem them family memories and would will them to them anyway.

√ If you collect newspapers, recipes, news clippings, and magazines or magazine articles, understand you are putting your family at risk by not storing these things properly. Paper can attract pests and pose a fire hazard. Cut your favorite recipes and articles out of magazines and newspapers and place them in binders with vinyl sheet protectors, organized by topic. It is much easier to find a recipe in a binder than in a pile of 10-year-old magazines! The sheet protector will also help you from getting gunk all over the recipe when you use it in the kitchen.

√ It's okay to get rid of photographs and recycle items your grandmother knitted or quilted, your kid's old schoolwork, and items you were willed. This is especially true if you are indeed a chronic clutterer; your family members would probably be happier that you took control of your clutter instead of keeping all of their old things.

√ Ask other family members or close family friends if they want to take mementos and tell them they must be picked up by a certain date. You are not required to be the historian for the entire family. Think about keeping just the items that are of use to you and that give you the best memories of your loved one. Consider having a yard sale with the rest and donating the proceeds to a charity in memory of your loved ones.

√ Experts claim that clutter is a depressant. It causes feelings or inadequacy and makes one feel as if they are not in control of their life. Getting rid of clutter will help you feel better.

√ Ask for help. A friend, neighbor, or family member would gladly help you out if you asked.

√ If you're into feng shui, decluttering is basic to a full life because it means you are ridding your home of stagnant chi, or life energy.

√ Join a declutter group. You can find one at **http:// declutter.meetup.com/groups**.

√ Avoid flea markets, garage sales, and thrift stores. You'll just buy more stuff you don't need.

GunkBuster's Notebook: Make Your Bedroom a Place to Relax

Since there really isn't much more to be said for bedrooms that hasn't been said for other rooms in the house, degunking your bedroom has been relegated to a short GunkBuster's Notebook. As with other rooms in the house, it's about making the room work *for* you, not *against* you. It's about uncovering problem areas and solving their related gunk. Here are a few ideas for the bedroom:

√ Place a laundry hamper well within reach of those who can never seem to find it; put a hamper wherever you find dirty clothes piled on the floor. Once it starts to catch on, slowly move the hamper to an area where it makes more sense.

√ Clean out what's under the bed and get rid of what you don't want. Then, use this new storage area wisely. It might make a good place to store sheets, blankets, and extra pillows.

√ Organize drawers and nightstands to hold what you need where you need it. You don't need old photos in your nightstand drawer; you need a TV remote control, earplugs, lotion, and a flashlight.

√ Use a shoe organizer or shoe shelf to keep shoes off the floor and organized.

√ Use an over-the-door shoe holder to hold anything that clutters up the bedroom, including flashlights, hosiery, sewing kits, lint brushes, travel kits, reading glasses, movies, jewelry, belts, scarves, and even wallets or keys. (Or even shoes.)

√ Invest in the bed. Make sure it's comfortable and clean and relaxes you. After all, it's where you'll spend almost a third of your life!

√ Do not be tempted by every white sale. You do not need dozens of sheet sets! If you decide to redecorate, consider donating your old sheets, curtains, and bedspreads to local shelters and halfway houses.

TIP: Learn to clean while you sleep. Soak your toilets in white vinegar once a week, flush the next morning, and you have a super-clean toilet with no hard labor. Line a white sink with bleached paper

towels, remove in the morning and you have a pristine sink. (Do not do this with colored sinks, as it may fade them.) Run white vinegar through a washing machine, coffee maker, or dishwasher; put lemon peels in the garbage disposal; let soiled dishes soak in Dawn Power Dissolver; purchase a RoboMaid or Roomba (these dust and vacuum on their own); and clean the air with an air purifier. You'll find these and other ideas in Chapter 11.

Control Clutter and Disorganization in Kids' Rooms

Kids' rooms hold special challenges for degunkers. Your child's room is not just a place to dress and sleep as your bedroom is for you; it's also a place to play, do homework, entertain friends, and store everything they own. A kid's room is their bedroom, dressing room, living room, playroom, storage room, and study room. Imagine if you only had one room for all of this and the mental abilities of a 5-, 10-, or 15-year-old; it would be quite difficult to manage. That's where you have to step up and make the task easier.

Apply the Four-Box Method

Twice a year, you should spend a half day or so in your kids' rooms and apply the four-box method. Let your kids and teens help, and decide together what clothes and shoes don't fit, what clothes and shoes they don't like, what toys they've outgrown or broken, what schoolwork and artwork they've saved that can be thrown away (yes, Mom, this may be hard for you, too), and how and where you'll get rid of this stuff. Let your children help you decide who you'll give the stuff to and teach them the value of giving along the way. Talk about charities and churches and how your used goods can help others. This can be a bonding time as well as a cleaning session. Also, don't insist they get rid of anything they really care about, no matter how silly the item may seem to you. If you are too harsh here, you may turn them into a pack rat—and you don't want that!

Make Cleaning Up Easy for Your Younger Kids

Once you've cleaned up the room (as you would any other room in the house using the four-box method), figure out what the problem areas are and work on those. Most kids have a hard time putting their toys away, and this is one task you can make easier with proper organization. Some kids can't seem to ever make their beds. Would you want to make the bed if you had to create hospital corners, fluff several pillows, and tuck in a comforter? No, and neither do they. In the following sections, you'll learn how to solve these dilemmas by making it easier for them to clean up, and thus, making it more likely they can stay on top of their required cleaning tasks.

TIP: *While most of the suggestions in this section are targeted at younger kids, some tips will apply to older ones. If you have teens, there's a section just for you later in the chapter.*

Toy Chests

Toy chests, if they have proper hardware to keep their lids from falling on a child's head, are a blessing for the messy child. If it isn't stuffed to the brim (and it shouldn't be after applying the four-box method), tossing all of the toys in the toy chest is a painless way to clean up. Unfortunately, it isn't the most organized solution, but for a problem child, it's a start.

Containers, Bins, Storage

There are a hundred ways to use storage containers, bins, and boxes to organize your child's room and make it easier for them to manage. Here are just a few suggestions:

√   Use containers and bins that you label to hold toys with multiple pieces. Once a toy loses too many pieces (a number you'll have to decide), tell your child you will have to get rid of it. That will help your child keep the toys in their proper bins.

√   Make sure toy storage options are well within your child's reach. Clear containers are best because they can see what's in them without opening them, and kids are more likely to keep containers that slide out of a cubby or are drawer-like where they belong. They know how and where it should be returned once they're finished with it. Label the containers with words or pictures. Make sure the lids are easy for little hands to open and close. Fancy latches and vacuum seals will only cause frustration.

√   When you purchase a toy, tell your child they must get rid of one they already own and no longer play with.

√   Keep books in a bookshelf, not stacked. This will help keep the books organized.

√ Keep arts and crafts together, preferably in a rolling cart. This way, any ongoing project can be moved to a family room (and then back to the bedroom) easily.

√ Install high shelves for beloved stuffed animals or collector dolls.

Easy-to-Make Beds

Most children (and teens) don't understand why their bed must be made every day. They don't care if you make it or not either, and they see no purpose in spending their own time doing it. After all, they're just going to mess it up again the next night. However, it's generally important to the parent, and it must be done under the general-cleanliness-principle rule.

In order to facilitate the bed-making part of life, take a moment to figure out what makes making a bed difficult. It's not the fitted sheet, but it is the additional sheets and blanket. They get all messed up and are hard to sort out in the morning. It's the half dozen pillows and 15 stuffed animals. It's stuff that doesn't belong on the bed to begin with, like a book or game. Solution? One fitted sheet and a comforter. One pillow. In the morning, the child hops out of bed, pulls the comforter to the top, and places the single pillow on top of that. It can be completed in 30 seconds.

TIP: A basket by the bed can be the daytime home for the stuffed animals, and they'll be easy to find to take to bed for a cuddle at night.

Clothes Hampers

As with spouses, kids sometimes have a hard time hitting the clothes hamper. Dirty clothes end up on the floor. If this is a problem, put a big-mouth tub or clothes hamper wherever your child usually changes clothes. If there is a way to make it a game, do so. For instance, you can put the clothes hamper against a wall and then put a large basketball net above it, and your child can shoot for the basket with his socks and underwear.

Use Lower Closet Poles

Lowering or adding a second closet pole can help younger children stay organized. You can't expect them to hang clothes on a pole they can't reach! Along the same vein, long and wide bookcases, shelves, and dressers are more easily accessed than taller ones. So if you can, think low and long, not tall and thin. Not only is it more accessible, it's safer. The chances of a short and wide bookcase falling on a child are much lower than a tall and thin one falling.

Dealing with Teenagers

If you have teenagers, you know that labeling containers, putting out a toy box, and offering a clothes hamper aren't solutions that fit their mindset. A teenager's messy room is an extension of who they are; it helps them assert their independence and allows them to show the world they are their own person and are separating themselves from their parents. So dealing with a teenager's messy room isn't nearly the same problem as dealing with a younger child's.

It isn't impossible to help your child become and stay organized, though. Here, I've collected some tips and tricks of the trade:

√ Make sure there are organizational units in place. A key rack for keys, their mail, and a cell phone is a necessity, as are a small filing cabinet, a desk with the proper supplies, and storage for those supplies. There should also be a filing system for works-in-progress and all of the paper gunk that goes with it.

√ Offer adequate shelving in closets and on the walls. Remember, this is really their only space. They need room to organize their things. These things include stuffed animals, trophies, plaques, books, electronics, and photos, as well as clothes and shoes.

√ Install CD, DVD, book, and game racks.

√ Put a clothes hamper in their room. Do not expect a teenager to put clothes in a community hamper that is not in their own room. The clothes hamper should not have a lid. That will only hinder the effort. Refuse to wash any clothes that are not in the hamper.

√ Create a place for their electronics. You may have to build something or purchase a small media center.

√ Don't go storming in and do the work for them. This is their private area and they probably won't appreciate you going through their stuff.

√ Make the bed easy to make. See the previous section.

√ Put a large wastebasket in the room.

√ Ask your teenager what you can do together to make the room more enjoyable. Can you paint it, create more shelves, or purchase a different comforter? Making the room more enjoyable can create pride in it, thus facilitating cleanliness. Kids like to have their own space to hang out and entertain friends. Large floor pillows are easily stacked, or consider using that small loveseat or overstuffed armchair from your newly degunked family room if there is space. An inexpensive slip cover will do wonders.

√ Apply the techniques in Chapter 5 to help them organize their closets.

√   If there is space, add a small coat rack. They are great for hanging school bags, accessories, jackets, and items like necklaces and bracelets for girls and baseball caps for guys. If there is no floor space for even a thin one, hang peg racks along one wall.

√   Let your teenager accept responsibility for their actions. If they can't find their keys and are late for school or work, if they can't find any clean clothes, if they can't find their homework, so be it. Tell them during a quiet moment that this happened because they are disorganized. Ask them if you can help.

Finally, and this is kind of fun, after you've told your teenager three times to do something—say, pick up all of their dirty clothes so you can wash them, get everything off of the floor so you can vacuum, or clear off their desk so you can dust—confiscate the offending items. Just walk though the room picking up everything you asked them to put away. After three times, it should have been done, so don't feel guilty about entering the room. Put all of the items in a brown grocery bag and hide it. Leave a note: "Your <insert items here> have been kidnapped. Please see me to work out the terms of its release." Then, work out a deal to get those items back. That might be vacuuming the house, washing the dog, or cooking dinner and then cleaning the kitchen. Once the chore is done, return the items. It works.

Create a Homework Area and an Area for Ongoing Projects

I've talked about this subject in several chapters, but your kids really need a designated place to do their homework and work on other projects such as science fair experiments, art projects, and papier-mâché volcanoes. If they're young, that area may be in a family room or kitchen, and if they're older, it'll likely be their own bedrooms or a game room. Wherever they do their homework and projects, though, there should be a space dedicated to that and nothing else. Creating a place for this in a small home or apartment might be difficult due to the lack of space. In contrast, creating a space in a large home within eyesight and earshot of the child may be an equal challenge.

For starters, then, ask your child where *they* want to study and work on projects. Wherever it is, see if you can create an area in that space. If it's the kitchen, perhaps a rolling cart is in order, one that can hold art and office supplies, pens, pencils, erasers, and staplers and also offers a place to store ongoing projects while at the same time making it easy to clean up once homework or project is done. Rolling the cart into a hall closet often works. If the child wants to work in their bedroom, make sure there's a desk with the required supplies. Usually older kids prefer this method, so add a filing cabinet too, along with other organizational tools.

Once you've established a place for working, you'll need to establish rules for keeping it clean and organized. It you are using a rolling cart or plastic organizers, make sure it's easy to put the items used back where they belong. Create a place just for the items being stored, and make sure they make it back there before bed.

Consider Captain's Beds or Futon/Desk Combinations

If you have the money, captain's beds with drawers underneath and futon/desk combinations are well worth the purchase price. With a captain's bed, you can store items that are rarely used in the drawers underneath. It makes a great place to store linens or off-season clothing. With a combination futon/desk bed, the bed is on top of the desk, as a bunk bed would be. The child climbs a ladder to get to the bed. With the bed off the floor, the room's real estate increases, allowing more room for the child and their belongings.

If you're not in the market for new furniture, though, you can always clean out from under the bed and add storage. If you can't get under the bed because it sits too close to the floor, you can purchase extenders to raise the height of the bed. You can also apply techniques detailed in this chapter, such as putting a skirt around a lamp table to provide under-the-table storage.

GunkBuster's Notebook: Reward Kids, Husbands, and Wives for Good Degunking Behavior

I know, I know, while it's pretty easy to degunk a home, the real challenge lies in keeping in that way. This is especially difficult if you have a lazy spouse, if your kids are slobs, or if everyone works until 5:00 p.m. and doesn't get home until 6:30. There's simply not enough time to keep everything clean. Or so it seems.

There actually *is* enough time when you know how to perform tasks quickly. You've learned how to organize your kitchen so that the dishwasher can be unloaded during a commercial break on television (Chapter 6), keep "move" boxes in every room (Chapters 4, 5, and 6), and throw stuff away as it accumulates to avoid gunk in the first place (Chapter 3). But how are you going to get your family to do this on a regular basis? The answer lies in rewards.

First, you'll need to tell your family what you expect. It can't be too much at first, but the process can be repeated as often as necessary. For instance, you can tell your five-year-old that you want everything off of the floor of their room before bed each night. Remind them gently each night about 30 minutes before bedtime. Each time they do it, you'll read a bedtime story. If they don't, you won't. You can then alter this as needed, based on rewards that he wants to receive.

Tell your spouse you want all of the newspapers in the recycle bin before bed each night, you want the coffee table clean, and you want all of the pet toys picked up off the floor. You promise that you'll unload and load the dishwasher while your spouse does that. This system will work only if your spouse agrees and only if they really hate loading and unloading the dishwasher.

You can tell your preteen that if they'll complete their homework before dinner, they can stay up a half hour later than usual. This tactic gets the homework out of the way first and encourages a new behavior and rewards the child all in one fell swoop.

There is no law that says housework has to be boring and done in silence. Let your kids choose some tunes they like and let them rock out while they clean. This is not the time to lecture them about musical taste, by the way. If they stop, the stereo goes off. If you and the kids want to dance around with the broom or emulate freakish pop stars, go for it, as long as it gets you all moving. You could also hold relay races for putting things away; get the family in teams with an extra reward for the winner. Take turns letting family members be the judge of when chores are done well. If your kids feel that their opinions count, they will take it seriously (an adult can be the co-judge to prevent sibling homicides). Your kids will love having the chance to bust their folks big time for sloppy housework, and you or your neatnik won't always be the house nag.

You can reward in other ways, too. Designate Saturday morning as cleanup time, and make a list of everything that must be done. As soon as it's finished, everyone gets to go to the movies, to the arcade, swimming, hiking, or to a friend's house. However, none of that happens until the list is complete.

Once your living areas are degunked, organized, clean, and rid of papers, things that don't belong, and useless items, how do you plan to keep it that way? Table 7-1 will help keep you and your family on track with everyday maintenance tasks for keeping rooms clean.

Table 7-1   Everyday Maintenance Tasks for Keeping Rooms Clean

Problem Area	Solution
The "move" boxes get full and stay full and create their own gunk. It's like a black hole.	Teach family members never to walk from room to room without carrying something. If moving from the family room to the kitchen, carry a glass or plate. If moving from the living room to the bedroom, carry the shoes that are on the floor.
The dining room table gets gunked up with newspapers, projects, and mail within a week of cleaning it.	Reconsider what tools are in place to hold this clutter. Is there a desk available for paying bills, a recycle bin for old newspapers, or a rolling cart for ongoing projects? Are those close by and easy to use and access? If not, you need to rethink this part of your degunking strategy.
DVDs, CDs, video games, and books and magazines are accumulating again, and they're everywhere.	Make sure a CD, DVD, or game tower is available or that a clear and precise location is nearby for these items. Remind your family of the new system. If it doesn't work, pick up the items and hold them for "ransom." Make the offending family member perform a task to get them back, such as dusting the CD or DVD tower or polishing the magazine rack.
The coffee table is covered with remotes, pens, telephone messages, and other items.	Make sure you've created an area for these things, either underneath the table or in an organizer. Remember, you can sneak storage under a couch or under a coffee table, too.
Knick-knacks keep piling up and you can't seem to gain control.	Insist that only three of these items remain out at a time. Put the others away and rotate them. If a new one comes into the house, an old one goes out.
Things keep accumulating in the bedroom that really don't have any other place to go, such as sewing kits, lint brushes, belts, and books and magazines.	If you do a lot of reading in the bedroom, consider putting a decorative recycle bin in the room. It should remind you to recycle what you've read. For the other gunk, either employ a "move" box or use an over-the-door shoe organizer to keep things tamed.
You can't get rid of your kid's artwork and old schoolwork and it's piling up.	Label a Ziploc bag with your child's name. Use additional bags for additional children. Put everything in there for one school year. At the end of the year, go through it and pick three things. Put those things in a photo album or
Your kids have toys with a thousand pieces, and those pieces are all over the place.	Collect as many pieces as you can, put them in a plastic container, and label it. Tell your child that this is where this toy belongs. If you find it out in a million pieces again, it's history.

Summing Up

In this chapter, you learned how to finalize the degunking of your living areas, including dining rooms, family rooms, bedrooms, and kids' rooms. Dining rooms and family rooms are hard to control because multiple people use them, they are used every day, and most are larger rooms with plenty of room to attract gunk. In order to control the gunk in these rooms, you have to put organizational tools and strategies in place and learn to use them. As with other rooms, a "move" box helps, recycle bins help, and employing family member's cooperation is important.

Chapter 8

Organizing the Home Office, Utility Rooms, and Bathrooms

Degunking Checklist:

√ Turn your office area into a functional working space.

√ Create a place for the paperwork you have to keep.

√ Use wall space effectively by adding corkboards, whiteboards, and calendars.

√ Reorganize your utility closets so you can more easily access and store what you want.

√ Get rid of bathroom gunk, including old medications, perfumes, razors, and lotions, and create a dedicated space for the items you need to keep.

√ Keep these rooms clean by uncovering and dealing with clutter as it develops.

There are really only three more places inside your home you need to organize and declutter: your home office (if you have one), utility rooms, and bathrooms. (Garages, attics, and basements will be discussed in the next chapter, which is about creating long-term storage solutions). Organizing and decluttering these rooms is the same as decluttering any other room in the house: Apply the four-box method, remove everything that doesn't belong and toss things you don't want or need, and then put what's left back in an organized and functional manner. Getting rid of stuff and organizing what you want to keep will free up extra space and allow you to create an organized, working plan for getting and staying degunked. Let's start with the home office.

Get the Most Out of Your Home Office

Whether you have an actual office, have transformed your breakfast nook into one, or are using a large closet, the organizational goals for taking control of any of these areas are basically the same. You need to be able to find a stamp and an envelope when you need one, you need a place to file the papers you want and need to keep, and you have to be able to find and mail bills when it's time for them to be paid. You need a system for staying on top of appointments, too. And of course, you need space to work. This is, evidently, easier said than done.

Getting Started and Finding Problem Areas

The first step, after applying the four-box method detailed in Chapter 4, is to use what's left to create a functional workspace. After getting rid of things you don't need, you still probably have a desk and chair, a computer, a file cabinet or a file drawer, and possibly a bulletin board or whiteboard. These are pretty much necessities for an organized home office, so if you're missing any of these items, see what you can do about obtaining them.

Next, decide how you work and what kind of space you'll need and list problem areas. If you write technical books or are a computer technician, for instance, your office will have to have a space for every type of computer and every operating system on the market, as well as tools, cables, and troubleshooting equipment. An example of a gunked-up office is shown in Figure 8-1.

There are multiple problem areas in Figure 8-1:

√   Unorganized bulletin board (1)

√   Books everywhere (2)

√   Computer equipment—including router, cable modem, and switch—that is hard to get to and stacked precariously (3)

Figure 8-1

Some offices require space to hold multiple computers.

√   Cables in the way of shelf (4)

√   Broken printer (5)

√   Unused computer (6)

√   Cat bed taking up desk space (7)

√   Cables on the floor (8)

√   Computer in a cubby making plugging in peripherals difficult (9)

√   Crooked certificates (10)

These problems can all be solved at no cost; it takes only a little time. The idea is to figure out where the gunk problems are and how gunk occurs. Once you know that, you can figure out a solution. In the office shown in Figure 8-1, that means dealing with the bulletin board, finding a place for the books to allow easy access, finding a new place for the computer equipment and hardware, getting rid of what doesn't work or isn't being used, and generally cleaning up the place. Figure 8-2 shows the "after" picture. Note that each problem is solved not only for the short term, but for the most part, for the long term as well.

Figure 8-2 shows that the computer and hardware have been moved out of the cubbies to allow easier access and to free up a space for the books. The unused

Figure 8-2
Often, you can degunk a room at no cost whatsoever.

computer and broken printer have been removed, and the place has generally been spruced up. Behind the scenes, the drawers are organized with (what else?) drawer organizers. There is a filing system in place, and the bulletin board only holds pictures and notes about current projects.

If computers aren't your problem, printers, work space, or papers may be. If you're an artist or graphic designer, for instance, you'll need room to work and a place to store multiple printers, papers, art projects, and catalogs. An example of a gunked-up artist's office is shown in Figure 8-3. It's easy to see the problem areas here: they include cable messes, printers, and paper gunk. In this case, it's either laziness, the result of a creative mind, or just someone who does not have the time to get or keep the place organized. In a case like this, it's best to remove everything from the room, apply the four-box method, and then put everything back in an organized and functional manner. Make sure to decide how to keep things organized in the short and long term, and then create a plan to keep it that way. Usually, this can be done at little or no cost.

Figure 8-3
Graphic artists' printers may be a gunk problem.

A Place for Everything and Everything in Its Place

Almost everyone has a problem with papers accumulating. That's why every home office needs a filing cabinet or a filing drawer. Even the most primitive system will work, like the one shown in Figure 8-4. In this figure, the filing system is in a single drawer of the desk, and files are handwritten and home-made. However, just because you have a couple of filing cabinets doesn't necessarily mean your problems are solved, as you can see in Figure 8-5. You actually have to use the space effectively.

If you need to set up a filing system, this should be your top priority. It's not that difficult or expensive; you only need to go through all of the papers you want to keep and sort them into like piles. Then, look at each pile and create a file (or files) for the paperwork you need to keep. Here are some ideas for file names, to help you create a filing system for papers you should hang on to for the long term:

√ Automobiles: service records, titles, maintenance schedules

√ Certificates: birth, death, wedding, graduations, certifications, stocks, bonds, passports, wills

Figure 8-4

Any kind of filing system will do, as long as it's alphabetized and organized.

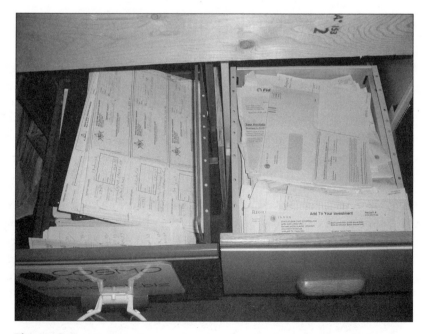

Figure 8-5

A file cabinet is sometimes just as gunked up as a junk drawer.

√ Credit: credit card information, saved bills, bills to pay, phone numbers to call if a card is lost or stolen, credit card numbers

√ Correspondence: family, friends, coworkers, business associates

√ Employment: resumes, photos, cover letters, IRAs, employee benefits

√ Health records: claims, reports, lists of medications and side effects, doctors' names and addresses

√ Insurance policies: health, home owners, auto, flood, disaster, life

√ Personal: nutrition, diseases, elder care, photos of possessions, hobbies, crafts, invention ideas, book ideas, personal property inventory list

√ Papers: divorce, custody, adoption, mortgage, loan, property deeds, social security card, voter registration card

√ Passwords and codes: software, Web sites, administrator passwords (just make sure to encode or hide them)

√ Tax records: copies of forms, receipts, past tax files

√ Warranties: receipts, warranty documents, phone numbers, serial numbers, and model numbers

√ User guides: yard equipment, kitchen appliances, computers, printers, scanners, sewing machines, hand tools

And here are some things you can throw away:

√ Newspaper clippings: articles, recipes, coupons, places you'd like to eat, and anything else you no longer need or want to file

√ Banking: old ATM receipts, deposit slips, bank and credit card statements over a year old (unless you need them for tax records), expired ATM or credit cards (be sure to cut in half)

√ Junk: grocery receipts, notes to yourself, to-do lists, honey do lists, expired paperwork for any kind of policy (especially auto and health), pay stubs, paid bills (phone, electric, water, and utility)

√ Memorabilia: ticket stubs, photos you never look at, letters, hotel keys, old car keys, dried flowers, old love letters, anything that's expired, things you've printed from your computer, old calendars

Once you've physically degunked the office and have a working file system, you can move on to efficiency-improvement degunking tasks.

Improve Efficiency in the Office

There are several ways to improve the efficiency of an office, and one of my favorites is adding a day planner. Having a day planner, either in printed form or on your computer, is a great way to store and recall appointments, meetings, and project due dates, and to map out whatever project you're working on. You can also use the planner to store phone numbers and addresses and to note birthdays, anniversaries, and things like yearly health exams. With a printed day planner, you can store physical things, too, like directions to your dentist's office (just stow it in the page on which your appointment is noted), envelopes and bills for quarterly tax payments, and printouts or clippings for trade shows or upcoming events. When you turn the page for the day or week, everything is right in front on you, so you never forget a thing.

In addition to keeping organized with a personal day planner, you can help organize your family with a family planner. This can be as simple as a whiteboard calendar, a calendar on a shared computer, or a shared day planner. You can also hang corkboards and whiteboards to keep notes and make notes to yourself. A very inexpensive alternative to a large corkboard if space is an issue is to use round cork trivets or plant pot "coasters," available at any home improvement or hardware store. They can be attached to a wall with (removable) double-stick adhesive. The round memo dots are a hip way to organize memos and they work great in home offices, over a desk in a kid's room or dorms, and in apartments where nails can't be used.

Here are some other ideas for improving office efficiency:

√ Unsnarl cables and cords. Use twist ties to manage computer cords and cables, use wall-mounted clips to hide cables and get them off the floor, and store cables and cords with their peripherals. An example of storing items together is shown in Figure 8-6.

√ Use desk organizers. Purchase or make organizers for pens and pencils, scissors, correction fluid, markers, highlighters, and erasers. You can even have your kids make them out of frozen juice containers, unwanted coffee cups, Tupperware, or LEGOs. Simple wicker silverware and napkin holders for picnics are great for this. (See Figure 8-7.)

√ Get some stackable trays. Use one for bills and mail you need to respond to, one for printer paper, one for coupons or promotional offers you plan to use, one for magazines you need to read (rotate these before the tray gets full), and one for invoices, faxes, or whatever else you collect in your business that needs to be filed or is waiting on a response or payment.

√ Hang a canvas shoe caddy over the door for a see-through holder for staplers, dry erase markers and eraser, office supplies, or even mail.

√ Use a Rolodex to hold business cards and store phone numbers and addresses.

√ Buy a keyboard tray for the computer keyboard. A tray keeps it off the desk and helps promote good posture.

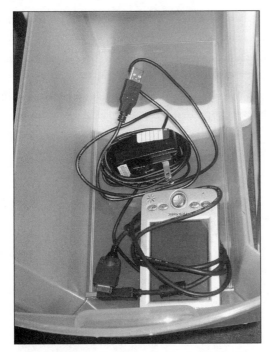

Figure 8-6

Store peripherals with their hardware, and
you'll always be able to find what you need.

Figure 8-7

Be creative with desk organization.

√   For wall organizers, use baskets to hold loose items, shelves for books, in and out baskets, and cabinets (or shelves) to house photos, trophies, or awards.

√   Buy a label maker to label stackable trays, cables, cords, desk organizers, files, shoe caddies, baskets, and stackable bins.

√   Use a memo book with carbon copies to write notes and take them with you and still have an organized copy in the memo book back at the office.

√   Recycle an old dresser and use the drawers to store those extra reams of paper, mailing supplies, and other bulk office items (See Figure 8-8.)

Figure 8-8

An old dresser can be jazzed up and recycled as office furniture.

Utilize Your Utility or Laundry Room

Utility and laundry rooms are often behind closed doors, making them the perfect place to hide and collect gunk. Whether your utility room is large or small doesn't matter; it's what collects there that does. Before you start this section, then, have a look-see at yours and write down what you collect. You'll have the usual, I'm sure: a broom and mop, detergents and cleaners, a few tools, and maybe some bulk items like soda, paper towels, and toilet paper. As always, you'll apply the four-box method, but before you do, decide what you really want in the room and what you don't.

Decide on the Room's Purpose

A utility room can serve many purposes; it's up to you to decide what purpose you want yours to serve. Perhaps it's only a laundry room and nothing else. If that's the case, get rid of anything that isn't laundry-related. Most utility and laundry rooms serve more than one purpose, though. Many are used to house all of the household supplies, some are makeshift repair shops, and a few are storage areas for bulk items, pet supplies, and sports equipment. Once you pinpoint what you want the purpose of the room (or closet) to be, you can better degunk and organize it.

Build Shelves

No matter what type of room or closet you have as a utility or laundry room, chances are good there's room to build a shelf or two. My laundry room originally came with one shelf, and I added another. That additional shelf added quite a bit of real estate to the room, offering a place to store items for which I could find no other place. Building a shelf is inexpensive, too, and creating one made of a single piece of wood cut specifically to serve as a shelf is simple:

√   Decide how long and wide you want the shelf to be, and purchase a piece of wood at the local home improvement center. Most have pre-cut shelves that are laminated. Also purchase two or three L-brackets on which to mount the shelf.

  √   Locate the studs in the wall by using a stud finder or by hammering a small nail into a hidden area. If another shelf exists, use the studs for that shelf as a gauge.

  √   Using a level, line up the L-brackets, mark where you want to attach them, and mount them to the wall using screws long enough to hold the shelf securely.

  √   Once the L-brackets are mounted, place the shelf on the brackets and attach them. An example is shown in Figure 8-9. You may also want to attach L-brackets to the top of the shelf for added support.

The bottom shelf in Figure 8-9 is the one that was added. From start to finish, the project took about an hour, not including the trip to the home improvement store.

There are other shelving options, too, including the popular wire shelving units. However, these are quite a bit more expensive and much more time consuming to install. If you just need a simple shelf that you can install quickly, a pre-cut piece of shelving and a few L-brackets are the easiest way to go.

Figure 8-9
You can build your own shelf quickly and inexpensively with pre-cut shelving.

Hang What You Can

Wall space is also good for storing things in a laundry or utility room. You can purchase hooks that are attached with a self-adhesive bond for less than a dollar, or use any old nail you have lying around your house for free. Figure 8-10 shows an example of the kinds of hooks you should look for when you need to hang lightweight items.

Figure 8-10
Hooks have multiple uses. You can use them to hang wet towels, brooms or mops, wet swim suits, laundry bags for the cleaners, whisk brooms, and more.

If you have a larger area, a manufactured tool holder can also come in handy, offering a place to hang mops, brooms, ceiling fan brushes, and other tall items, or you can make your own with a strip of metal and hooks. A peg board is another good option, as are stackable bins or wicker baskets on the floor. You can also purchase a rolling cart at your local home improvement store that fits in-between the washer and dryer for even more storage. Don't forget about recycling things, too. A large, plastic coffee container can hold loose items like scrub brushes, old toothbrushes, and sponges, and empty plastic detergent containers can be used to stabilize mops and brooms resting against a wall.

Wire metal organizers are easier to install than wire shelving, and they also make good storage options. To hang wire organizers, you only need to line up the holes with studs in the walls (or use special screws for Sheetrock), drill starter holes, and then attach the organizer with the provided screws. Figure 8-11 shows an example.

Figure 8-11

Wire organizers are easy to install and can hold bulk items, cleansers, or other objects.

Organize the Space You Have

Laundry and utility rooms are generally small. Figure 8-12 shows a fairly un-cluttered laundry room, hopefully what yours looks like after applying the four-box method. With the extra space you've freed up by getting rid of what you no longer want or need, and by putting misplaced things where they be-long, you should now have room to organize what's left.

There are a few problem areas shown in Figure 8-12, and they are noted here:

√ The laundry basket has items in it that are not clothes. The basket belongs in another room to collect clothes, in this room with clean and folded clothes, or in another room and used to put away clothes. (1)

√ There's a wet mop leaving a stain against the wall. (2)

√ Recycled plastic bags are in a bucket that is not labeled and precariously perched. (3)

√ Bleach goes by the washer, not the dryer. (4)

√ There is no hanging rod for clothes that need to be air-dried. (5)

√ Bulk items are not organized. (6)

√ Wall space is wasted. (7)

In Figure 8-13, you can see the same area with problem areas solved. Here, labeled organizers now hold plastic bags, party supplies (including cups and

Figure 8-12
Even utility and laundry rooms have problem areas.

Figure 8-13

This organization was achieved by purchasing $15 worth of plastic bins and a $10 clothes pole. No tools were needed, and it only took 30 minutes to organize it.

plates), light bulbs, and small tools; the bulk items are stored somewhere else. The laundry detergent is stored on the floor, and bleach and other cleaning supplies are grouped together in an easy-to-reach bin. There's now a pole to hang shirts and items that need to air-dry. Note that there is room in-between the washer and dryer now for a rolling cart, too, which can hold even more cleaning supplies. In Figure 8-13, you may be able to see that the plastic organizers are labeled.

GunkBuster's Notebook: One Woman, One Weekend, One Hundred Dollars: A True Story

Figures 8-14 and 8-15 show a typical problem laundry area; it's small, gunked up, and unsightly, but there are extenuating circumstances. The owner of this home only has 1,000 square feet and no basement, garage, or attic for storage and, therefore, no really good place to store the stuff she needed to keep.

She needed an area that was not only a functional laundry area but could also provide storage for paint, tools, and household maintenance items, too all in the space of a modest walk-in closet.

Figure 8-14
A problem laundry can be caused by of lack of space.

Figure 8-15
Laundry rooms sometimes serve as utility rooms, too.

She admitted that some of the paints and tools had been in the area when she moved in—more than 10 years ago. While she would love to have stacking appliances, they simply were not in her budget, so existing ones would have to be worked around. There was no room to store necessary items like mops and brooms, and laundry often fell behind the washer and dryer, never to be seen again. She needed a quick fix that could be done over a weekend with minimal cost. It was done by using existing items and supplementing them with low-cost organizing tools. She did it and you can, too!

How She Did It

First, everything was removed from the room and the four-box method was applied. Old paint and chemicals were safely disposed of (see Appendix C) and broken tools and sagging shelving thrown away.

Next, the now empty room was cleaned and painted. The owner hated the cinder-block wall, so she indulged her love of animal prints by "wallpapering" the wall using tissue paper from the local dollar store, gluing it on with strippable wallpaper paste for easy removal later. The sagging ceiling tiles were replaced with a sheet of beadboard paneling. The existing shelf struts and brackets were in good condition, so they were left as is.

Finally, the items that needed to go back into the room were evaluated, along with the space. She decided to purchase new shelf boards. A hanging rod was added in the dead space above the washer to air-dry clothing. A rack now holds the mops and brooms in a tiny bit of wall space. Using baskets from the local charity thrift shop is an inexpensive way to keep like items together. A simple bulletin board holds messages and extra keys. A clip "pins" stray socks on the donkey until their mates are located. All items are now within easy reach and everything from paint to extension cords to lightbulbs can be found quickly.

And, she didn't spend an arm and a leg to do it, either:

√ Paint and supplies: $30

√ Shelving, mop rack, and clothes bar: $35

√ Paneling for ceiling $20

√ Baskets: $15

Figures 8-16 and 8-17 show the after shots.

Figure 8-16
A lot can be done without spending
much money.

Figure 8-17
Shelving and wicker baskets brighten
up any laundry area.

Keep Cleaning Supplies Together

Finally, if you have room in your laundry room, create or purchase something to hold all of the cleaning supplies you need when you clean the house. If you don't have room in the utility closet, still keep all of your cleaners together in something you can carry. Anything will do, from a recycled plastic detergent container to a recycled plastic kitty litter container. I have one and I call it my Saturday Morning Cleaning Carrier. I have everything I need to clean the house stored in a single, organized unit, and it's shown in Figure 8-18 (more about this in Chapter 11). This is another good item to have in your utility room.

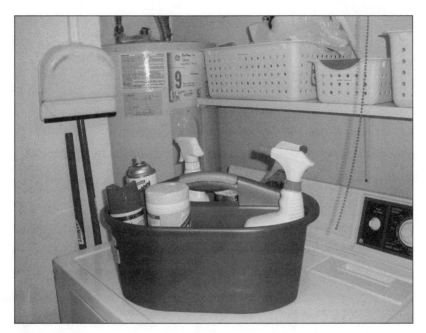

Figure 8-18
Minimize your steps by keeping cleaning supplies together and where they're needed.

GunkBuster's Notebook: Creating a Toolbox

You'll always have a need for a basic set of tools, and everyone should have a toolbox. When a toolbox isn't handy, looking for and finding the tools you need to do a job often takes longer than doing the job itself. If possible, the toolbox should be kept in the laundry or utility room. You can put it under the sink though, and you might have to put it in the garage, but the laundry or utility room is best. There's nothing worse than needing a screwdriver or hammer and not being able to find one.

You probably have most of the things you'll need to create a basic tool set scattered about your home, garage, or shop, but if you don't, you can probably ask your parents, kids, or neighbors for any extras they have. Here are the things you'll need to create a basic tool set:

√ Toolbox. This can be a real toolbox handed down from your dad or a recycled sewing kit or fishing lure box.

√ Hammer. 16 ounces is a good starting point, and make sure it has a claw on the end to pull out nails.

√ Tape measure. 25 feet is a good length.

√ Utility knife and X-Acto knife. Don't forget the extra blades.

√ Tape. Electrical, duct, masking, and clear.

√ Wrench. Adjustable and large enough to get around the largest pipe in your home.

√ Screwdriver(s). Philips and flat, but preferably one with interchangeable bits and multiple bit options.

√ Staple gun. Don't forget the extra staples; 1/2-inch staples are probably large enough.

√ Level. 24 inch is best, but a smaller level will do in a pinch.

√ Pliers. Needle nose and adjustable.

√ Cordless drill. Preferably a rechargeable one with lots of interchangeable bits.

√ Sandpaper. Simply attach sheets to a standard office clipboard.

√ Eye protection.

Clear Out Your Bathroom

The bathroom isn't the biggest room in the house, but it certainly gets its share of traffic. Every family member uses the room, not only for bathing, grooming, and other daily rituals, but also as a private place to take a long bath or contemplate the state of the world. In many families, it's the library, too. Because of this, it's important that the bathroom be user friendly, so to speak. It should not only be organized, it should also offer a tranquil place to escape, if only for a few minutes.

Get Rid of Unnecessary Items in Your Bathroom

As with all of the other rooms you've tackled, the first step is to empty out the shelves, drawers, medicine cabinets, counters, and any other storage areas and put back only what you need to have in the bathroom. You should get rid of expired medications, makeup, and perfumes; throw out old magazines, puzzle books, and catalogs; and then move whatever doesn't belong somewhere else. With all of the gunk gone, you can then concentrate on organizing the room and making it more livable and enjoyable.

Here are a few things you should consider moving out of the bathroom and into a designated area of a hall or linen closet, cabinet, or utility room:

√ Medications and vitamins that should be stored in a cool, dry, place, not a moist, hot, humid, wet place like a bathroom. Other items (like diabetes test strips) may need to be stored in a dark, cool, place, such as a drawer or cabinet.

√ Extra (surplus) bath towels, hand towels, and washcloths.

√ Superfluous soaps, toothpaste, toothbrushes, dental floss, hair spray, gel, makeup, shaving cream, razors, and so on (purchased as bulk or sale purchases).

√ Bathroom cleaners that should really be stored out of reach of children and away from any medications, toilet paper, and personal products. Integrate these products with other cleaning supplies in one large carryall and store them in a utility room. Also, buy multiple-use cleaners. You don't really need a different cleaner for each room of the house; many serve multiple purposes and can help you degunk the amount of cleaning supplies you buy and store.

√ Travel kits that contain sample size products or travel toothbrushes that could be stored in a suitcase or travel bag (already taking up space somewhere else).

√ Jewelry you don't wear often or that is expensive or an heirloom. Ideally, get rid of jewelry you no longer wear, and put expensive pieces in a safer place.

√ Any perfumes, soaps, makeup, or shaving cream that's more than a year old.

√ Any item whose label can't be read.

√ Multiple shampoos and conditioners. Pick one and get rid of the rest. In a best-case scenario, everyone in the family would use the same shampoo, conditioner, lotion, shaving cream, and toothpaste. If that is not possible (and this is likely), assign a small storage container to each family member.

Add New Items to Your Bathroom

And here are a few things you can add to assist in organizing what you want to keep:

√ Hooks or towel racks for wet towels.

√ Hamper for dirty clothes

√ Scented soaps, bubble bath, or a fragrant candle for the times you need to relax.

√ Shower sprays for the shower walls and doors. Using these after each shower (yeah right) can eliminate soap scum buildup.

√ Recycled jars from candles or food products to hold cotton balls, cotton swabs, and other products.

√ Toilet paper holder for multiple rolls, which serves as an attractive storage option. You can make one on the cheap using supplies from a craft store.

√ Wall mounts for hair dryers, electric shavers, and curling irons next to an electrical outlet, but away from the sink, shower, or tub.

√ Shower caddie to hold shampoos, conditioners, soaps, razors, and other bath accessories.

√ Low hooks or towel racks for children.

√ A bath net that can hold children's bath toys and be hung from the shower rod or towel rack (inside the shower).

√ A clear, plastic shoe organizer to hang on the back of a door (preferably not in the guest bathroom, though).

√ Pump dispensers for soap and lotions you buy in bulk, or just to keep the messy soap tray off the counter.

√ Pullout plastic bins or stackable organizers for the cabinets.

√ Corner organizer.

√ Soap dishes, or that ashtray your kid made at camp 15 years ago that you can't seem to part with, to hold earrings, buttons, safety pins, and other small items. Drawer organizers for brushes, combs, makeup, and shaving supplies. Don't be afraid to use a kitchen organizer

√ A pad and pencil for those moments of inspiration.

TIP: The next time you empty the bathroom trash, put an extra trash bag or two underneath the new one. It will make it a bit easier the next time you take out the trash.

GunkBuster's Notebook: Twenty-Five Uses for Ziploc Bags

Ziploc bags, those clear, plastic bags that zip closed, have a million uses. They come in sizes from small to extra large and can store everything from apples to, well, other Ziploc bags! Here, I've listed my top 25 uses for Ziploc bags. Oversize bags are now available that will hold a complete change of clothes and more! Use a Ziploc bag to hold these items:

1. Anything that could leak in your suitcase.

2. Dirty gym clothes.

3. Extra cotton balls and Q-tips for low-profile storage in cramped bathrooms.

4. A small child's clothing for every day of the week; imagine, no lost socks or underwear in the morning!

5. Minor health emergency supplies, including Ace bandages, alcohol, extra medications, Visine, anti-itch creams, and Band-Aids.

6. Minor clothing emergency supplies, including a shoe shine towelette, sewing kit with buttons, and clothing stain remover.

7. Minor car emergency supplies, including $1.25 in quarters, mini flashlight, map, a $20 bill, and emergency phone numbers.

8. Minor hair and nail emergency supplies, including travel size hairspray, clear nail polish, a nail file, tweezers, and clippers.

9. Loose parts when assembling something.

10. Cosmetics like eye shadow and powders that get crumbly in your cosmetic bag or purse.

11. Packed clothing for travel. You can buy the expensive vacuum ones at the travel store, or you can just use the ones in your pantry. Put your shirt, pants, and so on in large bags and push down to squeeze out air and seal. This saves room in your luggage and can be marked for each travel day.

12. Ice for a cooler, or to keep a pitcher of beer cold.

13. Cords, cables, and cards for your digital camera.

14. Your kids' artwork.

15. Opened food items, including cheese, lunchmeat, and candy.

16. Emergency food for long trips, including small bags of nuts, granola bars, and hard candy.

17. Straws, toothpicks, salt and pepper packets, lens cleaners, and other small items you keep in the glove box of the car.

18. Matchbooks, candles, a small flashlight, and any other item you'll need if the electricity goes out in your home.
19. Twist ties, rubber bands, and garbage bag ties for the pantry or junk drawer.
20. Game pieces.
21. Highlighters, pens, and pencils in a book bag or back pack.
22. Toiletries for the trek to the shared bathroom in the college dorm.
23. Cell phone and keys when you're on a boat or in the rain.
24. Screws, nuts, bolts, and hardware in your shop.
25. Pet treats for on-the-go training.

Everyday Maintenance Tasks for Keeping Rooms Clean

Once these last few rooms have been degunked, organized, cleaned, and rid of papers, things that don't belong, and unworthy, broken, duplicate, or useless items, how do you plan to keep it that way? With Table 8-1, I hope to keep you and your family on track by helping you find problem areas and dealing with them before you get gunked up again.

Table 8-1   Everyday Maintenance Tasks for Keeping Rooms Clean

Problem Area	Solution
Paperwork still collects in the home office and is always all over the place.	Create a *working* file system. Create files for ongoing projects, bills that need to be paid, and open invoices, and have and use an inbox, outbox, and immediate attention box.
You need to store bulky items like reams of paper, extra office supplies, books and mailing supplies in a small space.	Consider using an old dresser. Deep drawers can hold large amounts of bulk supplies.
Spouse or family members won't or can't put paperwork away in a file or stay on top of the family's shared paperwork.	Attach a paper holder to your office door. Tell family members to use it for paperwork they want to keep. This includes user guides for new appliances, voter registration cards, and warranties. You file the papers yourself.

(continued)

Table 8-1   Everyday Maintenance Tasks for Keeping Rooms Clean (continued)

Problem Area	Solution
Family members never know where other family members are; you miss appointments or forget to pick up junior from soccer.	Hang a whiteboard with a calendar in the entry area. Have family members write down appointments and meetings on the calendar. Have each member check the board before leaving and upon arriving home. (You won't get a ride home from soccer practice if it's not on the board!)
You or family members never put things back where they belong in a utility room, so after a week or so, everything is gunked up again.	Put labeled bins in the utility room on the available shelves. Add so many organizational bins that it's hard for dad to put the screwdriver anywhere else but the Tools bin.
No matter how much degunking you do, you still don't have enough room in the utility closet or laundry room.	You probably still have some wall space left. Build more shelves or hang a wire organizer.
There are cleaning supplies all over the house, but you can never find what you need.	Gather up all of the cleaning supplies in your home. Combine half bottles of the same cleanser into one. Throw away any cleanser that doesn't work. Put all cleansers together in a single carryall. When the cleansers are gone, purchase multiple-purpose cleansers to keep what you have to a minimum.
The bathroom won't stay degunked, and there's always stuff on the counter.	If you or your family members simply can't put things back into drawers where they belong, consider a compromise. Use counter organizers instead. Small soap dishes can hold earrings; an office organizer can hold toothbrushes, dental floss, and toothpaste; and glass jars can hold cotton balls or Q-tips.
There always seems to be dirty clothes and wet towels on the bathroom floor.	If you can't get yourself or your family members to walk the extra 15 steps to the laundry hamper or laundry room to put away dirty clothes, you'll have to put a clothes hamper in the bathroom or just outside of it. As far as the wet towels, generally, offering hooks usually solves that problem.

Summing Up

Home offices and laundry, utility, and bathrooms are the last rooms inside your house you have to degunk. They pose special challenges, though, because these rooms are generally small or have to house more supplies than there's really room for. Therefore, when degunking these rooms, it's especially necessary to get rid of everything that you can. With that done, you can then begin to organize what you want to keep. For smaller rooms such as these, that includes employing stackable bins, hooks, and other containers to hold things. Once these rooms are degunked, putting things back in their proper places becomes much easier, so staying degunked is possible, even for the messiest family members.

Chapter 9

Create Long–Term Storage and Maintain Storage Spaces

Degunking Checklist:

√ Gut the garage and remove everything you don't need or use.

√ Organize the garage for long-term storage and ease of use.

√ Get all of your lawn equipment together and get rid of what you don't need and what doesn't work.

√ Consider using an outbuilding to help you get and stay degunked.

√ Create useful storage areas in small living spaces.

√ Prepare for an emergency by allotting some long-term storage space to disaster preparedness.

√ Learn how to maintain storage areas.

Like you, I've been degunking, too. Before I tackled any chapter in this book, I degunked the area I was planning to write about first. It's a "practice what you preach" thing. I wanted the experience of actually doing it, step-by-step, so I could tell you, the reader, what really goes on during the degunking process. This process also helped me to decide what did and didn't work so I could state exactly the best way to go about degunking.

Unfortunately, a rather large problem arose. The garage became a gigantic gunk room. All of the stuff I really needed to keep but didn't need inside the house had to go somewhere, and it landed in the garage. I just threw it in there, including a Crock-Pot, bread maker, food sealer system, extra silverware and dishes for holidays, sports equipment, holiday decorations, craft supplies, tools, board games and puzzles, outdoor shoes, and furniture. Combine that with what was already there—lawn equipment, two cars, three sets of golf clubs, craft supplies, luggage, and tons of gardening tools—and you could hardly move around in there. My garage was a disaster area. If you've been playing along, your garage probably looks like mine did before I started this chapter: a huge mess!

In this chapter, then, we'll tackle the garage first, if you have one. If you don't have a garage, you'll want to apply these suggestions to a shed, shop, outbuilding, carport, or whatever else you have outside your home that collects gunk. You can also apply these suggestions to your basement.

After you've degunked your garage, created storage spaces, and learned how to organize them effectively, you might be interested in purchasing or building an outbuilding, which I'll also cover in this chapter. Perhaps you just need to keep too much stuff and don't have enough space. Finally, you'll learn about storage options for smaller areas, such as apartments, studios, and lofts.

Use the Garage Effectively

I'm going to be honest. Degunking the garage is going to be a long process. You'll probably need an entire weekend to complete this task, maybe more. However, the effort you put into it will produce results you could never imagine, results that will stay with you for years if you do it right.

Degunking the Garage

As with all other degunking tasks, you really need to remove everything from the garage and go through it. This is easier said than done because if it takes you more than a day, you'll have to leave your stuff outside overnight. If that's the case, you may want to concentrate on one side of the garage one day and the other side the next. Whatever you choose, though, you need to go through everything in your garage, touch everything once, and get rid of everything you can.

Going through your stuff doesn't mean just looking at what's written on the outside of a cardboard box and saying, "Oh, I want to keep this box; it contains my <insert anything here>." You need to actually go through each container. This includes toolboxes, too. You won't believe the rusty tools, broken garden tools, dried-up paintbrushes, cracked figurines, lawn attachments and hardware for equipment, and, well, junk you'll come across. I found concert ticket stubs from the '80s, cassette tapes, and old love letters. Just make it a rule that you'll get rid of all of the old cardboard boxes and storage containers and store the stuff to keep in see-through plastic bins, recycled milk crates, or new boxes. This will force you to go through everything.

Once you've worked through this phase, applying the four-box method to everything in the garage (see Chapter 4), decide how you want the garage to look. You may need to tear down old shelves and build new ones, for instance, and you may need to get both cars in the garage. Figure 9-1 shows an example of just how gunked up a garage can get; it's not hard to see there are problem areas.

Figure 9-1
Gunk in the garage is common.

In this garage, there are several things to tackle:

√   Disorganization. Things are thrown everywhere.

√   Dangerous conditions. Boxes are stacked hazardously and there are many things to trip over.

√   Unnecessary items. The hammock, ski boots, cat litter box, leaky water hose, and boxes of trash should be discarded.

√   Shelving. The shelving is useless because it's only a few inches deep. It also sags and is in danger of falling.

√   Cardboard boxes. Each box is a mini-gunk warehouse. Each should be thoroughly degunked.

Figure 9-2 shows the work in progress. Everything is off the shelves, and most of the things that need to be thrown away, recycled, or given to charity have been removed. These shelves are about to be removed and new ones built.

Storage Options

Once you know what you want to keep, you'll need to figure out what storage option is best for you. You can choose from plastic bins or shelving that you'll

Figure 9-2
Remove everything from the garage first; this will force you to do a good job.

probably need to purchase; you can use recycled book cases, drawers, or cabinets that you've acquired or no longer need; and you can hang items from walls and the ceiling with inexpensive hooks and brackets. Figure 9-3 shows an example of a degunked garage. Compared to Figure 9-1, it's not too shabby. Everything is categorized into bins, paints are together, furniture is stored out of the way, the wood is together, and a work bench is handy. The nuts, bolts, screws, nails, picture hangars, washers, and other small hardware are organized in bins as well. Arts and crafts are also stored effectively.

Figure 9-3
This garage is functional, neat, clean, and organized, and is set up to remain that way in the long term.

Storing Bulk Purchases

When cleaning out the garage, attic, outbuilding, or basement, leave extra space for storing bulk purchases. Buying in bulk can do more than save you money; it can lessen the amount of time you have to spend shopping for stuff (or looking for it). I sure do dislike running out of toilet paper and having to search the house for it or spending $4.00 for a few rolls at the convenience store in an emergency. You can purchase and store many bulk items in the garage or attic without any harm coming to them (unless you live in a climate where it's extremely hot or extremely cold). Here are some things you may consider purchasing in bulk:

√   Toilet paper

√   Water

√   Detergents for the dishwasher and washing machine

√   Printer and office paper

√   Canned food

√   Soda

√   Pasta (Store in airtight glass or plastic containers to avoid attracting pests)

√   Auto supplies

√   Paper towels

Bulk items can be stored on shelves, in bins, or in a makeshift pantry in the garage. The best way to go about keeping things degunked is to install a shelf that is empty. As you acquire bulk items, you can put them there.

Controlling Lawn Equipment

If you live in a house with a yard, chances are good you have quite a bit of lawn equipment. If you're a gardener, you have even more. Lawn equipment becomes gunk quickly, though, mainly because of its size and bulk and how much equipment you need if you have a large yard. Lawn mowers and edgers are big, fertilizer spreaders are bulky, and Weed Eaters and leaf blowers come in odd shapes and sizes. Along with all of that, though, are oil, gas, extension cords, chargers, and other items that make the equipment run. Combined with shovels, rakes, snow blowers, tree trimmers, brooms, and hoes, you've got yourself an entire room full of stuff.

Organizing all of this can be quite difficult. If the lawn equipment is the only thing in your garage or outbuilding, or if you have a two-car garage and only one car, it's not too bad. You can apply the organizational techniques you've learned so far in this book to get everything in order. But if you don't have this much space, it can be difficult to handle.

If you have a lot of equipment and not enough space, consider these options:

√   Put equipment you use don't every week on a hook attached to the ceiling. Fertilizer spreaders and snow shovels are light enough for this option.

√   Purchase or build a rack for hanging garden tools. These are inexpensive at the local home improvement store. (I got mine for under $10.)

√   Store fertilizers, sprinklers, bug killers, extra sprinkler heads, work gloves, and plant foods and sprays together on a shelf safely out of reach of children and pets.

√   Store small garden tools in a plastic container or hang them from the wall.

√   Place larger items like the mower and edger against a wall.

√   Give away or sell large items you don't use, including broken lawn mowers. You won't need a part from it, trust me.

√   Hang bulky items such as Weed Eaters and leaf blowers on the wall from large hooks.

√ Consider an outbuilding, detailed in the next section.

√ Consider using overhead rafters in the garage to store items. There are racks and bins at the hardware store made especially for this area.

Consider an Outbuilding

A friend of mine recently built a lean-to behind the shop in his backyard. That particular area was always collecting gunk, including a ladder, garden tools, and buckets. Anything that was used in the yard found its way back there eventually. Figures 9-4 and 9-5 show the before and after photos. Adding this lean-to not only solved his gunk problem, it also gave him plenty of room to store his lawn equipment. Look around your yard and see if there's an area you could build something like this.

If you are considering a building, there are lots of options, including some buildings that just snap together, requiring no building knowledge at all. Others can be purchased on the cheap if you can put them together yourself, including an 8-x-10-foot metal building for under $200 I saw recently at my local home improvement store. You may be able to find a used one, too, by looking in the classified ads of your local paper. If you have the money and you don't have enough room for your lawn equipment, this might be the perfect solution.

Figure 9-4
Any area that you can't see from the house or yard quickly collects gunk.

Figure 9-5
The new lean-to houses the lawn equipment.

TIP: Outbuildings that are tall enough to be seen over your backyard fence may require a building permit. Check with the local authorities before you build anything that is permanent.

Making Use of the Basement

Basements can be excellent places for storage, but they can also easily become gunk magnets if you aren't careful. The biggest mistake most people make is that they throw everything they don't want in their house down there and they forget about it. They only realize what a mess it is the next time they visit basement. It's the same thing people do with their garages.

If you have a sizable basement that you use for storage and you are doing a major "degunk" of your house, a good place to start is the basement. By getting rid of big and bulky things that are taking up unnecessary space in your basement, you'll free up some valuable storage real estate that can be later used as you degunk the main part of your home.

Here are some tips to help you make the best use out of your basement storage space:

√ Be mindful of moisture. Many basements are damp (especially if they are unfinished) and precautions need to be taken to keep your possessions safe. You'll first want to make sure that you don't store anything in an area that could be damaged by flooding. If the moisture level is high in your basement, consider getting a dehumidifier. A good dehumidifier can work wonders.

√ Determine a plan for using the space. You should decide if you plan to use the basement solely for storage, or if it needs to have multiple functions. For example, you might want to use part of the basement as the family game room and another part for storage. Once you have a plan, make sure you configure your basement with proper partitions and storage units so that the stuff you store doesn't take over the entire space.

√ If possible, improve the basement by cleaning and painting the walls and floors, applying a waterproofing sealant, cleaning the drain (if you have one), installing a smoke detector, and try to keep the temperature around 65 to 70 degrees. All of these things will help protect what's down there and encourage family members to keep it tidy.

√ Install shelving to store bulk items or wine racks to hold wine.

√ As with the garage, use clear plastic containers and label them so you can find things easily.

√ Hang as many items as you can and make sure to hang a flashlight by the basement steps.

√ If your laundry room is in the basement, vent the dryer to the outside.

√ Spray the basement for spiders and other bugs at least twice a year.

Making Use of the Attic

Most people don't think twice about the attic, or they throw stuff up there haphazardly and hope to remember to get it down when they move. Most of the items people store in their attics are the kids' old toys or clothes; things such as knick-knacks, commemorative plates, balls, or other memorabilia; or things they think they'll need later such as skis, ski boots, old sets of golf clubs, old sets of luggage, or small kitchen appliances. As with most stuff you save in long-term areas, though, it's mostly gunk and disappears in the abyss, never to be seen again.

The attic can offer gunk relief, though, if you handle it as you would any long-term storage area. Go through it as if it were a garage, and then create some sort of floor, shelving, or storage system that works and can be used effectively for the long term. For the most part, an unfinished attic can be turned into a functional storage area by putting down a plywood floor and installing a light. Attics can fluctuate greatly in temperature in winter and summer. An exhaust fan is helpful to cool the attic in the summer. Items such as old photos, delicate items (such as wedding dresses and materials such as silk and fur), valuable wooden antique furniture, and antique books and documents should not be stored in the attic if at all possible because the fluctuation of temperatures can create fading, swelling, and cracking.

GunkBuster's Notebook: Using Long-Term Storage for Disaster Preparedness

It's imperative in this day and age to be prepared for an emergency. It's not just tornadoes, hurricanes, floods, and earthquakes; being prepared now also includes protecting your family from the results of acts of terrorism. You can use part of your long-term storage system to house the disaster preparedness supplies every family should have, including water, food, a first-aid kit, a battery-powered radio, flashlights, and more. Usually a single shelf will do, either in the garage or somewhere inside the house. To put together a disaster supply kit, you'll need the items outlined in Table 9-1. At the very least, create a kit that can last three days. Figure 9-6 shows an example.

Figure 9-6
Emergency supplies should be stored with long-term storage items.

Table 9-1   Disaster Preparedness Checklist

Category	Supplies Needed
Water	One gallon for each person per day
Food	Energy bars, cereal, peanut butter, nuts, crackers, powdered milk, juice, vitamins, and ready-to-eat canned meats, fruits, and vegetables
First-aid kit	Aspirin, antihistamines, stomach medications, antacids, antibiotic ointment, hydrogen peroxide, razor blades, bandages, burn ointment, sterile gloves, thermometer, eye wash, and at least a three days supply of prescribed medicines
Clothing	Jacket, pants, long-sleeve shirt, boots, gloves, changes of clothes
Suggested additions	Copies of family documents, insurance papers, compass, signal flare, personal hygiene items, bleach, baby items such as formula and diapers, lists of emergency contacts, generator
Miscellaneous	Cell phone, Ziploc bags, battery-powered radio, laptop and connection to the Internet, battery-powered TV, boat horn to signal for help, can opener, garbage bags, life jackets, sleeping bag for each person, pup tent, fire extinguisher, dust masks, extra glasses and contact lenses

If there's a biological attack, tornado, fire, volcanic eruption, or any disaster that creates fine particles that could cause lung damage, you'll need additional supplies. Nose and mouth protection are important. You can purchase professional masks or cover your nose and mouth with a dense fabric such as heavy cotton. Anything is better than nothing when trying to keep biological particles out of your nose, mouth, and lungs. You'll also need plastic sheeting and duct tape to cover doors, air vents, and windows. It's best if you pre-cut and label these items, but if you don't, make sure you've got a pair of scissors handy.

If you think you'll have to evacuate quickly, make sure you have a tent and sleeping bags, a compass, and other camping supplies, along with water and food. If you store your camping supplies in the garage, make sure they're easily accessible.

Tip: Never let your gas tank get below one half a tank. In an emergency, you'll need every drop.

Consider Storage in Small Spaces

Creating storage in small areas such as dorms, efficiency apartments, studio apartments, and small lofts can pose quite a challenge. You have to know how to use every inch of space you have, including walls, closets, cabinets, drawers, bookshelves, and even seating areas. It's important to incorporate walls in the mix because many items can be hung, especially if you use the wall space to add shelves. Throughout this book, I've told you about ways to get more space from what you have, and all of those ideas can be applied here.

You also have to be creative when purchasing furniture, though, always being on the lookout for items that can double as storage. Piano benches, old trunks or cedar chests, and chairs with flip-up seats and storage underneath can all be used as seating in an emergency, and some for the long term. A decorative wooden ladder can hold quilts and blankets; bulletin boards, cork boards, and whiteboards double as calendars, makeshift filing systems, and day planners; coffee and end table drawers and shelves can store small items; and vintage suitcases can hold mementos and photos. The next time you're looking to add furniture or replace what you already own, make sure you go for something that offers storage as well. When space is at a premium, look down—can you store items in boxes under beds and furniture? Look up—shelving, peg racks, and decorative hooks on the walls can add extra space. Simple shelving units and bookcases can be used as room dividers and storage in small studio apartments, especially important if you aren't allowed to poke holes in the walls.

More Storage Additions for Small Areas

In addition to replacing and using furniture to increase your storage room, you can add smaller organizers. There are several options to consider, and most are inexpensive, can be purchased used, or can be created from recycled boxes or other storage containers.

Here's a list of some other items to use as storage in small areas or anywhere storage space is difficult to come by:

√   Shelving, either wooden or wire

√   Stackable baskets, boxes, or bins

√   Wall files

√   Over-the-door hanging plastic shoe organizers

√   Hooks and pegs

√   Screens to separate the living area from the storage area

√   Chests of drawers

√   Trunks or cedar chests

√   Decorative boxes

√   Skirts around tables

√   Closet, drawer, and pantry organizers

√ Bookcases for wall or corner

√ Decorative glass jars

√ Plastic bins that fit under the bed

> ### GunkBuster's Notebook: Use a Move to Degunk Your Home
>
> If there's a move in your future, you can use that opportunity to degunk your home. You can get rid of commemorative coffee mugs, awful gifts from relatives, clothes that don't fit, and weird stuff you've collected. The motivation is there; you're going to have to pack it up anyway, so why not pack it in a box for charity? You might even be able to have a garage sale and make a few bucks!
>
> If you're not going to be moving anytime soon, though, you can still apply the principles here. Just *pretend* you're moving. That's right, pretend that you'll be moving in three months and tell yourself you want to get a head start on the process. Pack up everything you know you won't need during that period. Box and label appropriately, and store the boxes in your long-term storage area. When three months has passed, look at the boxes again. Ask yourself, "Would I want to haul this box to a new house, unpack it, and find a place for it?" If you answer no, then get rid of the box.

Maintenance Tasks for Storage Areas

Table 9-1 Maintenance Tasks to Keep Storage Areas Degunked

Problem	Solution
Family members do not put items back in their proper places after using them.	Make it easier for them to do so. If the sports equipment is in a bin with a lid and you find sports equipment next to the bin, move the equipment to a big bucket without a lid. If craft supplies end up all over the place, make the container that holds them easier to move. Perhaps putting the materials on a rolling cart would be better.
Stuff continues to collect and there's no place to put it, creating disarray in the garage or storage area.	Add another shelf that will be used to house only new things. Once a month, go through what's on the shelf and move it to the proper area of the garage or home.

(continued)

Table 9-1   Maintenance Tasks to Keep Storage Areas Degunked *(Continued)*

Problem	Solution
There isn't enough room for two cars, lawn equipment, bulk supplies, and other items in the garage.	You have four choices. You can leave a car outside, get rid of some of your stuff, rent a storage space, or build an outbuilding. This assumes you've added as much shelving, hooks, and organizational containers as you can fit in the garage (and can afford), though. Because your car is worth much more than most of the stuff in your garage, leaving the car outside is probably not a good option, and neither is renting a storage space. Weigh the value of the items in the garage against the value of your car or the cost of a storage space or outbuilding. Then see if you can add more storage to the garage or employ the attic.
You can't remember what's in each box or storage container and you end up opening all of them to find the item you want.	Open each box and see what's inside, then label the box. Put holiday decorations, ski equipment, and other seasonal items up high so you know not to go through them when looking. Or take a photo of the items in the box and paste it on the front for a quick view.
The things you use once a month or less are hard to find and access.	Items in long-term storage that you use once a month or less should be on bottom shelves or at eye level.

Summing Up

It's imperative that you have some type of long-term storage, no matter how large or small your home is. For most people, the garage, attic, outbuilding, closet, or pantry serves as this storage space. To get the most out it, you'll need to apply the four-box method, remove everything you want to keep, and then put it back in an organized fashion. When working in a large area that has served as a gunk-holder for many years, the job could take a weekend or more.

Chapter 10

Taming Daily Tasks through Organization

Degunking Checklist:

√ Know what chores must be done every day and create a plan for doing them.

√ Run errands efficiently and share the tasks with other family members.

√ Manage your mail, pay bills on time, and keep the mail gunk factor low.

√ Meet due dates to save time and money.

√ Streamline your morning routine.

I f you've been playing along, it's likely you've cleared out all of the trash in your home, given a third (or more) of your stuff to charity, put misplaced items where they belong, and created long-term storage areas for the things you need to keep but don't use every day. You've minimized what you have to clean around too and created new spaces to hold and hide things you use regularly. You feel great. There's nothing better than being out from under all of that clutter. You feel free, happy, and good about yourself.

Hopefully you've also gotten your family involved. Perhaps you've trained them to put things back after using them, to put dirty clothes in hampers, and to keep shoes in shoe racks. Maybe you even had a little luck getting your slob or pack rattie converted to something a bit more normal by creatively placing hooks, bins, and boxes where they usually just toss stuff. With any luck, they were also involved in some of the degunking. Whatever you've achieved though, whether it was degunking one closet or your entire home, you should be proud. Any large or small steps can lead you to becoming a life-long degunker, and every accomplishment counts. Now it's time to move forward. With your house degunked (or with improvements made), it's time to take control of the tasks involved in everyday living. Managing daily tasks is one of the keys to maintaining your degunked home.

TIP: If you haven't achieved all you want to achieve, you can always go back and repeat any chapter or any step in areas you feel still need work.

In this chapter you'll learn how to tame daily chores. This is an important concept because daily chores must be done, well, daily or your home and life will get gunked up all over again. You must do dishes and laundry, you must dust and vacuum, you must run errands, you must meet deadlines, and you must get through your morning routine with as little stress (and as successfully) as possible. That's what you'll learn in this chapter—how to manage daily tasks and create a working daily routine. With that done, the book will take a turn to *cleaning* your home.

List, Organize, and Manage Daily Tasks

As previously mentioned, there are several tasks that must be done daily, or nearly every day, to keep a degunked home in order. Since these are things you *must do*, anything to streamline the tasks, share them, make them fun, or include them as part of an exercise program helps. The first step to degunking daily tasks though is to know exactly what must be done every day. With a list in hand, you can then create a plan for doing them.

Know What Chores Must Be Done Every Day

The following list contains chores that most families and households must do every day, or at least every other day, to keep their home running efficiently. If you live by yourself, eat out a lot, travel a lot, or hire someone to cook or clean, you'll have different needs and requirements, but for the most part, these are things that must be done on a daily basis for most families:

√   Load and empty the dishwasher or wash dishes by hand

√   Gather, wash, dry, fold, iron, and/or put away laundry

√   Put away stuff that accumulates in "move" boxes, on the floor, and on counters

√   Make breakfast and/or pack lunches

√   Walk the dog, feed pets

√   Wipe the counters and stove top, and generally clean the kitchen, including clearing breakfast and dinner dishes

√   Move newspapers to a recycle bin

√   Make beds

√   Put kids' toys and pets' toys away

√   Go through the mail

√   Put away dirty clothes

√   Set the table, make dinner, and clean up afterwards

√   Get the kids bathed and to bed

There are also things should be done weekly. You don't have to set aside an entire day to do them though; they can be spread out a few at a time as part of your daily tasks. Just figure out which day each of the following tasks will be done and who will do it:

√   Take out the trash

√   Tidy up the living room, family room, bedrooms

√   Put the newspapers or recyclables in the proper bin outside

√   Dust

√   Sweep and vacuum

√   Clean up after the pets, including vacuuming up pet hair, sanitizing the cat box, or picking up dog poop from the yard

√   Water plants

√   Run errands

√   Change the bed linens

√   Pay bills

√ Mop floors

√ Clean bathrooms

√ Empty wastebaskets

√ Clean mirrors and large glass doors

√ Clean the refrigerator and go through the pantry before grocery shopping

√ Mow the yard; weed the garden

√ Perform the weekly tasks detailed in the chapters of this book

You'll probably have chores that apply specifically to you and your family too, and you'll need to add them to this list. These may include feeding fish, visiting an elderly parent in a nursing home, passing out or taking medications, cleaning the swimming pool, cleaning the game room, taking care of an elderly parent who lives with you, and driving children to practices and games. Before moving to the next section, list all of the extra chores that are specific to your family.

GunkBuster's Notebook: Tackling Daily Food Tasks

If you and your family take their own lunches to work or school, you know how time consuming it can be to make and pack them. It's also time consuming to make dinner every night, especially if you work all day and don't get home until 6:00 p.m. or so. With a little organization, though, and a little effort on the weekends, you can make quick work of these tasks.

Figure 10-1 shows one of my Sunday afternoon activities. After grocery shopping for the week, which I do every Sunday, I lay out all of the vegetables and make salads. These are used in lunches and are easy to pack and carry. I place fruit in the refrigerator on a shelf specifically noted for lunch items to make creating and packing a lunch simple. This is shown in Figure 10-2. I also cut up vegetables for dinner entrees, like stir-fry, soups, and salads. I separate snacks like nuts and chips into baggies for easy on-the-go snacks and lunch additions) and keep granola bars, yogurt, and energy bars on hand. Sometimes, if I'm feeling especially motivated, I'll even put together a soup to store in the fridge, create and freeze a casserole, or make tuna or chicken salad for sandwiches. Allotting part of a Saturday or Sunday to prepare food for the week can save lots of time during the week, when time is scarce. If you can get your family involved in your Sunday cooking tasks, it can even be fun!

Figure 10-1

After grocery shopping and before putting food away, pack a few lunches.

Figure 10-2

Designate a shelf in your refrigerator for lunch choices; kids and adults will make quick work of packing their own lunches.

Create a Chore List for You and Your Family

After looking at the list of tasks that must be done daily and weekly, it's no wonder your house gets gunked up! It's so easy for the sink, and then the kitchen counter, to get cluttered with dirty dishes because you didn't have time to empty the dishwasher or pick up after breakfast. It's also easy to accumulate newspapers when there's no one to take them to the recycle bin. A family room can get cluttered in no time when no one picks up after themselves and there's no plan to put everything in its proper place before going to bed or before leaving for work each day. To stay degunked, a plan *must* be put into place to handle daily chores and daily debris.

Table 10-1 lists the everyday tasks and chores from the previous section and offers ways to incorporate them into your daily routine. Use this list only as a guideline and create a table of your own that applies to you or your family. You can create a table by using a spreadsheet program on your computer and printing it out each week; by writing it on a whiteboard and hanging it in the kitchen, entryway, or family room; or by using the old-fashioned pen-and-paper method.

Table 10-1   Required Daily Tasks and Suggested Days and Times for Performing Them

Daily or Weekly Task	Assign To	Suggested Day	Suggested Time	How Long the Task Should Take
Load and empty the dishwasher.	Anyone over the age of 10.	Every day.	In the morning while the coffee brews, during a commercial break on television, while a frozen dinner cooks in the microwave, while waiting for water to boil on the stove.	5 to 7 minutes.
Gather laundry.	Anyone old enough to understand what clothes can and cannot be washed	Every other day.	When walking past the laundry hamper in any room, when that hamper is full enough to create a load of like colors or clothing types, clothing types gather a load and put it in the washing machine. together.	If there are clothes in there and they've been washed, put them in the dryer. less than 5 minutes.

(continued)

Table 10-1   Maintenance Tasks to Keep Storage Areas Degunked (continued)

Daily or Weekly Task	Assign To	Suggested Day	Suggested Time	How Long the Task Should Take
Wash and dry laundry.	A family member that is 12 years old or older.	Every other day.	Fill and turn washer on before going to to bed. In the morning, put clothes in the dryer and turn the dryer on. Go on about your morning routine. Designate a family member to fold the clothes when the drying completes. Use a hanging rod and hangers to hang clothes on a laundry room clothes pole until they can be put away. When folding clothes, put each person's clothing in a separate pile.	Verifying clothes are like colors and that pockets are empty, washer, 5 minutes. Folding the clothes in the dryer in the morning, 10 minutes.
Fold and put away laundry.	Anyone capable of putting away clothes.	Every day.	During a commercial break on television, while waiting for water to boil on the stove, or when waiting for a spouse to finish getting ready to go out. If possible and the laundry room is big enough to store folded clothes, let each family member gather their own folded clothes and put them away.	Depends on the number of family members, but generally, 5 to 7 minutes per person.
Iron clothes.	Adult.	Sunday.	Set aside a time each Sunday to iron the clothes for the week. Do your best to replace items that need to be ironed with no-iron fabrics. Consider sending items that need to be ironed to the dry cleaner for washing and pressing. The cost is small in comparison to the time you save. Kids' play and and school clothes should not need to be ironed; instead, buy no-iron options if at all possible.	Varies, but generally 3 to 5 minutes per garment.

(continued)

Table 10-1   Maintenance Tasks to Keep Storage Areas Degunked *(continued)*

Daily or Weekly Task	Assign To	Suggested Day	Suggested Time	How Long the Task Should Take
Put away stuff that accumulates in "move" boxes.	Every family member as an ongoing project.	Every time you pass a "move" box.	Every time you pass a "move" box, pick up something and carry it with you. As you pass by the room where it belongs, put it away. When going from one room to another, always carry something.	3 minutes, maximum.
Pack lunches.	Adults and eventually, children.	Every day.	Pack lunches the night before with your kids' help, or pack them in the morning while making breakfast. You can include prepackaged salads, fruit, small bags of chips, and other time-saving products to make the task go faster. By packing lunches with your kids, you can teach them to make healthy choices, and they can eventually make their own lunches.	If you dedicate one shelf in the refrigerator for appropriate lunch entrees, fruit, and refrigerated snacks and one shelf in the pantry for appropriate dry foods, any lunch can be packed in less than 3 minutes.
Take something out for tomorrow night's dinner.	Whoever's job it is to cook the next day.	Every day.	At night, remove items from the freezer and put them in the refrigerator so the meat has time to thaw. If you want, you can also group the veggies you plan to eat, make a salad (minus the dressing), put together a casserole, or get out canned food to speed things up the next day.	1 minute to an hour depending on the amount of preparation.
Walk the dog.	Best done as a family, but if a child does it, a parent should accompany.	Every day.	After dinner, while another family member cleans up the kitchen. This "chore" could be rotated or assigned as a reward for good behavior.	10 to 20 minutes or more.

(continued)

Table 10-1   Maintenance Tasks to Keep Storage Areas Degunked *(continued)*

Daily or Weekly Task	Assign To	Suggested Day	Suggested Time	How Long the Task Should Take
Wipe the counters and stove top, and generally clean the kitchen, including clearing breakfast and dinner dishes.	Anyone over the age of 12.	Every morning before leaving for work and school, and every night after dinner.	Put away cooking utensils and pans as you finish using them. For instance, after sliding an omelet off the frying pan, rinse the pan and put it in the dishwasher (or sink). When family members finish eating, they should put their own dishes away as well (if appropriate for your family and the meal being served). Assign one person to put away milk, butter, and other perishables and another to wipe down the counter with a disposable wipe or wet paper towel. Assign dishwashing chores as well.	Varies, but cleaning the kitchen after breakfast, if the proper tasks were completed the day before, should take no more than 15 minutes. Dinner dishes may take up to 30 minutes.
Move newspapers to a recycle bin.	Youngest school-age child.	Every morning before school.	On the way out the door or before leaving, the youngest school-age child should take the newspapers to the recycle bin.	If your family reads the paper at night, leave the papers by the door and have junior take out yesterday's paper each morning. 3 minutes.
Make beds.	Every family member.	Every morning.	The last person out of bed makes it. Children make their own beds.	5 minutes, maximum.
Put toys away.	Whoever played with them.	This includes kids' toys as well as adults'.	Before bed, every family member picks up their toys.	5 minutes to pick up, 5 minutes to put away properly.
Go through the mail.	An adult.	Every day.	Upon coming home from work and before doing anything else. If this isn't possible, every night after dinner, or while relaxing before going to bed. It will go very quickly if you stand near a garbage can or recycling bin. You can even sort by the garbage cans outside so junk mail never makes it into the house.	5 minutes to open and view, 1 minute to throw away what isn't necessary, and 5 minutes to file or put in the appropriate holding place.

(continued)

Table 10-1   Maintenance Tasks to Keep Storage Areas Degunked *(continued)*

Daily or Weekly Task	Assign To	Suggested Day	Suggested Time	How Long the Task Should Take
Put dirty clothes away.	Everyone.	Every day.	After showering or changing clothes, put worn clothes in their proper places. Stress that the proper place is not where the wearer took them off but is instead a clothes hamper or closet.	If you only have one or two family members, carry clothes directly to the laundry room. 1 to 3 minutes.
Set the dinner table.	Youngest child capable.	Every night.	When a parent starts dinner, the child sets the table. If there aren't any children around, put out plates and silverware buffet style.	5 to 10 minutes.
Make dinner.	Teenager or adult.	Every night.	Always try to multitask, save time, and reduce cleaning tasks while you cook. Make the salad while waiting for the water to boil; microwave vegetables in the dishes they'll be served and stored in; serve meals buffet style so meats and entrees don't have to be transferred to another dish; put away blenders and food processors when you're finished with them; soak pans while you eat; put soiled pans and utensils in the sink or dishwasher when you're finished with them. Save time with prepackaged meals; cook and freeze entrees over the weekend; order take-out as a special treat.	15 minutes to 1 hour.
Get the kids bathed and ready for bed.	An adult or older sibling, until children are capable of doing it themselves.	Every night.	Perform these tasks at the same time every night and do what you can to multitask. You may be able to lay out your children's clothes for the next day while they get ready for bed or clean the bathroom counter and toilet while they're in the bathtub. You can always fold laundry while keeping an eye on them, put away things from the "move" box, or straighten the gunk on the counters or dressers.	30 minutes.

(continued)

Table 10-1 Maintenance Tasks to Keep Storage Areas Degunked *(continued)*

Daily or Weekly Task	Assign To	Suggested Day	Suggested Time	How Long the Task Should Take
Gather and take out household trash.	Anyone over the age of 7.	The night before trash pickup day.	Carry an empty plastic garbage bag from room to room and empty all of the trash cans in the house. Remove the trash bag from the kitchen and take both to the trash bin outside.	10 minutes.
Gather and take out recyclables.	Anyone over the age of 7.	The night before recyclables are picked up.	Newspapers, plastics, and glass should already be sorted in their own bins. Carry the bins to the recycle area outside.	Less than 5 minutes.
Dust.	Anyone 12 or older.	Monday	Carry the proper dusting tools detailed in Chapter 11 from room to room and dust appropriate areas. Dusting chores should be kept under 20 minutes. If it takes more time, perform the task over two days.	Varies, but generally no longer than 1 to 2 minutes per item to be dusted.
Sweep.	Anyone capable of sweeping.	Tuesday.	Start at the corners and walls of the room and work inward. Keep a dustpan handy to sweep up the dirt.	No more than 10 minutes per room.
Vacuum.	Anyone capable of vacuuming.	Wednesday.	Vacuum slowly enough to get the grime but quickly enough so you don't spend unnecessary time on the task. Keep one attachment handy for couches and chairs, and read the manual for the best settings for your vacuum cleaner.	No more than 10 minutes per room.
Clean the cat box or pick up dog poop.	Whoever is the pet's "owner," or rotate among family members.	Day before trash pickup for emptying, sanitizing, and refilling the cat box and for cleaning up after, the dog, daily for maintaining the cat box.	Keep the proper tools handy and near the tasks, including cat box liners, dog and cat poop scoopers, fresh kitty litter, and plastic bags. Don't use recycled grocery bags for this purpose; often they have holes in them and will create a mess of their own. Take the refuse to the outside trash can immediately.	15 minutes.

(continued)

Table 10-1 **Maintenance Tasks to Keep Storage Areas Degunked** *(continued)*

Daily or Weekly Task	Assign To	Suggested Day	Suggested Time	How Long the Task Should Take
Run errands.	Anyone who has a driver's license.	Friday and Saturday.	Read the next section, "Manage Errands," for tips. The short version is to plan your route carefully, which may include going to the bank, the dry cleaners, the movie rental store, and the grocery store.	Varies by task.
Change bed linens.	Anyone capable of the task.	Sunday.	If you only have one set of sheets per bed, you can eliminate the task of folding clean linens. On Sunday morning, strip the beds and start a load of laundry. Do your normal Sunday morning activities, but make time to transfer the sheets from the washer to the dryer. When the sheets are out of the dryer, place them on the bed to which they belong. Whoever sleeps in that bed gets to make it up. That may be you.	5 minutes to strip the bed and start the laundry, 3 minutes to transfer the sheets from the washer to the dryer, 3 minutes to put the sheets on the proper bed, and 5 minutes to make it.
Pay bills.	Adult.	Monday.	Go through your mail in box and pay any bill that is coming due the next week. Put the mail by the door in its proper container or pay the bills online. See the section "Manage Mail, Bills, and Deadlines" for more tips.	20 minutes.
Mop floors.	Adult.	Thursday.	Keep all supplies together and perform the task when others are not home so the floor has time to dry.	Varies, but generally no more than 30 minutes.
Clean bathrooms.	Anyone over the age of 12.	Saturday.	Keep cleaning supplies together and choose supplies that perform multiple cleaning tasks. Use disposable towels or ones you can wash (instead of a sponge); check toilet paper and tissue supplies; clean toilets last to avoid spreading germs from surface to surface. Avoid gadgets to make cleaning the bathroom faster; they usually do not save time.	15 to 20 minutes.

(continued)

Table 10-1   Maintenance Tasks to Keep Storage Areas Degunked *(continued)*

Daily or Weekly Task	Assign To	Suggested Day	Suggested Time	How Long the Task Should Take
Clean mirrors and large glass doors.	Adult, preferably a tall one.	Friday.	Use a squeegee and proper cleansers to clean large glass doors on the front or back of the house and to clean full-length and bathroom mirrors in the home.	5 minutes per door or mirror.
Clean the refrigerator.	Adult or as a family.	The day you grocery shop, preferably the day before trash pickup.	Check all dates and throw away anything that's expired. Throw away leftovers more than two days old and put their dishes in the sink to soak. If items are out of place, such as ketchup that wasn't returned to the door, or if anything has spilled, remedy the situation now. Wipe down the shelves with a damp cloth.	15 to 20 minutes.
Mow the yard.	Adult or teen.	Saturday or Sunday, after 10:00 a.m.	Mower, edger, gas, oil, Weed Eater line, extension cords, and other supplies should be easily accessible. Edge first, then mow. Run the mower over the sidewalk when finished to blow the grass clippings back in the yard (eliminating the need to get out the leaf blower).	1 to 2 hours.

<Add other tasks specific to your family here>

When you create your list, create another column for the person who performed the task to sign off on it. This will allow you, in one quick glance, to see if the day's chores were done.

TIP: Mom or dad should check, maintain, and manage the daily task table while watching television, reading, or relaxing at night. Anything that wasn't done during the day will have to be done by the assigned person while other family members are relaxing.

Manage Errands

Sometimes I'm amazed at how families with children and those in which both parents work outside the home ever get their errands run. I'm equally amazed at how single moms or single dads do it. There are so many errands to do and seemingly never enough time to do them. While running errands is a necessary part of life, there are ways to do it more efficiently and more quickly. And, you don't have to do it all yourself.

Make a List

Keeping a list of errands that need to be run serves many purposes. Having a single list on a whiteboard allows you to jot down things as you think of them and to copy the list before you go out to run errands. You'll never forget an errand again, providing you look at this list daily. However, keeping a list of errands can serve many other functions:

√   Family members can be taught to run one errand each time they leave the house. This may eliminate the need to specify an actual day and time to do them. You can even require it if there are enough errands.

√   You'll always know what day DVD rentals are due, when dry cleaning can be picked up, and when you're photos are ready if you make a note of them on the whiteboard.

√   A list will remind you to go to the bank, buy stamps at the post office, or pick up take-out for dinner.

√   A list will allow you to write down things as you think of them, such as purchasing a gift for your brother's birthday.

√   A list will help you plan the order of errands you need to run on "errand day."

TIP: If a whiteboard doesn't work for you, consider sticky notes. You can stick them to an "errand area" and grab one when you leave the house to remind you to run the errand before or after work. You can even attach sticky notes to a family member's keys or cell phone. Stick the note on your dashboard to keep you from forgetting.

Run Errands Efficiently

Part of running errands is avoiding the backtrack syndrome. You pass the post office to go to the bank and then remember you should have stopped to get stamps. Before heading out on an errand-running, look at your list of all of the places you have to go. Organize these places so you make a circle when running them and so you don't have to backtrack. Make sure to plan your errands so the grocery store or ice cream store is last to keep perishables safe.

There are a multitude of errands you may need to run, and I've listed the places you may need to go for many of them next. When you look at the list, consider the location's proximity to your house. Devise a plan now, pretending you have to go to each of these places. Put a 1 by the place you'd go first, a 2 by the place you'd go second, and so on. The next time you run errands, take a look at this list to plan your route. Remember, you're trying to not backtrack. You can add additional items to the list too. Here are the more common places for the errands people run weekly:

√   Post office

√   Movie rental store

√   Dry cleaners

√   Bank

√   Charity to drop off donations

√   Where the kids are to pick them up or drop them off

√   Pet groomers

√   Doctor, dentist, vet, pediatrician

√   Grocery store

√   Drug store

√   Department store

√   Shoe store

√   Fast food restaurant for take-out

√   Hospital to visit a friend or nursing home to visit an elderly parent

√   Library

√   Any other place you may need to go

With your list in hand and numbered, you can probably save quite a bit of time.

TIP: Create an errand supply list too. You may need deposit slips, grocery list, coupons, ATM card, checks, a calculator, receipts, or other items.

Multitask While Running Errands

Although I don't like to see people talking on the phone and driving at the same time, it is one way to run errands while taking care of other business. I won't promote it, but I will say that talking on the phone while running errands, when appropriate, is a great way to multitask. If you must attend to business while you're running errands, at least try to do so when you're not driving and only when you're out of earshot of other people. That's common courtesy.

Besides talking on the phone, though, there are other ways to multitask while running errands:

√   You can do many of your errands in one place if you shop at a store that has a branch of your bank or an ATM inside. Most grocery stores carry postage stamps at the checkout, and some stores even have a dry cleaner on-site. Think about other places where you can combine errands.

√   If you have to drop off your kids for soccer practice and pick them up in one hour, use that time to talk on the phone, balance your checkbook, or run other errands. Ditto for kids' doctor and dentist appointments.

√   If you have to wait in a doctor's or dentist's office, take along your laptop or even a pad and pen and get some work done.

√   If you have to wait while getting your hair cut colored, styled, or dried, make a grocery list, or if you are a catalog shopper, bring them along and shop.

√   If you have to wait while your dog is groomed, make that phone call you've been putting off, or if the groomer is at a pet store purchase food and necessities.

√   If you need to get pictures developed, drop them off at a store that has one-hour processing and also offers one hour's worth of shopping, such as a grocery store or drug store.

√   If you're waiting one hour for your new prescription glasses, use that time to run another errand in the area.

√   If you have to wait for take-out, organize the items in your car's glove box.

√   When getting your car's oil changed, take a short walk to get some exercise, or bring along birthday, holiday, or greeting cards you need to write and stamps and mail them.

Learn to Avoid Running Errands

There are ways around doing many of the errands mentioned in this chapter. Most involve the Internet, although some errands can be eliminated by paying a little extra for delivery or shipping. If you're interested in completing errands from home, perhaps at night or on the weekends, there are many ways to get started. Here are some examples:

√ Do your banking and bill paying online.

√ Use delivery services for grocery shopping. (Schwan's is one example.)

√ Shop online for drugstore items, holiday gifts, books, clothing, shoes, airline tickets, and pet supplies.

√ Have your dry cleaning delivered.

√ Rent DVDs by mail. (NetFlix is one example.)

√ Use online postal services that allow you to print postage from your home computer, or order stamps by mail.

√ Download books, music, videos, and movies that can be saved, played, and watched on a computer, MP3 player, or iPod.

√ File insurance claims online.

√ Obtain or manage health, life, home, and car insurance online.

√ Call on the phone or order online for take-out instead of picking it up on your way home.

√ Send gifts from online sources such as FTD, Red Envelope, and Amazon.

√ Order digital prints online by uploading pictures and having the prints mailed to you. (Shutterfly is one example.)

√ Book vacations and business trips online.

√ Obtain information about drugs and health issues online.

√ Get information from government sources, print tax forms, and file taxes online.

√ Obtain birth records, naturalization records, divorce certificates, and death certificates online. (Government Guide is an example.)

Manage Mail, Bills, and Deadlines

Although I've written a little in this chapter and others about managing mail, paying bills, and running errands that have to do with deadlines (like getting movies back on time), it's likely still a problem area. It's an important issue to revisit because being unable to manage the bills, return rentals on time, deal with and file insurance paperwork, and respond to personal correspondence can cost you quite a bit of money in late fees and missed opportunities. And, if you don't have the time to work through your bank statements and health insurance papers and read the small print on credit card statements, you'll probably end up getting scammed one way or the other as well. Although it's difficult to stop for 15 minutes go through the day's mailbag, it's extremely vital, if only to double-check what you're being billed for. For these reasons, I've included the following sections to create a concise guide for managing these tasks.

Manage Mail

You need to have a few things in place to manage the flood of mail you'll get and have to deal with every day:

√   A filing system (see Chapter 8).

√   A place to sort mail, preferably by a trash can and shredder.

√   In the sorting area: three baskets or bins, one for incoming mail for other family members, one for bills that need to be paid, and one for outgoing mail.

√   A plan to sort mail immediately. Junk mail should be thrown away, bills should be filed or put in an in box specifically created for them, and papers you need to keep should be immediately filed.

√   A place for storing magazines and catalogs you want to keep. Move magazines immediately to their proper place, and put them on top of the other magazines in the pile. Once a month go through the pile and get rid of anything over three months old.

√   A nearby shredder or scissors. Cut up or shred unwanted credit cards, blank checks from credit card issuers, and anything you don't need to file that contains sensitive information like Social Security numbers. Many shredders feature an option to shred stiff items like credit cards.

√   A unit to weigh packages. If you send out many packages, consider a unit to weigh them. One is shown later in Figure 10-3. This will end your trips to the post office.

√   Remove your name from junk mail lists on www.dmaconsumers.org.

Manage Bills

If you've put into place the three bins mentioned in the previous section—one for incoming mail for family members, one for bills that need to be paid, and one for outgoing mail—you're already halfway there to never being late paying a bill again. All you have to do now is take the system a few steps forward:

√   If possible, teach family members to go through the mail basket once daily and remove what belongs to them. If they can't, don't, or won't, distribute the mail for the others in the household to their personal mail area. This may be a dresser in their room or an in box. Once it's out of your hands, it's their problem, not yours, and any blame for late fees will fall on them.

√   Once a week, go through the basket that holds the bills that need to be paid. Pay them. Then, on the back of the envelope, write the latest date they can be mailed. Put the envelopes in the out box.

√   Make sure the out box contains pens, pencils, tape, and stamps.

√   Each morning on your way out the door, check to see if there are any bills that need to be taken to the mail box and sent out.

There are organizers you can purchase too, organizers that hold bills by date and offer a place to store stamps and other supplies. If you find one in your price range, buy it and hang it by the door. Some organizers even have places to hold mail for different family members, a place to hold keys, and a place to keep outgoing mail.

Figure 10-3 shows a mail sorting station. On the far left is a unit to weigh outgoing mail; in the middle, a desk organizer that holds return address labels, tape, scissors, pens, pencils, markers, and paper; and on the right, four shelves that are labeled. Figure 10-4 shows a close-up of the labels. Under the desk where these sit is a shredder and trash can, and one drawer of the desk doubles as a file cabinet.

Figure 10-3
A mail sorting station contains a filing system and supplies.

Figure 10-4
The best systems are labeled and offer plenty of space.

Notice in Figure 10-4 that there's no area for *outgoing* mail. That's because there's an area next to the door to hold all outgoing mail. Having an area by the door makes remembering and taking the mail to the mail box simple.

Manage Returns

The only way to never be late with a VHS, DVD, or game rental is to have a system in place for knowing where they are, when they're due, and who's going to return them. The same is true of things you borrow from friends and books you borrow from the library, as well as things you've purchased but want to return within the 30 day return window. Usually, creating a system for making this happen requires quite a few changes to the current one.

However, you can use the system you've put in place for managing your mail as a start. You can put rented or borrowed items you need to return in the same place you store your outgoing mail. Designate a basket or box for items like books, DVDs, clothing, and so on. And, as with the bills you need to put in the mail box, you can make a note on the rented items stating the last day they can be returned. Keep some sticky notes by the door to do this.

While this system might work if everyone in your home is organized and on top of things, it probably won't work if the person playing the rented video game is your 8-year-old son and he has an Xbox 360 in his room. It also won't work if your spouse borrows the neighbor's tools without your knowledge. If that's the case, you've got some changes to make.

The only true way to control never being late with a rental or borrowed item again is to write down everything you borrow or rent on a master calendar, noting specifically the day it's due back. When anyone goes out to run errands, they can check this list to see if anything needs to be returned while they're out. This will take some doing, especially if your family isn't used to such a system. But it'll be worth the time and effort if you're constantly paying late fees or ticking off the neighbors.

TIP: *I have a small family and work at home, so I handle all of the errands myself. I put anything having to do with an errand, rental, or return in the front seat of my car, plus any packages that need to be taken to the post office and any coupons I cut from newspaper or mailing circulars. Because I'm in my car at least once a day, I never forget an errand.*

Streamline Your Morning Routine

There's one more thing to consider when it comes to managing daily tasks, and that's streamlining your morning routine. Every morning's the same: you're tired, you're late, your kid is moving slower than a sloth, you can't find what you want to wear (or your keys, money, shoes, or tie), and the cell phone is dead because no one's plugged it in for days. You also forgot to sign your kid's field trip papers and box up that item you have to take to the post office, and you have no idea what you'll take for lunch, much less what you'll have for dinner. Having a harried transition between getting up and heading to work or school can ruin the entire day, or at least the morning.

If this sounds like you, you need help learning how to start the day off right, not just for you but for your entire family. Making the morning routine pleasurable will carry good feelings over to the entire day. It will also reduce your morning stress, and perhaps also lead to better health. Less stress in the morning helps by keeping your blood pressure down and allows you time to eat a healthy breakfast.

For the most part, streamlining your morning routine consists of two things: what you can do the night before to prepare and what you can do in the morning to make the transition from home to work or school smoother.

The Night Before

First things first. If you and your family feel hurried in the morning, change the alarm clocks so that everyone will get up 15 minutes earlier than they do now. Your family members won't like this, but assure them that they can all change their alarms back as soon as the morning routine is under control. Tell them they may even get to sleep longer than they do now if they help you in getting mornings under control. With that done, let's look at some things you can do at night, starting tonight, to shave some time off of tomorrow's morning tasks.

At dinner tonight, list all of the things you do in the morning. Have family members do the same. Look carefully at the lists and see if you can cross off anything tonight. Can you do any of these things before you go to sleep tonight, or is there any way you can make tomorrow morning's tasks more efficient? Usually, you can find several things that can be done at night to streamline the morning routine. Table 10-2 lists some ideas, and you may have more.

Table 10-2   Things You Can Do at Night to Streamline the Morning's Routine

Morning Task	How to Perform It at Night
Make coffee.	Make coffee at night and use your coffeepot's timer (if you have one) to automatically start the coffee before you wake up. You can make this task part of cleaning up after dinner.
Shower.	Kids can bathe at night, and men can too. Women generally have hair styling tasks, but if possible, shower before bed.
Iron clothing.	Set aside one day a week for ironing, such as Sunday afternoon. You'll never have to iron in the morning again.
Pick out clothes to wear.	Lay out clothes the night before for yourself, and have your spouse and your kids do the same. You can even perform this task for the entire week on Sunday when you iron
Make breakfast.	Buy healthy breads, cereals, yogurt, breakfast bars, and drinks and make on-the-go breakfasts available. There are a few healthy microwaveable choices available too. Once you've gotten the morning routine under control, you can return to home-cooked breakfasts.
Gather keys, cell phones, money, briefcases, purses, wallets, PDAs, laptops, backpacks, glasses, jewelry, watches, and lunches.	Designate an area in each person's room or by the entryway for family members to gather items or store them. Family members can each have a designated space to put cell phones, keys, money, etc., making them easily accessible in the morning. Pack lunches at night while someone else is cleaning up the kitchen.
Deal with paperwork.	Before bed, ask everyone if there's anything that needs to be signed, taken to the post office, or otherwise looked at.
Feed the dog or cat.	Assign this task to a family member, and put Rover's bowl someplace where you'll see it in the morning.

(continued)

Table 10-2   Things You Can Do at Night to Streamline the Morning's Routine *(continued)*

Morning Task	How to Perform It at Night
Take medications and vitamins.	If possible, leave medications and vitamins on the kitchen counter to remind family members to take them.
Avoid last-minute emergencies.	Check your calendar and to-do list before bed; keep emergency cleaners and sewing supplies handy; plug in your cell phone before bed and keep a car charger in every vehicle; set an alarm to go off 15 minutes before you have to leave the house.

The Morning Of

If you did some of the things in Table 10-2 last night, chances are that this morning will go a lot more smoothly than yesterday morning. You'll find yourself with a few extra minutes on your hands. You can either use that time to work through some of the daily chores listed earlier or spend it using even more tricks to hasten your morning routine.

Table 10-3 offers some ideas for ways you can shave time off what you have to do in the morning. Applying these ideas can really help streamline morning tasks.

Table 10-3   Things You Can Do in the Morning to Streamline the Morning Routine

Morning Task	Ideas for Performing the Task More Quickly
Read the paper.	If you commute, read the paper then. If you don't commute, read the paper during your first coffee break at work. You can also read the front page in the morning and the comics at night.
Apply makeup.	Work with a professional to help you limit the time you spend on this task.
Shave.	Purchase a shaver you can use in the shower or an electric shaver that does not require shaving cream.
Shower.	Take a shorter shower. It's easy to save 3 to 5 minutes by having a shower caddie handy, avoiding conditioner that has to stay on for three minutes, and taking a shower instead of a bath in the morning.
Run the dryer or empty the dishwasher.	Set the alarm 15 minutes early and perform these tasks while others are sleeping, or assign the task to family members on a rotating basis.
Get dressed.	Lay out clothes the night before.
Brush teeth.	Use an electric toothbrush and brush your teeth while checking your email, or brush your teeth in the shower with a regular toothbrush.
Have coffee.	Keep all coffee supplies together, including sugar, stirrers, and add-ins.
Clean up the kitchen.	If you empty the dishwasher before bed or first thing in the morning while the coffee is brewing, it won't take long to clean up the kitchen. Insist that every family member put away their own breakfast dishes and cereal and clean up their own mess.

Summing Up

The daily art of living creates its own debris and gunk. There are almost always newspapers, coffee messes, dirty dishes, dirty clothes, and daily dirt and grime to deal with. There's also breakfast, lunch, and dinner and all of the debris that comes along with that. Finally, there are bills, errands, groceries, and mail to deal with every day of the week. A big part of staying degunked is about staying on top of these things.

In this chapter you learned some tricks for taming daily debris, running errands, and staying on top of mail and bills. If you can learn to use the charts presented in this chapter, you can become the master of your home and your life while at the same time reducing your stress and creating a better environment for your family.

Chapter 11

Cleaning Efficiently and Successfully

Degunking Checklist:

√ Keep and follow a to-do list to promote productive cleaning sessions.

√ Dress properly for cleaning.

√ Clean efficiently by avoiding backtracking.

√ Don't perform unnecessary tasks or create more work for yourself.

√ Purchase and organize the cleaners you'll need to do the job right.

√ Clean while you sleep with tips and tricks from the experts.

Now that your house is organized and your daily chores manageable, it's time to address cleaning tasks. Cleaning in this chapter isn't about emptying the dishwasher or putting in a load of laundry though; it's about the cleaning tasks you perform once a week after work, on Saturday or Sunday in longer cleaning sessions, or the first weekend of every month in marathon ones. This chapter is about how to make these types of cleaning sessions more productive by having your to-do list written and up-to-date, learning and applying the tips and tricks the experts know for working quickly, and having the tools you need readily available and organized.

Promote Productive Cleaning Sessions

Unless you have hired help, it's likely you spend time every day, one day a weekend, and one day a month really getting after clutter, dirt, and grime that collects in your home. (If you don't, you should.) This can be stuff you do once a week, like cleaning the bathrooms, scrubbing the shower stall and tub, and scrubbing fingerprints off the walls and light switches, but it can also include things you do monthly, such as cleaning behind the washer and dryer, cleaning the top of the refrigerator, getting the dust off the ceiling fan blades, and clearing out old magazines and other long-term clutter. You probably have to dedicate time to pick up after kids and spouses too, carry boxes and larger trash to the curb for pickup, wash or dust mini blinds, or vacuum curtains.

To make these cleaning sessions more productive and to perform the tasks more quickly, you need to streamline your to-do list, dress properly, learn how to clean a room quickly, and avoid performing unnecessary tasks or creating more work for yourself than necessary. In the following sections, we'll look at these topics in detail.

GunkBuster's Notebook: Never Get Gunked Up Again

As you already know, gunk is going to continue to collect no matter what you do or what system you have in place. Small appliances and electronics are going to break, clothes are going to go out of style, shoes are going to be sent to the garage to be used as "garden" shoes, and paper is going to accumulate. And, either you or a family member is going to be unwilling or unable, for whatever reason, to throw this gunk away. So, before starting any weekend cleaning spree, follow this advice: Take a garbage bag and a cardboard box from room to room

and collect anything that is trash, anything that's broken, anything missing necessary parts or pieces, and anything you've outgrown or no longer want. Immediately do something with the items you collect. This will help you stay on top of gunk and, hopefully, prevent it from ever taking over your home again.

Keep a To-Do List

Writing an effective to-do list will save you time; that's all there is to it. It may also reduce stress, save money, and save gas, and it may even help you sleep better. How many times, in the middle of the night, have you thought of something you *had* to do the next day? Knowing you'd forget, but not wanting to get up, find a pen and paper, and write down your thoughts, that nagging thought prevented you from getting the rest you needed. And how many times have you gotten home from running errands only to realize that what you really went out for didn't get done? Finally, how many times have you started off on a cleaning jag and gotten so wrapped up in the medicine cabinet that you completely forgot about the other chores you wanted to get done? It happens to the best of us, and a good to-do list is just the thing we all need to stay on track.

Before you start haphazardly creating a to-do list though, spend some time matching the type of to-do list you should create with your own personality and needs. Here are some questions to consider:

√ Would you feel most comfortable writing your list on a yellow legal pad and crossing items off as you do them?

√ Would you prefer using sticky notes or index cards so you can put one task on each, carry them around with you, and then physically throw away the note as a reward?

√ If you are a long-term planner, would you prefer using a large calendar?

√ Do you share to-do lists with others? If you do, perhaps a whiteboard is in order.

√ Do you prefer spiral notebooks? You could carry a spiral notebook around with you and cross items off at the same time. When an entire page is crossed off, you could tear out the page and throw it away as a release.

√ Do you use a PDA or computer program to manage your to-do lists?

√ Are you more comfortable haphazardly writing down thoughts on the *TV Guide*, phone book, the back of an envelope, or whatever else is handy because you don't want to invest in a legal pad, spiral, or sticky notes or you know you will never able to find them when you need them anyway?

Be honest about the type of person you are; it's okay to be messy, quirky, or the type who keeps lists of your lists. Decide on the type of list you think will work for you, and make a commitment to that type. If you need to buy sticky notes, legal pads, new software for your PDA, or small writing tablets you can leave all over the house, buy them. If you want to write your to-do lists on the backs of used envelopes, that's fine too. Just make sure you have a place for those used envelopes, that there's a pen nearby, and that you can find them when you need them. You can even hide your used envelopes in a drawer, on the coffee table shelf, or even in a decorative box beside the television, right out in the open. Whatever you decide though, get a pad and pencil for the nightstand. I promise you'll sleep better when you can make a note at 3:00 a.m. to pick up toilet paper on your lunch hour tomorrow.

Here are some tips for writing a successful to-do list once you've decided on the proper medium for keeping it:

√   Create categories for cleaning chores. Chores can be categorized by room, my personal favorite, or by the day of the week you'll perform them.

√   Prioritize the items. If it's more important to clean the bathroom because your mother-in-law is coming for dinner, put that ahead of another less important task, like cleaning up the dog poop from the yard (unless you're going to be eating outside on the patio).

√   Categorize your to-do list by how long you think each task should take. This will not only allow you to clean when time permits, it will also to help keep you on track when cleaning. There's no reason to leave the kitchen a mess because all of a sudden you saw grime on the cabinet doors, got out the orange wood cleaner, and started scrubbing. There will still be the issue of the other grime in the kitchen and cleaning the cabinet doors might be better suited for a weekend job.

GunkBuster's Notebook: A Not-To-Do List

There are a million ways to get distracted while cleaning the house. Checking and responding to e-mail is a real showstopper. So is surfing the Web, even if you were looking for something to clean red Kool-Aid out of the carpet (it's club soda, by the way). Surfing always leads to ego-surfing, Googling an ex, or updating your NetFlix queue anyway. In the interest of fun then, let's look at some other things that should be included on your *Not-To-Do List*. You should not do any of the following while you're cleaning the house:

√   Sit down to read the magazines you collected to throw away.

√ Organize a medicine cabinet, drawer, spice rack, or CD or DVD rack when dusting or cleaning; that's degunking and should be done another time.

√ Embark on *self-cleaning*, including clipping or painting your nails, flossing, coloring your hair, looking for gray hair, clipping your nose or ear hair, or trying a new hair style because you thought you saw a pimple (or egads!, a mole) when cleaning the mirror in the bathroom.

√ Start an argument about who left the empty juice carton in the refrigerator while you are walking around with your trash bag collecting trash.

√ Think a beer will make the tasks you need to perform more pleasurable.

√ Stop to have a cup of coffee or take a nap.

√ Collect ATM receipts and decide to balance your checkbook, or decide that now is the time to sign up for that online banking and bill paying thing your bank keeps offering.

√ Decide that this is the last time that cat is going to spray your favorite chair, and write an ad for the paper. (And call it in.)

√ Take a dog or cat to the groomer.

√ Research a maid service.

√ Get sucked into a television show on which all kinds of people are screaming, *"Who's my baby's daddy?"*

√ Write an angry letter to the comptroller stating that your house can't be worth what it's recently been appraised for.

√ Decide now that you absolutely must go immediately to the 12-hour sale you just read about in today's circular.

Dress the Part

Before you clean anything, be it after work or on Saturday morning, make sure you've dressed for the part. Wear something that's comfortable and baggy and that you don't mind ruining. Bleach and other cleansers can be hazardous to your clothes as well as your health. Make sure what you're wearing won't be too hot either; you'll work up a sweat once you get started. Whatever you choose should move with you too; you'll be doing a lot of bending and reaching. You'll need rubber gloves and a dusting mitt too, and maybe even an apron to hold supplies and tools.

TIP: Turn on the stereo, iPod, TV, or DVD or VHS movie so that you have some kind of media on in all of the rooms you'll be cleaning. You can even record your tv show during the week and play that back while you clean. Do not stop to watch when you are finished with that room though!

Make the Most of Your Time

Chances are you backtrack a lot when cleaning. Perhaps you get sidetracked or forget what you entered a room to do, but most likely it's because you don't know how to clean in such a way that you don't have to backtrack to get things done. You probably make multiple trips across a room to clean it. In the kitchen, you may walk back and forth to put clean dishes away and then back and forth again to load dirty dishes in the dishwasher. Collecting the dishes may even take you to other rooms and then back to the kitchen to cross it again.

Backtracking gets worse if you don't have a work apron or a carryall to keep your supplies in. If you have to walk to and from the bathroom to keep retrieving supplies from the kitchen or the utility room, you're wasting steps, and thus you're wasting time. Shaving time off of your cleaning tasks is the best way to lessen how long it takes to get the tasks done, and it's all about learning to make precise, thoughtful movements.

Make Every Move Count

To make every move count means you can't backtrack. To keep from backtracking, make sure you have all the supplies you'll need to clean a particular area with you. These tools can be in a carryall or work apron, as mentioned earlier. With the right tools in hand, make sure to also do the following in each room:

√ Circle the room once cleaning from outside in. Clean the floor last.

√ Clean from top to bottom. Don't clear the spider webs in the corner of the ceiling or wipe the dust from the knickknacks *after* vacuuming or mopping; do it *before*.

√ Don't keep cleaning if something is clean. If there's no dust on the television screen or grime on the outside of the refrigerator, don't clean it just because it's part of your current routine.

√ Clean the walls, light switches, doors, and shelves only when they're dirty.

√ Clean countertops with a cleanser and cloth, not a sponge. Sponges have lots of nasty germs. If you must use a sponge, put it in the microwave for 30 seconds first.

√ If something isn't working to get up a stain, switch to a stronger cleanser. Don't waste time scrubbing when another cleanser will work better.

√ Buy the best supplies as detailed in the next section, in Chapter 13, and in Appendix B.

√ Learn to express-clean as detailed in Chapter 12.

√ Learn what cleansers are must-haves, as detailed in Chapter 13 and Appendix B.

Avoid Unnecessary Tasks

In this book I've written a lot about getting and staying degunked. While degunking a home takes a lot of time, keeping it degunked is really only a matter of staying on top of things with a system. The same can be said for cleaning. There are things you can do to keep a freshly cleaned area dirt free longer, just as there are ways to keep a degunked area from getting gunked up again.

Although I'll only list a smidgen of what you can do to keep your clean home clean, there are entire books written on this subject if you're interested. By putting the tools detailed in Table 11-1 in place though, you can make a big difference and you'll see it immediately.

Table 11-1   Staying Clean, a Room-by-Room Guide

Room	Tools to Make Available (They can be hidden if applicable.)	When to Use Them
Entryway	A shoe rack and floor mats outside and inside	Wipe feet and/or take off shoes upon entering the home.
Kitchen	Paper towels, disposable cleanser towels (like Clorox), cloth rags, spray cleansers	Anytime there's a spill and after each meal.
Living, family room	Feather duster, coasters, disposable cleanser towels, cotton cloth	Anytime you're in the room and notice dust or grime, on the tables or TV, or anytime there's a spill. Use coasters under drinks to avoid rings and moisture.
Pet area	Pet cleaning supplies such as cat box liners, pet sprays, poop-pickup bags, plastic bags for food cans, and grooming supplies	Clean the pet area anytime it's soiled, preferably each day before feeding the animal.
Bedroom	Scent packets or plug-ins for stuffy areas, including clothes hampers and wherever shoes are stored	Leave on daily.
Bathroom	Cleansers you can spray on and leave if you can remember to use them every day, toilet cleansers that work each time you flush if you don't have pets, a plunger, disposable cleansers, or a sponge and powdered cleanser	Use automatic cleansers daily, or wipe up scum and grime as it appears.
Office	Feather duster, coasters, small vacuum	Use as dirt appears and to avoid rings on furniture.

Have and Organize the Right Tools for the Job

Just as important as performing cleaning tasks daily, weekly, and monthly is having the right tools at your disposal when doing so. I've written a little about this already and will discuss it again in Chapters 12 and 13 and Appendix B. As noted, you'll need a carryall or cleaning apron, multipurpose cleansers, and tools in place for quick cleanups. You can use the carryall or apron to take everything with you that you'll need to perform the job at hand. Having these tools handy prevents backtracking and helps you perform tasks faster than you could otherwise.

There are some things you absolutely must have in your cleaning arsenal, in the tote you carry around with you when you clean: a toothbrush, a scraper, mild household cleanser, bleach in a spray bottle, a feather duster, furniture polish, a polishing cloth, powered cleanser, a small broom and pan, glass cleaner and squeegee, disinfectant cleanser, a toilet brush, a scrub pad, a mop, floor cleanser, rubber gloves, a vacuum cleaner, a rug cleaner for stain removal, garbage bags, and paper towels. Of course, you might not need to carry all of this around with you every time, so separate the tools listed here into what you need for short cleaning bursts and what you need for long cleaning jags. You may want to store all of the garbage bags in a utility room and only put a few in your carryall when you clean, and store a toilet brush and disenfecting wipes in each bathroom.

TIP: *Recycled grocery bags, both paper and plastic, make nice inserts for smaller trash cans positioned around the house.*

GunkBuster's Notebook: What's Hot and What's Not

There are a few things that are really hot on the cleaning scene—Dyson vacuums, for example. Sure they're expensive, but if you ever get a chance to use one, you'll never want to use anything else. It's the bomb, as my teen would say.

Roombas are hot too. These are automatic vacuum cleaners that vacuum and then return to their charging station all by themselves. These are perfect for those who have mobility problems or anyone with hard to reach areas that rarely get vacuumed.

Roomba, made by iRobot, also makes the Scooba. This is a floor washing cleaner that preps, washes, scrubs, and dries your floors, making mopping a task you can cross of your to-do list.

Another way to minimize your chores is the RoboMaid. RoboMaid is an automatic sweeper for your floors, and it's cheap. For hardly anything, you can get the RoboMaid sweeper, the ball that moves it around, and the built-in rechargeable battery and charger and eight electrostatic pads. Turn it on and it will sweep your tile, marble, granite, wood, or linoleum floors on its own, picking up dust, pet hair, and other small pieces of gunk. Figure 11-1 shows my RoboMaid in action; you can tell it's been used a lot, and you can also see it's one of my cat's favorite toys.

Figure 11-1
RoboMaid is cheap and reduces your sweeping chores.

Swiffer Dusters are hot too. They work well and there are several varieties, depending on the type of floor you need to clean. There's a Swiffer for dry floors, one for wet, one that sweeps, one that dusts, and even one for carpets.

There are some other items that, although popular, are not on my personal must-have list. One is the bathroom spray you use every time you finish taking a shower (don't bother, it's going to be very hard to get your family on this bandwagon). There are tons of rechargeable bathroom scrubbing brushes too, but storing them, getting them out, using them, cleaning them, and restoring them is much more trouble than it's worth. There are also cleansers that promise to do the work for you, using scrubbing bubbles or some such, but in my home I still have to get out the trusty powered cleanser and a sponge to get the bathtub clean. Just make sure to research before you buy. If you have specialty tubs and sinks (such as marble, acrylic, glass, specialty ceramic, or a resurfaced tub), make sure the cleanser you use won't mar the finish. There are many nonabrasive and nonbleach cleansers that work on a variety of materials.

Clean While You Sleep

There are lots of things you can do while sleeping to aid in your quest for a clean home. Several of the items mentioned in the GunkBuster's Notebook "What's Hot and What's Not" can be used, including the Roomba, Scooba, and RoboMaid. If you can afford any of those items, you're well on your way to reducing how much time you spend cleaning.

There are many less-expensive ways to lighten the load though, and lots of things you can set up and let work while you sleep. I'm sure what first comes to mind is soaking the dinner pan overnight in hot water. That's a classic. If the stain is stubborn though, add a used fabric softener dryer sheet. Just lay it on top and let it soak up the gunk. That's not so classic. There are lots other tricks to saving time by letting things work overnight or automatically. Here are some of my favorites:

√ Cleansers that you can drop in the tank of a toilet and that work all of the time, by dispensing bleach to keep the toilet clean (don't use this if you have pets that might drink out of the toilet, or look for nontoxic ones).

√ Deodorizers you can plug into electrical outlets or set out to absorb unwanted odors, including those found near shoes and dirty clothes and near recyclables and pet food.

√ Bathroom sprays that attack mold and mildew in caulk.

√ Overnight spa and hot tub filter cleaners.

√ White vinegar to remove mineral deposits from around drains, or use to deep clean your toilet bowl.

√ Talcum powder to remove oil and grease from clothing.

√ Oxy-Boost to remove yellow stains from clothing on collars and under the arms.

√   Baking soda to remove grease from carpets, give a fireplace a nice smell, remove a stain on a countertop, or clean a burnt pan.

√   Powdered dishwashing soap to remove burnt-on food.

√   Vinegar (in an open bowl) to absorb odors.

There are thousands of other tricks too, and I'll address as many as pages permit in Chapter 13 and Appendix B. This is just a teaser!

Summing Up

In this chapter you learned what measures you need to put in place to facilitate effective cleaning sessions. You need a productive and working to-do list, and then you need to have the tools you need readily available, know what products really work and which don't, and apply some tricks to let cleansers work for you overnight (instead of having to scrub the offending gunk away yourself). You'll learn more tips and tricks for cleaning house in the next few chapters, so keep reading!

Chapter 12

Express Cleaning

Degunking Checklist:

√   Learn the 12 steps to express cleaning and apply them.

√   Know what tools are must-haves and what should be in your cleaning apron or tote.

√   Practice express-cleaning the bathrooms first (they're the smallest rooms in the house); then apply what you've learned to other rooms.

√   Clean from top to bottom and in a circular manner in every room.

You just got home from work after a long commute only to realize it's Thursday and the bathrooms need cleaning. That's what the schedule says. The microwave is too dirty to cook anything in though, and the kitchen counters are stained with blueberry syrup from breakfast. There's another couple of chores. Time is tight and you have dinner to make, and you really don't feel like doing anything at all, much less clean the bathrooms or the mess in the kitchen someone else created. You know that if you don't stay on top of the daily chores though, your house will to turn into a pigsty.

Although you can work with your family to get them to clean up after themselves (including wiping up stains as they happen), ultimately, someone has to clean (and deep clean), and cleaning is a chore. And the longer you put it off, the longer it's going to take when you finally do get to it.

Wouldn't it be nice if you could make those chores go a little faster? If you could, you might be more motivated to perform them. It is possible if you know a little about express cleaning. Express cleaning can motivate family members too. Once my spouse figured out it really only took five minutes to empty the dishwasher, it seemed like a much smaller chore than it once was. Five minutes is only five minutes; it's only one commercial break.

What Express Cleaning Is

Express cleaning is about learning how to clean an area in less time than it takes you now. Successful express cleaning requires using a lot of tactics, including having tools handy, having tools that work, and knowing how to work a room (or a house) so you don't waste time. For instance, the next time you put away folded clothes you've taken from the dryer, gather up any dirty clothes you find on the way back. Put those clothes in the washer right then. Another way to shave off some time is to only clean what needs to be cleaned. Just because you see one sticky spot on a cabinet door doesn't mean you need to clean the entire thing. One more way is to always carry something with you when you move from room to room. Finally, if you work a room in a circle, you'll spend less time cleaning it. It's all about making the most of your time.

TIP: The more people you can get involved in the cleaning process, the faster it will go. Assign a "kitchen" person, a "bathroom" person, a "dusting" person, and a "vacuuming and mopping" person.

Twelve Essentials of Express Cleaning

There are a few rules you'll have to follow if you're going to make express cleaning work for you. Express cleaning is all about making the most of each footstep and the most of each scrub. That means putting several things in place first and performing cleaning tasks in a specific order, no matter what room you're cleaning. Here are the 12 things you need to remember or put in place to become successful at express cleaning:

1. Complete daily chores every day.

2. Keep a to-do list.

3. Wear an apron if you don't have supplies, or carry a tote if you do, depending on the job at hand of course.

4. Know the best order for cleaning rooms in the house, and clean clockwise, working from high to low as you clean. (Clean the floors last.)

5. Learn to clean with both hands. (Pick up an item with one hand and dust with another; spray a cleanser with one hand and wipe with another.)

6. Use the right tools and cleansers and avoid gadgets.

7. Don't clean areas that aren't dirty.

8. Shift to stronger cleansers if the current one isn't working.

9. Stay focused on the job at hand; know how long you want to allot to a task, and keep track of the time.

10. Never move from one room to another without taking something with you.

11. Don't repurchase cleansers that don't work, and store cleansers in their original containers.

12. Know when to call a professional.

Express Cleaning Tools

You should have certain cleaning essentials in your cleaning apron or tote, and these were noted in Chapter 11. In a nutshell, you'll need a toothbrush, scraper, feather duster, and whisk broom for small physical messes and multipurpose cleansers to clean counters, windows, stoves, and bathrooms of dirt, fingerprints, and grime. You'll also want something that contains bleach, some paper towels, a scrubbing sponge and rags, and a powdered cleanser to get up tough stains. For dusting furniture, you'll need dusting polish and a polishing cloth. Carry a trash bag too. You can't express-clean if the tools you need aren't readily available.

Order Counts

The order in which you clean is very important. You want to clean from the top to the bottom of every room, and you want to clean in a circular fashion. That means knocking down cobwebs first, dusting shelves second, cleaning the counter third, wiping off the coffee table fourth, sweeping the hearth of the fireplace fifth, and vacuuming or mopping last. Dirt will fall down, it will not creep up. Higher places will have less dirt than lower ones, just by the law of gravity. Additionally, while your teenagers won't put their feet on the ceiling, they may put them on the coffee table!

The order you clean the house matters too, especially if you're off on a Saturday morning cleaning jag. In that case, clean the outer rooms first, such as the bedrooms and bathrooms. Carry your supplies with you, and pick up items that need to be dealt with when you go to each room. For instance, as you clean the bedrooms, throw all of the dirty clothes you find into the hallway. When you clean the bathrooms, throw all of the dirty towels there too. When you're finished cleaning both rooms, pick up the entire mess and take it to the laundry room. If you've stripped the beds, wrap the bedding all up in one of the sheets. In doing so, you'll save hundreds of steps you would have taken walking back and forth, performing the single task of gathering up the laundry and doing nothing else.

You'll find all sorts of things that will need to be moved besides laundry though, including dirty dishes. After cleaning the bedrooms and bathrooms, head toward the other outer rooms, including family rooms and game rooms. While cleaning those rooms, gather the dishes the same way, by setting them in the hallway or in the corner of the room, and carry them to the kitchen when you're on your way there. When you get to the kitchen, all of the dishes that need to be washed will be there, again, saving you hundreds of steps walking from room to room collecting them while performing no other task.

Bathrooms

If you dislike cleaning the bathrooms as much as I used to, it's probably because it takes way too long or you put it off longer than you should and the collection of filth grosses you out. If you're like I was, you may also have cleansers everywhere, cleansers that didn't work, and a lack of the proper tools. You also have to deal with the "ick" factor, especially if you have to clean up after teenage boys or teenage girls, sometimes making it an agonizing task. Before I wrote this book I had all kinds of "miracle" cleaners and even a few bathroom scrubbing gadgets too. None of them worked, and I finally got rid of them during a degunking session. And it took me forever to clean this tiny room; way longer than it should have. However, after a lot of research and trial and error, I found a way to make it go a lot faster. I'll share those tricks with you here.

Use the Right Cleansers

Bathrooms are mostly cleaned by spraying something and then wiping it up. That may mean a powdered cleanser for the tub, a mold/soap scum remover for the shower stall, glass cleaner for the mirrors, wood cleaner for the cabinets, and a disinfecting cleanser for the countertops. You'll also need something to clean the floors. Wow, you'd have to be Superman to carry all of this stuff around and Catwoman to figure out where you're going to keep all of it in the bathroom while you use it (and where to store when you're done). Get away from all of that! Look for and purchase a cleaner that can be used on multiple surfaces.

Pledge makes a multipurpose cleaner that works on wood, metal, glass, and electronics, and it could be one of the cleaners you use not only in your bathroom, but also in many other areas of your home. There are multipurpose cleansers that work on other combinations of surfaces, including those that work on mirrors, windows, stainless steel, appliances, *and* kitchen countertops. (Remember, if something can be used on a kitchen countertop, it can likely be used on your bathroom countertop too.) These multipurpose cleansers can make your cleaning tasks go faster because you won't have to keep switching products and cleaning towels. Multipurpose cleaning and disinfecting wipes that come in pop-up plastic containers are a must-have. They will clean everything from kitchen countertops to toilet seats. They are great for small spills and big messes because they are disposable and don't spread germs as sponges do.

Stand in One Place as Long as You Can

Spray and wipe, spray and wipe. That's really what you do in the bathroom when you clean it. You're going to spray and wipe the mirrors and countertops, spray and wipe the toilet, and spray and wipe the tub and shower. You can get more spraying and wiping done in less time though if you don't have to take any steps. So, go into your bathroom, put a cleaning towel or sponge in one hand and spray in the other, and stand in front of the sink. How many things can you spray and wipe from that one area? That's what you'll do. Just because you've always cleaned the mirrors first and then the countertops, the toilets, the tub, and finally the floor, and all with different cleansers, doesn't mean that's the way you have to keep doing it. Remember, you're trying to see how much you can clean without moving a step! If the only thing you do is switch to a multi-purpose cleanser, you'll save several minutes right there.

Let the Cleansers Do Their Work

Spraying and wiping is all well and good if you let enough time pass between the spraying and the wiping so the cleaners have a chance to work. Many shower stall cleansers have to be left to sit a few minutes so they can loosen what's on the walls. Some toilet bowl cleansers are created to work for a while, too, before you wipe them off. You'll need to read the packaging. If you find that your shower stall cleanser needs to sit for a few minutes, spray down the shower stall before doing anything else. The same is true for any specialty toilet cleansers (although I'd avoid those because there are multipurpose cleansers than can do the job just as well). By the time you get to it, the cleanser will have done its job, making yours easier.

CAUTION! Some cleansers don't play well with others, and some create a noxious odor. Never mix bleach with an alcohol-based cleaner. Be careful and always read the packaging. Make sure that a room has good ventilation if you are using certain soap scum and mildew removers. There are also many organic-based multipurpose cleansers available that are less toxic and environmentally safe.

Kitchens

Since the kitchen has to be cleaned often, it's important to know some tricks for making that chore go a little faster. As with other rooms, carry a plastic tote that contains all the cleaners, towels, and sponges you'll need for the job so all of your tools are handy. (You can also use an apron.) Make sure you've arranged your kitchen in the ways outlined in Chapter 6 to facilitate ease of use (and ultimately, ease of cleaning).

With that done, employ these tricks when cleaning:

√ Empty the dishwasher first. After emptying the dishwasher but before closing the door, load the dishwasher. This will clear the countertops and make them easier to clean.

√ Clean and put away any small appliances that have storage places.

√ Work from back to front and top to bottom. That means clean the stove knobs first, the stove top next, and the stove front last; clean under small countertop appliances first and work toward yourself; and clean the higher shelves and backs of shelves first when cleaning the refrigerator. The dirt and grime will move toward you in all instances and ultimately into a cleaning rag or on to the floor.

√   Keep a toothbrush handy to clean up stuck-on grime.

√   Clean the sink and rinse *after* cleaning the kitchen.

√   Sweep and mop last.

Living Areas

Living areas need different cleaning strategies than bathrooms and kitchens because they need vacuuming, they acquire cobwebs, they require dusting, and there are small items that must be dealt with such as pictures, porcelain keepsakes, art, and lamps. Again, it's important to work from top to bottom in a circular two-handed fashion. When dusting, use one hand to lift an item and the other to dust it or dust underneath it. You should dust cobwebs and shelves before dusting the glass on the coffee table; otherwise, the table will just get dirty with falling gunk! Always vacuum last.

Summing Up

Express cleaning is learning how to clean faster than you do now. For the most part, it's all accomplished by having the correct cleansers and tools available and easy to get to and learning how to multitask. You have to make the most of every step and every scrub. You can do this by using multipurpose cleansers and working a room from top to bottom, back to front, and in a circular fashion, all to avoid backtracking. You can decrease the time you spend now on a particular cleaning task; you just have to figure out how!

Chapter 13

Prepare Yourself for Cleaning Emergencies

Degunking Checklist:

√ Know what cleaning emergencies can (and will) occur.

√ Arm yourself with the cleansers you'll need to recover from these emergencies.

√ Understand that the longer a stain sits, the more likely it is to become permanent.

√ Learn how everyday items such as vinegar and baking soda can be used in cleaning emergencies.

Poop happens. Well, if you have a dog or a cat it does. If you have a pet, one of these days you'll come home all happy to see Rover and there you'll be, with poop on the carpet and a cleaning emergency on your hands. Poop isn't the only emergency you'll run into though; there's vomit, blood, and skunk and other smelly mishaps. There are sticky ones too, including gum, spilled beer or wine, kitty hair balls, and Kool-Aid. When these emergencies happen, you won't have time to figure out what product will clean it up and then run out to get it; you really need to be prepared for it ahead of time by having some things handy just in case. Remember, the longer a spill sits, the more likely it will become a stain!

TIP: In this chapter I've categorized cleaning emergencies by type. There are sections for pet, adult, kid, laundry, and food emergencies. However, since some of the sections overlap, you might need to find your adult blood emergency in the kid's section. Don't worry though, it'll be easy to find. The sections are alphabetized by topic to allow you to find your answers quickly.

Pet Emergencies

Pets can really only do so much damage. They can chew stuff up, pee, poop, and vomit. They shed of course, and you have to pick up their toys, but as far as emergencies go, they are pretty much limited to whatever your pets can excrete, one way or the other. Some emergencies can be caused by a curious cat though (or a mad one) and often an extremely happy, tail-wagging Labrador retriever. However, those emergencies and their solutions are scattered about the other sections.

Pee on the Carpet

Dilute the spot using a cloth dampened with water or club soda. Dab up as much as you can. Then clean the area with a solution specially formulated for pet urine. You can buy a cleanser or create your own by mixing a quart of water with 1/3 cup white vinegar. Apply a pet enzyme digester to keep the animal from using that spot again (try Quick'n Brite from **www.quicknbrite.com** or purchase a similar product from your local pet store). Follow the directions on the container.

Poop on the Carpet

Remove any solid waste first. Blot the area with a paper towel. Soak the stain with a pet enzyme digester that you purchase from a pet store. Soak it thoroughly and follow all directions. Retreat if necessary.

Pee and Poop Changes the Carpet Color

If, after cleaning up a pet's mess, you find that the carpet color has changed, dab the area with a mild ammonia solution. You can also try lemon juice or hydrogen peroxide, but these are really best used only on light-colored carpets.

TIP: *Always test any solution in an inconspicuous area first, just in case the solution itself will stain or change the carpet's color.*

Vomit and Hair Balls on the Carpet

For some reason, cats like to cough up hair balls under beds and in hard-to-reach places. Dogs don't seem to care where they throw up, as long as they're on your best carpet, couch, or Persian rug. Cleaning up this kind of mess requires some discipline.

First, don't wipe or rub any liquid part of the mess, but do gently pick up any solid waste. Sprinkle baking soda on what's left and let it sit. Once it's dried, vacuum up the mess. For whatever is left, use the tricks in the previous tips.

Pet Mishaps on Upholstery or Other Furniture

Cleaning upholstered furniture depends on what type of furniture you have. You'll have to figure out what type of material you're dealing with and go from there. If you can use water on the stain, try that first. Before applying any other cleansers, test them in an inconspicuous area first. As with other material, you'll need to apply an enzyme to soak up the smell and all traces of the incident to keep the pet from going there again.

Adult Emergencies

There are a few things that only (mostly) adults get into. Coffee, tea, beer, cosmetics, and correction fluid are a few of them. Here, I'll offer tips for some of the adult mishaps you may encounter. In general, these are tips to remove stains from counters and carpets; however, some stains, such as those caused by lipstick, are found almost exclusively on clothes. If you can't find what you need here, check the section on laundry emergencies.

TIP: *Always blot with a clean, white cloth to avoid transferring the cloth's dye to the material you're cleaning.*

TIP: Although I've done my best to make sure the following stain removal tips are accurate, your fabric may differ from the fabric on which I've tested these tips. Sometimes cotton reacts differently to a product than carpet does; sometimes polyester reacts differently than linen. No matter what, always test in an inconspicuous spot first.

Beer

Blot up all of the excess liquid with a damp, white cloth. You can use water, but club soda is better. Continue to blot until you've gotten up all, or at least most, of the liquid. You can also try ammonia or white vinegar if club soda isn't available or doesn't seem to be working. Next, use a carpet remover to get out the rest. I prefer Spot Shot Instant Carpet Stain Remover.

Candle Wax

Carefully scrape up as much of the wax as possible. Fill a Ziploc bag with ice and set it on top of the affected area. This will freeze the wax and make it easier to remove. Try again in a few minutes and remove as much as possible. Repeat this until you can't remove any more wax. Next, put several white paper towels over the area and use a warm iron to heat it. Lift up the remaining wax as it melts. You can also use a hair dryer to produce heat. (If the wax is on a tablecloth, put paper on top of and underneath before heating.)

Coffee and Soda

Club soda, water, or hydrogen peroxide on a clean, damp cloth is the best solution. Blot up any spill quickly, though, because the longer you leave it the more likely it is to leave a stain for good. If you've spilled on a countertop and can use a bleach product, by all means, do so. If you've spilled coffee on your keyboard or laptop, immediately flip it over and let it drain. Sometimes even a laptop can be saved from the trash heap if you do this quickly enough.

Correction Fluid

Spray WD-40 or rubbing alcohol on the stain and dab the spot until the stain begins to loosen. You may also want to use a brush to gently remove the flecks.

Cosmetics

On clothing, it's best to spray the spot with a pretreatment detergent, let soak, and then wash. On other surfaces, use a dry cleaning solvent, or mix one teaspoon of a mild detergent (no bleach) and blot the area. You can also use commercial products though. Again, Quick'n Brite is perfect. This stuff cleans anything, is a nontoxic enzyme cleaner, and will even remove set-in laundry stains. You'll find listing of more great commercial products in Appendix B.

Glue, Adhesives, and Rubber Cement

White school glue is the easiest to remove. Usually rubbing with a mild detergent and water mixture will get it up. If that doesn't do the job, mix a tablespoon of ammonia with a half cup of water and blot. Adhesives and rubber cement are a bit more stubborn though. Acetone usually works on stronger glues, but make sure you always test in an inconspicuous area first. (Never use on synthetics such a nylon or polyester; it will eat through the fabric.) Finally, for dried-on glue stains, boil one part vinegar and four parts water and soak for an hour.

Grease and Oil

Grease and oil come in all forms. Butter, hand cream, cooking spray, salad dressing, vegetable oil, automotive oil, and animal oil all apply. Removing oils usually takes more than one step. For all oils, remove as much as possible with a dry paper towel. Then use baking soda or cornstarch to draw out the oil that's left. Let it sit for a half hour, brush off, and check the stain. If this doesn't work, spray the stain with WD-40. After 15 minutes of soaking, use a mild detergent and water mixture and rub the stain with your fingers. Rinse with hot water.

TIP: A toothbrush is a must-have for gently rubbing stubborn stains.

Lipstick

Since lipstick is found almost only on clothes and napkins and is oil based, you need to treat it as an oil stain. As with all other oil stains, WD-40, mineral oil, alcohol, or a commercial product like Shout should get the stain out. Remember to always test the product in an inconspicuous area. Let any of these solutions sit for 10 minutes before working the stain with a mild detergent and water. On carpet, try Spot Shot Instant Carpet Stain Remover. (However, if you're getting lipstick on your carpet, you may not have much time available for cleaning, and you might need to consider a housekeeper!)

TIP: Don't dab oily stains with water; this will spread the stain.

Paint

There are many kinds of paint. Before deciding what to use to clean it up, make sure you know what kind of paint you're dealing with. For water-based paint, remove what you can with a paper towel (by dabbing) and then apply a small amount acetone and let sit for 15 minutes. Flush with water or dry cleaning fluid. For latex, flush the area with water to get out as much as possible, and then treat the stain with a mild detergent and water solution. For oil-based paint, try turpentine. Get out as much as possible and then rinse the item thoroughly. Soak overnight if necessary. (I prefer and suggest commercial productions such as, Oops! All Purpose Remover and Goof Off, which you can buy at the hardware store.)

Rust

If the item is white, blot the area with water and then squeeze lemon juice on the stain and salt lightly. Either dry the stain in the sun or place the item over a pot of boiling water. Rinse and repeat as needed. If that doesn't work, or if you can't use lemon juice on the fabric, try a commercial rust remover such as Rust Magic.

Shoe Polish

There are many kinds of shoe polish, but for the most part, polishes are oily. That means no dabbing with water! Try working in laundry detergent or sponging with alcohol. You can also try WD-40 if all else fails. If the polish is on clothes, you can also try a mixture of one part water to two parts alcohol.

Tea

First, flush the spill with water and blot up all you can. Tea responds best to a vinegar solution. Combine one teaspoon liquid detergent, one tablespoon vinegar, and one quart of water, put some on the stain, and then soak for 15 minutes and rinse. If that doesn't work, you'll probably need to use a bleach or bleach alternative product on the stain.

Wine

One solution is to use Wine Away. This commercial product is simply amazing. If you don't have that handy, mix one teaspoon mild detergent with a cup or so of warm water. Blot the spill with this mixture. Next, apply a vinegar and water mixture, a one part to three parts mix, and blot again. If none of this works or if you're in a hurry, you can pour white wine on the spill if you do so immediately. If no white wine is available, sprinkle with salt and flush with club soda.

Kids' Emergencies

Some things only kids get into, such as crayons, Silly Putty, and Kool-Aid. Here are some tips for dealing with emergencies only kids bring home.

Blood

First, flush with club soda if you have it, or apply cornstarch to the surface and then flush. Then, create a mixture of one teaspoon mild detergent and a cup of cold water, and rub gently into the stain and let sit. Rinse. Follow that with a few drops of ammonia and rinse again. If that doesn't get the stain out, pour hydrogen peroxide on the stain and flush with water. Launder items as soon as possible. (For dry-cleaned clothes, sprinkle with salt and take to the dry cleaner immediately.) You can also use commercial enzyme cleaners. They work by eating proteins in the stain. Finally, and believe it or not, saliva works. Just put as much as you can on the blood and rub and rinse.

Crayons

Sometimes, simply sponging the mark with a dry-cleaning solvent works to get rid of a crayon stain. Other times you may need to blot with some WD-40. Either way, you'll need to follow up by flushing with a mild detergent and water and launder immediately. Since crayons can melt like candle wax can, if the stain is persistent, even if it's been washed and dried, using the ironing trick noted earlier in the section on candle wax will sometimes work.

Gum

Gum can be removed best by freezing it first. Either put the item in the freezer in a plastic bag or fill a baggie with ice and lay it on the gum. Scrape the gum with a butter knife after it's hardened. This works on hair too! Peanut butter will get gum out of hair also, as will fabric softener liquid.

Kool-Aid

Immediately blot up anything you can. If you have a Shop-Vac, use that to pull the spill from the carpet and thus keep it from settling deep in the rug or upholstery. Then apply club soda and rinse under cold water if possible. If the stain remains, try a mixture of Dawn dishwashing detergent and water (one part to five). Dampen a cloth with it and lay it over the stain to help soak up what's left. Repeat as needed; it will eventually work. Wine Away also works.

Markers

Washable markers are just that, washable. Flush with mild detergent and water. Permanent markers are a bit more trying. For those, try something stronger, like alcohol or a non-oily hairspray. Use a white cloth to blot. If the stain is on a carpet and it remains, it is okay to use tweezers to pull out a few of the carpet's fibers to lighten the color and size of the stain. Rubbing alcohol or hairspray with a high alcohol content will remove ballpoint pen ink too. A big, cheap, can of Aquanet is great to have on hand for ink.

Mud

Always let mud dry first, and then get up larger pieces with a dull knife. Use a vacuum cleaner to pull up the rest. Use an old toothbrush to loosen anything that remains and vacuum again. For what's left, on carpet, try Spot Shot Instant Carpet Stain Remover. On clothes, mix laundry detergent and cool water and let soak for 30 minutes before laundering.

Silly Putty

Usually, Silly Putty will come off with some gentle scraping using a butter knife. WD-40 can be used to get off any that remains. If there's a stain, blot with rubbing alcohol. Peanut butter will do in a pinch, especially if the Silly Putty is in your kid's hair. (Do not ask me how I know this!)

Skunk

I'm not sure if this should go under kids' emergencies or pet emergencies. Usually it's a dog that gets into it with a skunk, but kids can be just as ornery. Either way, on a kid or a dog, tomato juice seems to do the trick better than anything else. However, a mixture of one quart of peroxide, one-quarter cup baking soda, and a dash of laundry soap (or Dawn dishwashing liquid) has been proven to work too. (Don't store this in a sealed container though, it could blow the top off of it!) On walls and in the house, use chlorine bleach or vinegar or a commercial odor-removing compound. Skunk-Off is a popular product.

Stickers

On glass, metal, or plastic, use nail polish remover or rubbing alcohol. Mineral oil or vegetable oil may also work. On paper products, try alcohol or use a commercial solvent like Goo Gone. On wood, use furniture polish. Heated vinegar also works, as does WD-40.

Vomit

Scrape up as much as you can and then flush the fabric with water. Make a paste of laundry soap and water and scrub the stain. To remove the odor on carpet, pour a small amount of ammonia on the stain, let sit, and blot up. Vinegar can also be effective on vomit stains if there are still remnants.

Laundry Emergencies

The following emergencies usually happen or are dealt with in the laundry room. Almost always, your first step should be to apply a stain removal product, such as Spray 'n Wash or Shout. You might also try applying a paste of mild detergent and water. Follow the directions and let soak as instructed on the packaging. If that does not work, and before putting the item in the clothes dryer, retreat and rewash with a bleach product or bleach alternative. If the stain persists, look to the following sections for further assistance.

TIP: There are several products on the market that contain enzymes. Tide is one example. However, much has been said about this type of detergent causing an allergic reaction such as a rash. Be careful!

Beverages and Fruit Juices

Pretreat the spot with white vinegar and Dawn; then launder as usual.

TIP: Quick'n Brite can be used on almost anything; you can even wash your hair and your dog with it. If you have sensitive skin, you might try this for stubborn stains. A tub is kind of expensive, but it lasts forever!

Bleeding of Colored Fabrics

If you've ever put a red sock in with a load of whites and turned everything pink, you may have thought your only option was to wear pink underwear until you could purchase new stuff. However, there are several commercial products available to undo it, and my favorites are Synthrapol and Carbona Color Run Remover. Follow the directions on the packaging.

Chocolate

Soak the item in cold water. Surprisingly, this often works. If not, let the stain soak in OxiClean, a commercial detergent.

Collar Stains

Shampoo works well to remove stubborn collar stains. Baby shampoo works well for me. Just rub in, let sit a few minutes, and launder again. There are also several commercial products available, including Wisk.

Deodorant and Antiperspirant

First, wash the garment as soon as possible in the hottest water the garment will allow using an enzyme detergent as a presoak. If the stain is still there after you wash the garment, treat with hydrogen peroxide. Vinegar and water may also work.

Gray, Dingy Socks

Let socks soak overnight in hot water with a squeeze of lemon juice Use the juice from two lemons.

Ketchup and Other Tomato-Based Stains

Sometimes, the only way to get out these stains is to use a product like Wine Away Red Wine Stain Remover. If no other options work, consider making this purchase (before putting any stained item in the dryer or letting it dry).

Lipstick and Chap Stick in the Dryer

Everyone's done it at least once. You open the dryer only to find a mess of Chap Stick or lipstick. To get it out of the dryer, wipe it down with WD-40 and wash with water and Dawn dishwashing soap.

Mustard

This probably won't come out, but if it's on your lucky game-day T-shirt, you can certainly make an attempt. If the clothing is colorfast, apply hydrogen peroxide and let stand for 30 minutes. If that doesn't (or won't) work, try an oxygen bleach, like OxiClean. You can also gently pull the fibers of the cloth to remove or break up dried-on parts.

Yellow Stains

Apply ammonia to new stains and white vinegar to old ones. If that doesn't work, try an oxygen bleach and wash in the hottest water possible.

TIP: Refer to Appendix B for must-have stain removers.

Quick Reference Chart

Table 13-1 offers a quick look at some of the most common spills and stains and how you should deal with them. This list has similar accidents, spills, and stains grouped together and solutions are in general terms. For more specific instructions, refer to the entries in this chapter. As always, test solutions in an inconspicuous area first because the solutions listed here may cause damage to your particular (or specialty) fabrics or carpets.

Table 13-1 Quick Reference Chart for Stains and Spills

Stain or Spill	Immediate Response	Second Response	Third Response or Response for Old, Dried, or Permanent Stains
Pet Mishaps	Remove solid waste with a paper towel.	Dilute the spot with water or club soda and blot.	Apply a commercial pet enzyme digester.
Beer, coffee, soda, tea	Blot up excess with a cloth or paper towel.	Dilute the spot with water or club soda. Tea responds best to a vinegar solution. Combine one teaspoon liquid detergent, one tablespoon vinegar, and one quart of water, put some on the stain, and then soak for 15 minutes and rinse.	Apply Spot Shot Instant Carpet Stain Remover on carpets or white vinegar or ammonia on light cloths.
Correction fluid, lipstick, shoe polish, crayons, Silly Putty.	Apply WD-40 and let sit for a few minutes. If the polish is on clothes, you can also try a mixture of one part water to two parts alcohol.	Brush lightly with a toothbrush and dab the spot with a paper towel.	Repeat.
Cosmetics	Spray a pretreatment detergent and let stand.	Launder in the hottest water possible.	Apply a commercial enzyme cleanser like Quick'n Brite.
Adhesives	Rub with a mild detergent and water mixture.	Use acetone on stronger glues.	Boil one part vinegar and four parts water and soak for one hour.
Oil and grease	Blot with a paper towel and apply baking soda.	Brush off what's drawn out with baking soda.	Repeat. Apply WD-40, let sit, and rinse.
Paint	Dab with a paper towel.	For water-based paint, remove what you can with a paper towel (by dabbing) and then apply a small amount of acetone and let sit for 15 minutes. Flush with water or dry-cleaning fluid. For latex, flush the area with water to get out as much as possible, and then treat the stain with a mild detergent and water solution.	

(continued)

Table 13-1 Quick Reference Chart for Stains and Spills (continued)

Stain or Spill	Immediate Response	Second Response	Third Response or Response for Old, Dried, or Permanent Stains
Paint (continued)		For oil-based paint, try turpentine. Get out as much as possible and then rinse the item thoroughly. Soak overnight if necessary. Apply a commercial paint remover such as Goof Off.	Use a commercial paint removal product such as goof off.
Candle wax, gum, and crayons	Either put the item in the freezer in a plastic bag or fill a baggie with ice and lay it on the spill.	Scrape with a butter knife once the item has hardened.	Peanut butter works on hair, as does fabric softener.
Wine	Mix one teaspoon mild detergent with a cup or so of warm water. Blot the spill with this mixture.	Apply a vinegar and water mixture, a one part to three parts mix, and blot again.	Use white wine or a commercial product like Wine Away.
Blood	Flush with club soda if you have it, or apply cornstarch to the surface and then flush.	Create a mixture of one teaspoon mild detergent and a cup of water and rub gently into the stain and let sit. Rinse. Follow that with a few drops of ammonia and rinse again.	Pour hydrogen peroxide on the stain and flush with water. Launder items as soon as possible.
Countertop messes	Wipe up spill with a cloth or paper towel.	Apply a commercial product like 409 or use a pop-up disinfecting wipe.	Apply a bleach product if possible.
Kool-Aid	Blot up what you can with water and a clean white towel.	Apply club soda and rinse with cold water.	Use a mixture of Dawn dishwashing detergent and water (one part to five). Dampen a cloth with it and lay it over the stain to help soak up what's left.
Markers and ink	Flush with water or club soda.	Use alcohol or a non-oily hairspray and blot blot with a white cloth.	Use a commercial carpet or stain removal product.
Stickers	On glass, metal, or plastic, use nail polish remover or rubbing alcohol.	Try mineral oil or vegetable oil.	Use a commercial product like Goo Gone.

(continued)

Table 13-1   Quick Reference Chart for Stains and Spills *(continued)*

Stain or Spill	Immediate Response	Second Response	Third Response or Response for Old, Dried, or Permanent Stains
Laundry stains	Apply a stain removal product, such as Spray 'n Wash or Shout. You might also try applying a paste of mild detergent and water.	Retreat and rewash with a bleach product or bleach alternative.	Refer to the specific stain in this chapter.

Summing Up

Although there are stains that can probably never be removed, including acid-based toilet bowl cleaners, alkaline drain cleaners, bleaches, many hair dyes, iodine, and mustard, almost all other spills and stains have stain-removing solutions. If you have a stain or spill not mentioned in this chapter, though, and you have access to the Internet, you can always look for new-found solutions posted by do-gooders. Take these with a grain of salt. In my research, I came across several odd solutions to cleaning tasks, including boiling potatoes and using the juice to clean silver, rubbing raw potatoes on mud stains, and removing ballpoint pen ink stains with nail polish remover. Perhaps all of these work; I haven't tried them. If you do look for help on the Internet, go to reputable sites, such as About.com or Cleaning101.com.

Chapter 14

Maintain a Degunked Home

Degunking Checklist:

√   Get rid of something every day.

√   Put things back where they belong.

√   Create working clutter areas.

√   Perform daily tasks.

√   Keep your family involved.

√   Stay on top of your cleaning schedule.

Congratulations. You've degunked your home (or at least you've learned how to)! You've thrown away stuff, given items you no longer need to charity, and organized and cleaned from top to bottom, literally. You've created schedules and put chores in the hands of family members. You have to-do lists and grocery lists all in one place. You even have your garage looking spiffy. Now what? Well, you're going to need to learn how to keep it that way. You want to stay *forever degunked*.

What You Know So Far

Throughout this book I've included tables at the end of almost all of the chapters, showing you how to find problem areas and deal with them before they get out of hand again. That's a good start to staying degunked. For instance, in Table 3-2 you learned that creating a space that's only used to hold newspapers that have yet to be read can permanently solve the newspaper crisis you had previously. You learned in that same table that you must get rid of a broken appliance you've replaced *immediately*. Waiting only causes the old appliance to become gunk. The other tables offer similar tips to staying degunked. The information in the tables in this chapter consists of a lot of the same information found in those chapters, not only to reinforce how important they are, but to get them to the forefront of your thoughts and to help keep you focused and on track. You can always revert back here if things start to get out of control.

Caution! I'm going to get a little hard-nosed in this chapter. That's because if you want to stay degunked, you have to really put your mind to it. You're going to have to sit on family members and force yourself to do things even when you don't feel like it. This chapter isn't for the wimpy or the faint of heart!

Continue to Get Rid of Things

Getting rid of things every day is the first and foremost way to stay degunked. You absolutely *must not* get attached to things that are broken, things that people give you but you don't want, or things that accumulate in piles, including magazines and books. You have to remember to stay focused on throwing stuff out. You're going to have to get used to that.

Table 14-1 sums up how to stay on top of various gunk that accumulates but should really be thrown away. When a room starts to get messy and disorganized, look here for telltale signs of developing problems and for ways to solve those problems in the short and long term.

Table 14-1   Things That Should Be Thrown Away Daily or Weekly

Clutter	To Prevent Gunk in the Short Term	To Eliminate Gunk in the Long Term
Newspapers, magazines, catalogs, mail	Create a space just for these items, such as a wicker basket, the bottom shelf of a coffee table, or an area of a bookshelf. Put new magazines and catalogs on top of old ones. Go through the stack when it starts to get large, starting at the bottom and throwing away anything older than three months. Go through mail daily.	Assign a member of the family to put the previous day's paper in the recycle bin or trash can each morning on their way out the door. When a new catalog comes in, throw one or more away. Pay bills weekly.
Appliances, electronics, toys	Assign a space for the new addition immediately. Remove what is being replaced.	Get rid of an item before purchasing its replacement. Spend time deciding if you really do need and want to purchase the item.
Cleaning supplies	Keep cleaning supplies together, in a carrying case with a handle. Purchase cleaners that serve more than one purpose to keep cleaning supplies to a minimum.	If it has three drops left it in but you can't get them to come out, throw away the bottle. Don't repurchase cleansers that don't work.
Broken items	When things break, throw them away (or get them repaired) immediately. This includes appliances, electronics, eye glasses, toys, dishes, and computer equipment.	Do not replace an item without throwing out the broken one.
Food and medicine	Check expiration dates on refrigerated food once a week. Check expiration dates on medication every two months.	Throw away expired food and medication immediately.

Put Things Back Where They Belong

Another *degunking-buster* is a failure to put things back where they belong. Kids make sandwiches and don't put the food back in the refrigerator, you use an appliance and don't put it back under the cabinet, and your spouse wears clothes and doesn't put them in the proper clothes hamper. This all causes gunk so fast that a house can go to spotless to a total wreck in only a few hours. Trust me on this, I know. And once it's a mess, who's going to clean it up? You? You're going to be really mad about that, I guarantee it. Figure 14-1 and 14-2 shows one day's worth of unattended dishes and messes. If only the people who lived here had emptied the dishwasher in the morning, and added dishes back as they were used!

Figure 14-1
A kitchen can go from pristine to a disaster area in a single day.

Figure 14-2
The TV watching area is often a disaster in the morning. Putting the dishes away and folding the blanket before going to be could have remedied this mess.

As you can see in Figures 14-1 and 14-2, family members have to be encouraged (and possibly forced) to put things away after using them. It's everyone's job and there's no way around it. Table 14-2 offers some strategies for getting your loved ones to put things away.

Table 14-2   Things That Should Be Put Back After They're Used

Item Usually Left Out After Use	Ways to Make Putting It Away Easier for You and and Your Family Members	What to Do If Family Members Still Won't Put Things Away
Toys, shoes, electronics, DVDs, magazines, books, CDs, papers, pens, pencils	Place move boxes between the family room and the bedrooms, by the entryway, and in the kitchen. Anything left out for <set time limit here> gets put in there. Tell family members to check the box every day before work or school or every night before bed (your choice), remove things that belong to them, and put them in their proper places.	Create a rule for things not removed from this box after the specified time limit. Perhaps you confiscate the items for a week, throw them out, or box them up until a "ransom" is paid in the form of a chore.
Dirty clothes, wet towels	If possible, place a laundry basket or hamper wherever you find clothes on the floor. If this isn't possible, put one as close as you can. Instruct family members to put clothes there. Hang hooks for the towels.	Don't launder anything that's on the floor or not in the hamper. In fact, you can refuse to launder clothes or towels for a person until they can learn where they should go all the time.
Small kitchen appliances	Make sure the storage solution is easy to reach and accessible. Ask the family member who uses this item where they would like it stored.	Move the appliance to the garage and leave it there until someone asks for it. Explain why it's there; there's no room for it on the counter. Tell them it'll be moved to the Give Away box if a proper place can't be found for it in the kitchen.
Food, food utensils, condiments	Put items family members use often within their reach. Make it easy for them to return the items they use, such as condiments, and insist they put used dishes in the dishwasher or sink. Consider paper plates and plastic spoons, and put a trash can in plain sight until they are trained.	Ground kids from the kitchen for a day each time they fail to clean up after themselves after a snack. Have a rule that whoever messes up the kitchen has to clean up after dinner.

(continued)

Table 14-2   Things That Should Be Put Back After They're Used *(continued)*

Item Usually Left Out After Use	Ways to Make Putting It Away Easier for You and and Your Family Members	What to Do If Family Members Still Won't Put Things Away
Pantry or refrigerator items	Consider labeling the shelves or putting pictures up for kids (they could even draw them), and make sure the spot you've chosen to house the cookies, crackers, and chips is easy for all family members to reach.	Don't buy what gets left out the most such as chips, cookies, or crackers until they promise to put the packages back where they belong.
Toys and pieces of toys	Collect as many pieces as you can, put them in a plastic container, and label it. Instruct your children as to where toys go, and put a toy basket in easy reach. Teach them to put away toys when they finish playing with them.	If you continue to find toys left out, confiscate them and hold them for "ransom. If that doesn't work, throw them away or give them to a child who would "appreciate it more than they do."
Utility room tools	Put labeled bins in the utility room on the available shelves. Add so many organizational bins that it's hard for anyone to put the screwdriver anywhere else but the tools bin.	Collect tools and put into move boxes. Create a rule for things not removed from this box after the specified time limit. Perhaps you confiscate the items for a week, throw them out, or box them up until a "ransom" is paid in the form of a chore.
Paperwork	Create a *working* file system. Create files for ongoing projects, bills that need to be paid, and open invoices, and have and use an inbox, outbox, and immediate attention box. Instruct family members on how to use it.	Collect paperwork from others in a special folder. You can't throw it away, but if they need it they'll have to search here for it.
Sports equipment, craft supplies	If the sports equipment belongs in a bin with a lid and you find sports equipment next to the bin, move the equipment to a big bucket without a lid. If craft supplies end up all over the place, make the container that holds them easier to move. Perhaps putting the materials on a rolling cart would be better.	Put the items in the attic or other hard-to-reach area. Tell the offending family member that you can't handle all of that gunk everywhere and they need to put it where it should go, or this will be its new storage place.

Create Working Clutter Areas

You're going to have clutter. There will always be keys, cell phones, magazines, DVDs, cat toys, kid toys, iPods, purses, and shoes. They're going to fall somewhere. People are tired when they get home from a long day at work; no one wants to drag their purse to the bedroom and hang it up, put their keys on a key rack, and walk across the room to put their cell phone in the charger. It has to be made easier to keep everyone on track and in the game, so put your organizing station in the area where most family members enter and exit the house.

In order to make working clutter areas work, then, they have to be easy on the eyes, close to the door, and big enough to hold what needs to be held. Table 14-3 includes some thoughts on creating good, working clutter areas.

Table 14-3   Creating Working Clutter Areas

Area	Ideas for Reducing Clutter
Kitchen counter and wall	Hang wicker baskets for each family member, build or purchase a key ring/cell phone/mail holder, and create a specific area for kids to sit and do homework and parents to read the paper, prepare mail, and pay bills.
Coffee area	Place a small "trash can" on the counter to collect small trash items. There are many decorative ones available. Also, get away from packets of sugar and creamer. Put those items in a holder specifically created for them.
Entryway	Install a coatrack for coats, hats, purses, backpacks, umbrellas, and other hanging items. Add a trash can for items brought into the house that should be immediately thrown away, such as junk mail, catalogs, empty fast food bags, and flyers that were placed on the door.
Hall closet	Install plastic hooks halfway down the wall for children's coats and backpacks. A shoe rack can hold shoes. Shelves can store books and paperwork.
Clothes closet	Put a trash can and a move box in the closet or just outside of it. Place things in there as they accumulate and deal with the items in these two containers weekly (or better yet, daily). You might also want to add a box for things that need to be mended and a box or hanging area for items that need to go to the dry cleaner. (If things aren't mended in a month, toss them.)

Complete Daily and Weekly Tasks with the Help of Your Family

When it comes to staying degunked, performing daily and weekly tasks is just as important as throwing things away, putting things back where they belong, and creating clutter areas. It's also important to share the chores with others so you don't feel overwhelmed or build resentment toward family members. Choosing the correct family member to do a particular chore depends on the age and maturity of a person, though, and sometimes their ability to sort laundry, handle glass dishware, go outside alone, or reach high places. You'll have to use your own judgment regarding what chore can be assigned to what family member.

Whatever you decide, remember that it isn't only up to you to keep the place neat and clean; that is, unless you're the only person that lives there! For that reason, I've included Table 14-4. Here, you can read some of the daily chores most people have to perform and write down your thoughts regarding who can do them and when.

Table 14-4   Complete Daily Tasks with the Help of Family Members

Daily or Weekly Task	Who Can Help and When They Can Perform the Task
Load and empty the dishwasher	(Example: A 10-year-old can load the dishwasher after dinner and the older sibling can unload it before school.)
Gather laundry	
Wash and dry laundry	
Fold and put away laundry	
Pack lunches	
Take something out for tomorrow night's dinner	
Walk the dog	
Wipe the counters and stove top, and generally clean the kitchen, including clearing breakfast and dinner dishes	
Move newspapers to a recycle bin	
Make beds	
Put toys away	
Go through the mail	
Put dirty clothes away	
Set the dinner table	
Make dinner	
Get the kids bathed and ready for bed	
Gather and take out household trash	
Gather and take out recyclables	
Dust	

(continued)

Table 14-4   Complete Daily Tasks with the Help of Family Members *(continued)*

Daily or Weekly Task	Who Can Help and When They Can Perform the Task
Sweep	
Vacuum	
Clean the cat box or pick up dog poop	
Run errands	
Change bed linens	
Pay bills	
Mop floors	
Clean bathrooms	
Clean mirrors and large glass doors	
Clean the refrigerator	
Mow the yard	
<Add other tasks specific to your family here>	

When you create your list, create another column for the person who performed the task to sign off on it. This will allow you, in one quick glance, to see if the day's chores were done. Think about consequences that the family member may have to face if they don't do the chore. Make each chore fit the situation. For example, you don't need to go grocery shopping until the fridge is cleaned and ready for new groceries. Do not nag if the chores aren't done; simply let the person know what the consequence of their inaction is. Remember, you are not in charge of "punishing" your family. They have made a choice not to do the chore and are choosing to take the consequence.

If you tend to be a perfectionist, you are going to have to bite your tongue sometimes. Yes, you probably can fold towels faster and better than your children or spouse, but doing things for them that they can do themselves only teaches your family that if they drag their feet long enough or do a poor job, you'll step in and do it yourself. That will make you resentful and doesn't teach your kids to be degunked adults. Your consequence for perfectionism may be that you get stuck doing everything.

TIP: Sometimes there are things that are better left to the experts. Find out when and what in Appendix A.

Summing Up

Maintaining a degunked home is not as easy you might think it should be. That's because the "stuff" that comes into your house every day always finds a way to pile up, family members will always forget to put stuff away, and it's difficult to keep everyone involved in performing the daily tasks that are required to run a home smoothly. However, understanding what can and will happen unless you stay on top of things might be enough to keep you on the straight and narrow. In this chapter, I hope to help you understand that, with a little heavy-handedness. You must do daily chores, family members must help, you must throw away things you don't want or need, and everyone must put back things after they've used them. If you can get there, you'll have a happy, healthy, and degunked home for life and more free time to enjoy your family, time with friends, and hobbies.

Appendix A

Checklists

You know by now you must perform myriad tasks to keep your home degunked. In every chapter in this book I've included tools to help you perform these tasks more efficiently. For the most part though, I've only talked about daily and weekly tasks, like washing the dishes and gathering and taking out the garbage. You can find checklists and tables regarding these types of tasks throughout the book. However, there's more to maintaining a degunked home than just staying on top of daily and weekly chores. There are chores you have to perform once a month too, tasks that must be completed once every season, and duties you have to perform once a year. You can't perform these chores if you don't know what they are though, and that's what this appendix is about.

General Housekeeping

In this section, general housekeeping chores are listed by what must be done monthly, seasonally, and yearly with regard to keeping a home organized and clean.

Monthly Tasks

- Dust ceiling fans and light fixtures.
- Dust window blinds.
- Dust air vents.

- Wipe down any dirty walls and clean corners and baseboards.
- Vacuum furniture.
- Change air filters.
- Replace the vacuum bag.
- Wash kitchen and bathroom rugs.
- Vacuum under furniture.
- Sweep and hose down driveways, patios, and walks.
- Clean sliding doors.
- Clean mirrors.
- Dust woodwork.

Seasonal Tasks (Spring and Fall Cleaning)

- Clean windows and doors and check weather stripping for cracks.
- Clean grills and outdoor furniture.
- Replace storm windows with screens in Spring and vice versa.
- Clean window screens.
- Clean gutters.
- Change smoke alarm batteries at Daylight Savings Time.
- Wash bedspreads and blankets.
- Clean out cupboards, wash, and reorganize.
- Clean your desk at work and home.
- Polish door knobs.
- Clean the oven before the holidays and in the Spring.

Yearly Tasks

- Clean drapes and curtains.
- Clean rugs and carpet and/or wax floors.
- Clean and reorganize closets.
- Run the dishwasher and coffee pot (without any dishes or coffee) using vinegar.
- Get rid of things you don't use or need.
- Check gutters and rain spouts for obstructions.
- After the holidays, put holiday decorations in clear, stackable, sealable, labeled bins. Do not leave yourself a mess for next season. Launder holiday napkins and tablecloths before putting them away.

- Update (or create) your address book using address labels from holiday cards and gifts.
- Thoroughly clean guest rooms including laundering linens, wiping baseboards, and washing down walls.
- Srub the refrigerator and freezer.
- Clean fireplace.

What to Leave to the Professionals

In this section, general housekeeping chores are listed by what must be done only occasionally, preferably by professionals. Table A-1 shows the task and when it should most likely be performed.

Table A-1   Tasks for Professionals

Task	Timeline
Vent cleaning	Once a year
Fireplace servicing	Before using it in the winter
Mold removal	As needed
Plumbing and leaks	As needed
Sewage maintenance and problems	As needed
Root removal	As needed
Pest control	Quarterly or as needed
Bee removal	As needed
Air conditioning and heating servicing	Seasonally
Clean dryer vents and inspect exhaust areas	Seasonally
Roof inspection	Anytime loose shingles, leaks, or other damage is noticed
Trim trees	Once a year
Landscaping (prune bushes and so on)	Once a year

Appendix B

Must–Have Stain Removers

As noted earlier in Chapter 13, you should be prepared for cleaning emergencies. People *will* spill red wine and kids *will* get gum in their hair and on furniture. There's always the chance you'll spill something too, perhaps coffee or tea on your new Berber carpet. Because of these unexpected spills and stains, I dedicated Chapter 13 to removing them. In that chapter I named several common household products that could be used in an emergency including cornstarch, salt, vinegar, lemons, and hydrogen peroxide. I also mentioned several commercial products including WD-40, Spot Shot Instant Carpet Stain Remover, and OxiClean, all of which are my personal favorites. I promised even more miracle stain removers in this appendix.

So, here it is; a complete list of common household products, miracle surprise products, and awesome commercial products to get you past any spill. It's in your best interest to have these on hand and know when to use them. Your carpet, clothing, counters, and floors will thank you!

CAUTION! *Always test your concoction of homemade stain removers on an inconspicuous part of the clothing, carpet, or fabric before applying it to the stain.*

Miracle Cleaners You Already Have or Should Purchase

I'll bet you already have a lot of these natural cleansers in your home. With a little practice, you can learn how to mix all kinds of concoctions for all kinds of stains, spills, and fabrics. Just remember to test it first; you wouldn't want to make the stain worse!

Alcohol (Denatured or Rubbing)

Use on grass stains, ball point pen ink, berry stains, mustard, pencil marks (try an eraser first), and difficult to remove stains. Depending on the stain and the fabric, you may need to dilute the alcohol with water or dishwashing detergent. Alcohol is often diluted before use, or, sponged or dabbed on full strength.

Ammonia

Use on blood, perspiration stains, deodorant and antiperspirant stains, mercurochrome, mustard, chocolate, fruit and berry stains, felt tip ink, lipstick and makeup, urine, vomit, and permanent markers. Generally the ammonia is mixed with alcohol, or vinegar and water to dilute it.

Baking Soda

Make a paste with 6 tablespoons of baking soda and 1/2 cup warm water. Use the paste to pretreat laundry stains such as blood, sweat, fruit, wine, and pet mishaps. Baking soda is also a good odor remover for carpets; just sprinkle on, leave as long as possible, and vacuum up. Use an open box in the refrigerator or pet area to absorb areas. Use baking soda as you would a soft-scrub cleanser. Great for burnt on food on pots and pans.

Club Soda

Club soda works on just about anything you can rinse with water. Use it at home to clean up anything spilled on tablecloths or carpets; use at restaurants to get up spilled food or drink; and never worry about ruining fabrics or making the stain worse.

Hydrogen Peroxide (3%)

Use to remove blood, to remove stains from white clothing or rugs, rings from shirt collars, or use on anything else you'd use bleach on. You can also use this product on mattress stains, carpet stains, and mud stains.

Lemon Juice

Great for clothing stains. Just rub on and wait. You can put the clothing in the sun if you'd like. Use lemon juice to dissolve soap scum and hard water deposits, or to shine copper or brass. Put lemon peel through the garbage disposal for a fresh, clean, smell. You can even get stains off of your hands with it.

Meat Tenderizer (Unseasoned)

Protein stains from blood, urine, food, and milk, can be removed with meat tenderizer mixed with water. Meat tenderizer breaks down the proteins making them easier to remove. Let the mixture work on the stain for about an hour before laundering.

Shampoo

Shampoo works on makeup and ring around the collar. It also works on protein based stains like sweat and blood. Just work into the fabric and rinse.

Shaving Cream

Use to get all kinds of stains up, including mud in carpets, spills on clothes, stains on carpets and upholstery, car rugs, and throw rugs. Works well on wine spills and light grease stains too.

Toothpaste

Toothpaste is the best safe and nontoxic silver polish available. It's great for silver jewelry too.

Vinegar (White)

Mix equal parts vinegar and water for an awesome window cleaner. Use in coffee makers, washing machines, and dishwashers to deep clean the inside of them. Use after waxing floors (mix with rinse water) for a super shine. Use to clean suede, or use in the washing machine during the final rinse. Vinegar can also be used to remove soap scum and mineral deposits, neutralize pet odors, and clean toilets.

Must-Have Commercial Products

If you don't have these products in your home, you should consider getting them. Don't gunk up your home with unnecessary products though; if you already have something that works for you, by all means continue to use it!

Biz Bleach

This is an enzyme presoak product that really works. Enzyme products break down protein stains such as blood, milk, or egg. Biz is a color-safe powder that can be used with detergent or on its own as a stain remover.

Borax (20 Mule Team Borax)

Use this product to clean fine china, cookware, kitchen appliances, showers, tubs, and tile, carpets, and laundry. Borax is a natural laundry booster, works as a water conditioner, and helps your laundry detergent work more effectively.

Carbona Color Run Remover

Use to get out dye and color runs from mixed-wash accidents. Follow directions on the package.

Clorox Bleach Pen

The Clorox Bleach Pen lets you "write" bleach on any fabric, grout, caulk, or countertop with precision. You can also use it to customize your own T-shirts, or, fade your jeans.

Dawn Dishwashing Liquid

Dawn comes in all flavors, from Ultra Dawn to Dawn Power Dissolver. Each Dawn product works to remove grease effectively. If you have a really nasty grease stain, or a pan you can't get clean, try Dawn Power Dissolver.

Goo Gone

Use to remove gum, tar, crayon, paint, tree sap, oil and grease, blood, ink, tape and tape residue, shoe polish, soap scum, bumper stickers, duct tape, and more. Use it on a variety of fabrics too, including carpets, upholstery, clothing, tile, glass, grills, appliance, vinyl, wood, draperies, and fiberglass.

Oxiclean

Oxiclean makes products for laundry, carpets, dishes, and more. Oxiclean is activated when added to warm or hot water. During this process, oxygen is released to target the stains (not the fabric) and can remove even the toughest stains. It is the oxygen that makes the product so powerful.

Quick'n Brite

This product is completely biodegradable and environmentally safe. It contains no toxic chemicals so you can use it on just about anything. Use it to clean windows, mirrors, showers, tubs, floors, walls, tires, stove tops, clothing, carpet, and upholstery.

Rust Magic

You won't need this product until you come across something rusty, but if you do need it, it's good. You can use it to remove rust from tubs and toilets, but it's usually used outside. Rust Magic works to remove rust on stucco, brick, concrete, stone, metal, tile, and more.

Shout

Shout is one of my favorite laundry cleaners. It's a concentrated stain-removing product that penetrates deep into fibers to loosen the stain. Follow directions on the package.

Spot Shot Instant Carpet Stain Remover

This product cleans better than any other carpet remover I've ever used. It can get up any stain, no matter how long it's been there. Use it on pet stains, makeup, food and drink spills, and anything else you can think of.

WD-40

Use WD-40 for grease stains, Chap Stick, lipstick, salad dressing, or anything else oil based. Spray it on and let it sit 15 minutes, then work in dishwashing soap to get it out. The stain should come with it. Launder as soon as possible.

Wine Away Red Wine Stain Remover

Use to remove red wine stains on carpets, tablecloths, and clothing. The product is made from fruit and vegetable extracts, contains no bleach, and is safe for use around children and pets. Wine Away also works on other stains such as tomato sauce and grape juice.

Zout Stain Remover

Another laundry stain remover that works wonders is Zout Stain Remover. Use to get out red stains such as tomato sauce and grape juice. www.Zout.com also offers an interactive stain guide that allows you to choose a stain and a fabric for specific instructions for stain removal.

Appendix C

What to Do With Items You No Longer Want or Need

There are numerous ways to rid your home of "useable" gunk. Usable gunk are things that you and your family no longer want or need, but stuff that could be useful to others. For instance, while you may no longer want your VCR (you replaced it with a DVD player years ago), a charity might be able to use it to show educational videos to its patrons, or someone might even buy it in a garage sale. And, while your old clothes may not fit you anymore, they may be the perfect items for someone else. Besides usable gunk though, you'll have gunk that can't be recycled. Old paint, chemicals, and bald tires must be disposed of properly. Here, I'll discuss options for getting rid of all of the gunk you've collected while working through this book; all of the gunk that is probably stored in boxes, in a garage, or in a storage shed.

Charities

There are numerous charities that will take your unwanted and usable items. Just make sure they are in good condition, and that the items are something you would use yourself. You don't want to burden any charity with items *they'll* have to discard.

TIP: *The www.justgive.org site offers donations pages to over one million charities. You can search by category too. Categories include Animals, Arts and Culture, Children and Youth, Crime Prevention, Disabled, Disaster Relief, Health and Disease, Homeless, Peace, and Women.*

Many charities offer free pick up services for your gently used goods, and others offer drop-off points. Some require you mail in your donations. Some popular foundations to make donations to include:

- Community Computer Foundation: Collects old computers and refurbishes them for underserved communities throughout Colorado. Call 303-570-1928 or visit **www.jaredpolisfoundation.org**.

- Donate a Cell Phone—Save a Life: Collects cell phones for victims of domestic violence. Call 202-785-0081 or visit **www.donateaphone.org**.

- Glass Slipper Project: Collects new and gently worn formal dresses and accessories. Call 312-409-4139 or visit **www.glassslipperproject.org**.

- Goodwill International: Accepts almost anything at local drop off areas in metropolitan areas and often picks up as well. Call 301-530-6500 or visit **locator.goodwill.org**.

- Humane Society of the United States: Accepts old leashes, food bowls, cages, and other pet supplies. Call 301-258-8276 or visit **www.hsus.org**.

- The Salvation Army: Collects used furniture, clothing, and household items. To schedule a pick up call 1-800-95-TRUCK. You can also visit **www.salvationarmy.org**.

- World Computer Exchange: Accepts computers for refurbishing and redistribution to connect poor youth in Africa, Asia, and Latin America to the Internet. Call 781-925-3078 or visit **www.worldcomputerexchange.org**.

Don't forget about the needs in your own area though. Consider giving to your favorite church, synagogue, or temple, and local libraries, schools, hospitals, nursing homes, veterinary clinic, public parks, and recreational facilities. Table C-1 offers other options.

Table C-1   Additional Charitable Options

Charity	What They Do	What They take	How To Reach	Do They Pick Up?
Donate a car.com	Provides a list of charities in your area that you can donate your vehicle to.	Cars, trucks, boats, RVs working and non-working.	www.donateacar.com	Yes
American Diabetes Association	Provides research into the cure of Diabetes and support for diabetics.	Cars, trucks, boats, RVs working and non-working.	1-800-ADA-6570 Or info@carprogram.com	Yes

(continued)

Table C-1   Additional Charitable Options *(continued)*

Charity	What They Do	What They take	How To Reach	Do They Pick Up?
Make-A-Wish Foundation.	Grant the wishes of children with life-threatening medical conditions to enrich the human experience with hope, strength, and joy.	Airline miles, stocks, cash donations.	1-866-880-1382 (toll-free) or www.wish.org/home/giving/	No
Lions Club International.	Lions are recognized worldwide for their service to the blind and visually impaired.	Plastic and metal frame eyeglasses.	www.lionsclubs.org/EN/ content/vision_eyeglass_ recycling Or call the local Lions Club in your area They are available worldwide.	No
Dress for Success.	Dress for Success is a non-profit that offers services to help clients enter the workforce and stay employed. Each client receives one suit when she has a job interview and a week's worth of separates when she gets the job. Also provides job counseling.	Coordinated, contemporary, interview-appropriate skirt and pant suits Beautiful, crisp blouses Gorgeous blazers and jackets Professional shoes They are particularly in need of larger-size suits.	To find and affiliate in your area: www.dressforsuccess.org/ where_we_are/affiliates.asp	No
Big Brothers and Sisters.	Founded in 1904, Big Brothers Big Sisters is the oldest and largest youth mentoring organization in the U. S.	Household goods, clothing, furniture, appliances.	www.hosted.bbbsa.org /agencyfinder/index.asp	Yes
wirelessrecycling. com.	In 2004, over 3.0 million wireless handsets were collected, refurbished, and resold or recycled by ReCellular throughout the world.	Cellphones chargers and accessories working or not.	www.wirelessrecycling.com	No Enter your zipcode for drop-off locations.
techsoup.org.	Provides tips on donating and recycling computers and other equipment.	Great site to determine what to donate and safe ways to recycle.	www.techsoup.org	N/A

Garage and Yard Sales

Having a successful garage sale takes a bit of planning. Although you can put out everything Saturday morning, pop up a few signs, and hope for the best, you'll do much better if you plan and promote your garage or yard sale effectively, and apply some tips and tricks of the trade.

To have a successful garage or yard sale, perform the following steps:

1. Place a classified ad in your local newspaper with your address, and the date and time of the sale. You may even want to add your phone number. Plan the sale for a weekend, but do not choose a holiday weekend.

2. Ask neighbors if they would like to have a sale too, or if they would like to join yours.

3. Call a local charity that picks up donations and schedule them to come the day after the sale to get whatever you didn't get rid of. If you don't have that option, the next day put everything in the car and drive it to a local charity drop off point.

4. The day before, place signs around the neighborhood with arrows and denoting the day and time.

5. When you are getting things ready, make sure everything is clean and organized.

6. Set up boxes, tables, or areas for things that are one dollar, five dollars, ten dollars, and so on.

7. Count on early birds; there will be some. Post a sign on your door that says "No early birds—we're still sleeping!" Do not answer if someone still knocks.

8. On the day of the sale, put out an extension cord so people can test electric items, and put gas in any yard equipment that requires it. Charge batteries if required.

9. Put larger items closer to the road so people will notice you.

10. Have plenty of small bills and change handy.

11. Remind yourself that whatever doesn't sell you're going to give away and get nothing for. Take what you can get!

12. Get rid of items that don't sell immediately after the sale is over, preferably the next day.

TIP: If you don't want to have the garage sale at your place, or your location prohibits it, perhaps your house of worship or club you belong to would like to put on a group sale to raise funds. In the case of a church or charity, the things you donate for the sale may be tax deductible. Organizations like the Junior League can make thousands of dollars with their annual sale. Doing a group sale is also more fun than doing it alone.

Classified Ads

If you have items that are worth something, selling them through a classified ad in your local newspaper could be worth your while. Some things you may consider selling in this manner include riding lawn mowers, push mowers, edgers, and other lawn equipment; used computers, like-new furniture, musical equipment, tools; wedding dresses and expensive formal wear, cell phones, MP3 players, video equipment, cameras, and other gadgets.

To place a classified ad, purchase a copy of the paper you want to advertise in (you might pick several), and contact them as denoted on the classified ad page. Visit your local grocery store and pick up any additional publications. In Texas, we have the Greensheet. It's a specialized paper that lets you place ads for around 50 cents a word. When people want to buy something around here, many times they're more likely to look in the Greensheet than in the local paper. These specialized papers may be a better option.

Sell Online

Selling online is another way to get rid of items that are valuable. Selling online is a better choice (over classified ads or garage sales) when you have items that are specialized, rare, and/or small enough to be shipped. If you have large items like furniture (or even a car!) to sell, you can specify the auction as a "local auction only" and require that the winning bidder pick up the item. Probably the best place to sell items online is eBay (you can sell your used books on Amazon), but there are also many up-and-coming auction sites like Bid-A-Lot (**www.bid-a lot.com**). You can sell virtually anything online from your classic Led Zeppelin concert shirt from the late 70's to a potato chip that looks like the state of Florida to the fine china you inherited 10 years ago.

Selling online takes a bit of setup time though, but no more than putting together a garage sale. Before you can sell anything online you'll have to create an account and create a payment method. You'll also have to take and post pictures of the item(s) to sell, and you'll need to create a write up of each product you want to get rid of. Then, you'll have to monitor the bidding and ship the item(s) out to the winner(s) of the bid(s). It's not as hard as it sounds though; these sites offer step-by-step guides to make the selling process simple. It's time consuming, but may well be worth it if your Led Zeppelin T-shirt brings in $500!

TIP: Don't forget about consignment stores. These stores are especially good for selling designer clothing/formal wear, baby clothes, maternity clothes, and sports equipment. To find one in your area, look in the phone book under "consignment stores" and call them to learn about their selling policies.

Dispose Of Properly or Recycle

The only things left to dispose of are items that you can't sell, can't give away, can't donate, but can't *throw away* either. For instance, where I live, you can't put old paint in the trash cans for pick up. You can't put it down the sink or storm drain either. It's considered hazardous waste and must be taken to the proper collection center. Hazardous waste is anything that could potentially harm the environment, combust, ignite, or produce gases. There are lots of items under the hazardous waste umbrella that you may not be aware of.

Hazardous waste includes but is not limited to:

- Acids
- Aerosol cans
- Anti-freeze
- Brake fluid
- Drain cleaners
- Fertilizers
- Car and truck batteries
- Motor oil
- Household chemicals
- Paint and paint thinner
- Pesticides
- Solvents
- Tires
- Varnish

While degunking, collect all of the hazardous waste into one area, but don't mix them together! Then, find out where you should dispose of the items by calling city services or visiting their Web site.

In addition, ask your community leaders the following questions:

- Do you have a facility that collects hazardous waste year round? Where is it?
- Are there any days designated for the collection of hazardous waste? Will a truck come by my house on those days or will I need to deliver the goods myself?
- Are there any local businesses that accept waste for recycling? What types of waste will they collect?

NOTE: *The average home can accumulate as much as 100 pounds of hazardous waste in basements, garages, and storage closets. (U.S. Environmental Protection Agency)*

Recycling is another way to rid yourself of gunk. Again, contact your city services department and ask about your recycling options. In some communities, recycling actually costs more than if you simply threw the item away, but recycling is an environmentally friendly act and keeps your landfills from filling up too quickly. It's always better to recycle if recycling is an option.

Some things you may be considering throwing away that can be recycled include:

- Newspapers and paper
- Cardboard boxes
- Steel from cans, steel sheds, and other products
- Yard trimmings
- Beer and soft drink cans
- Magazines
- Plastic including milk, soft drink, and water bottles
- Glass and glass bottles

NOTE: *The most frequently encountered item in most landfills is paper. On average it accounts for 40% of a landfill's contents. Newspapers don't degrade quickly either; it's best to recycle.(U.S. Environmental Protection Agency)*

Tax Deductible Worksheets

When you donate an item to a charity you'll almost always be given a tax deductible form. If you aren't, you can usually print one from the organization's Web site. However, on the slim chance you can't or don't get one, the one in Table C-2 will do in a pinch.

Table C-2   Tax Deductible Form for Donated Items

Item Donated	Approximate Value	Charity it Was Donated To

Items you can deduct as charitable contributions include money or property you give to churches and other religious organizations, federal, state, and local governments if it is solely for public purposes, nonprofit schools and hospitals, public parks and recreational facilities, Salvation Army, Red Cross, Goodwill Industries, Girl Scouts, and similar groups, and war veteran's groups. The group needs to be religious, charitable, educational, scientific, or literary, or, for the prevention of cruelty to children or animals.

Items you cannot deduct as charitable contributions include items given to civic leagues, sports clubs, labor unions, chambers of commerce, most foreign organizations (contact your CPA, there are exceptions), government lobbyists, homeowner's organizations, groups run for personal profit, and political groups or candidates. That means while you can give your used sports equipment to Goodwill Industries and write it off, you cannot give the equipment to your daughter's for-profit gymnastics club and take the deduction.

TIP: To read all about tax deductions for charities visit www.irs.gov/pub/irs-pdf/ p5626.pdf.

Whichever way you choose to go though, the object is to get rid of the gunk! Whether you give it to charity, sell it, or donate it to a local group doesn't matter. Just keep at it, and happy degunking!

Index

More Than 500 Step-by-Step Instructions for Everything from Organizing Your Closets to Planning a Wedding to Creating a Flawless Filing System

The Ultimate Guide to Getting It All Together!

how to organize *just about* every-thing

Peter Walsh

Professional Organizer from TLC's hit series *Clean Sweep*

For more great organizing tips, check out *How to Organize Just About Everything* from author Peter Walsh, Organizing Expert seen on TLC's Clean Sweep.

Available in bookstores

fP **FREE PRESS**
A Division of Simon & Schuster
A VIACOM COMPANY